the Kingdom Agenda

the Kingdom Agenda

Experiencing God in Your Workplace

Mike C. Rogers & Claude V. King

Saratoga Press, P. O. Box 369
Murfreesboro, TN 37133-0369

96 97 98 99 00   9 8 7 6 5 4 3 2 1

ISBN 0-9651288-0-6

For seminar information write:
Kingdom Agenda Ministries
P. O. Box 747
Murfreesboro, TN 37133-0747

Illustrations from the workplace are true stories Mike Rogers has encountered. Some names
have been changed to maintain confidentiality.

CONTENTS

FOREWORD

*N*ever have I sensed a more urgent call than the call to return to the New Testament truth of the Kingdom of God. The Kingdom of God was the heart of Jesus' teaching and preaching. The Kingdom and Christ's righteousness were to be sought first and above all else (Matt. 6:33). Never has there been a greater need for a clarion call to experience the Kingdom of God in the workplace than today. This truth has been uppermost in my thinking, my preaching, and my ministry from the very beginning.

This new and fresh work by Mike Rogers and Claude King is a very welcome "word from God" to our generation. The format is exceptional, and the content biblical and practical. We must have our theology right. Then we must be able to put into practical application this truth in our daily lives. Every person who studies this material will be confronted with a biblical and practical encounter with Christ in their workplace.

I personally know Mike Rogers. He is a man of integrity, and he is one who is well qualified to write on this biblical truth. He has lived it as a layman, as a missionary, and as a pastor. He has faithfully taught others what he shares here. I've been in the church he pastored in Kentucky and have been with his people. That church was built on this truth, and the excitement of experiencing God daily was very real.

Of course, I've known Claude King for years and worked closely with him in developing *Experiencing God* and *Fresh Encounter* resources. Together, Claude and Mike have given to the people of God a very timely and valuable tool by which we can experience God as He intended—in every aspect of our lives. In the Scriptures God confronted His people most often and most significantly in the workplaces where His people were to be found. May God use this work to profoundly affect our nation and our world through a people on mission with God in the workplaces of our world.

Henry T. Blackaby
Office of Prayer and Spiritual Awakening, SBC

AUTHORS

Mike Rogers is founder and President of Kingdom Agenda Ministries. He leads conferences, seminars, and other training sessions to equip people in all types of job assignments to live by God's Kingdom Agenda at work. His burden is to help pastors equip their people for effective ministry in their workplaces.

Mike is a Vietnam veteran with 7 years of service in the United States Marine Corps. He worked for 5 years in personnel management and training. During this time, Mike became a Christian. Later, he sensed God's call to the pastoral ministry where he served for 10 years. Mike and his wife Debi also served for 4 years as missionaries to Venezuela.

Mike is a graduate of Chaminade University and holds a Master of Divinity degree from the Southern Baptist Theological Seminary. Mike has been a contributing writer for *Experiencing God Magazine*.

Mike and Debi are parents of two grown children: Corey and Summer.

Claude King serves as a Mission Service Corps consultant and writer for the Office of Prayer and Spiritual Awakening, Southern Baptist Convention. For eight years he worked at the Sunday School Board of the Southern Baptist Convention developing and editing self-paced interactive curricula for the Lay Institute for Equipping (LIFE®) and the LIFE® Support Group Series.

Claude is a graduate of Belmont College and holds Master of Divinity and Master of Religious Education degrees from New Orleans Baptist Theological Seminary. Claude has co-authored several books and courses, including *Experiencing God* and *Fresh Encounter* resources with Henry Blackaby, *The Mind of Christ* and *In God's Presence* with T. W. Hunt, and *WiseCounsel: Skills for Lay Counseling* with John Drakeford.

Claude and his wife, Reta, have two daughters: Julie and Jenny.

PREFACE

You hurriedly shower and dress as you mentally prepare for the day that awaits you. The caffeine from your first cup of coffee begins to kick in as you maneuver your way into traffic on the interstate that carries you into the heart of the city. It's only Tuesday and already you are feeling exhausted from the pressure of surviving another competitive day at work. You deliberately fight back the temptation to take another "mental vacation" so that you can get focused on your priorities. There is no time to think of anything else—only the tasks that lie ahead.

As you pull into the parking garage, you begin to feel the adrenaline surge to which you have become addicted. You're off to start another day of "slaying the giants" and proving yourself to be a worthy adversary. As you sort through the details of the day, you block-out that nagging empty feeling that your life is really not making any difference in this world.

Unfortunately, this will be the best work has to offer so long as you shape your life around any agenda other than the "Kingdom Agenda"!

Jesus said, "Come to me, all you who are weary and burdened, and I will give you rest. Take my yoke upon you and learn from me, for I am gentle and humble in heart, and you will find rest for your souls. For my yoke is easy and my burden is light" (Matt. 11:28-30).

This book is written with the belief that there is a better way to work in this world. It is written with the belief that God is offering each one of us a dynamic opportunity to join Him as He actively works to carry out His Kingdom Agenda to redeem a lost and dying world.

This is a book about God's agenda for all people in the workplace. I challenge you to open your heart and mind to let God teach you how to "color outside the lines" of conventional thought and the patterns of human traditions. Our primary teacher and model is Jesus Christ, and our primary source will be the Bible.

Nothing less than a paradigm shift in your thinking will be asked of you and me. Jesus said, "If anyone would come after me, he must deny himself and take up his cross daily and follow me" (Luke 9:23). I believe God is calling each of us to work according to a radically different agenda than one that has been fashioned by the heart and mind of man! This paradigm shift in our thinking and living requires us to:

- abandon those priorities, principles, and practices of man that are in conflict with the revealed will of God
- abandon a self-focused life and become God-focused
- accept the sovereignty of God in our work
- adjust our lives to God's Kingdom Agenda
- allow God to mold our character into the likeness of Christ
- accept and depend on God's provision for our lives
- allow God to demonstrate His wisdom and power through us
- build redemptive relationships through which God shines light into the darkness
- trust that following God's agenda will ultimately bring God's blessing on our workplace

It is my prayer that this radical shift in your perspective will be like leaven in the lives of those who work around you. I pray that people will "see your good deeds and praise your Father in heaven" (Matt. 5:16). I pray that you will choose to work according to God's Kingdom Agenda!

Mike C. Rogers
January 1996

"In the beginning God created the heavens and the earth" (Gen. 1:1).

*E*ver since that first day, God has been on mission in His world. He created all that exists including the human race. It was a good and perfect creation until Adam and Eve sinned. Corruption and death entered the world God had created. Since that day "the whole creation has been groaning" for its redemption (Rom. 8:22).

God did not remove Himself from the scene. He has always been at work, and in Christ He was present reconciling the world to Himself. God is on a redemptive mission to draw sinful men and women back into a right relationship with Himself. He invites you to become involved in His mission, and He gave to you the ministry and message of reconciliation (2 Cor. 5:19). "We are therefore Christ's ambassadors" (2 Cor. 5:20).

God has not limited His work to church buildings. He is at work throughout His creation. He is at work in your workplace. He is on mission to redeem your workplace and the people who labor there. You are God's ambassador there. God desires to work through you and other believers to bring His kingdom rule in the hearts of those who work there. God has an agenda for your workplace. He has a plan for establishing His kingdom rule there. He has chosen you to be involved with Him in His Kingdom Agenda.

Many people, however, have difficulty living out their faith on the job. Consequently they come to the place of separating their faith and church experience from their work and their workplace. If you are one of these people, I have good news for you. God has a plan for your workplace. Better still: "It is God who works in you to will and to act according to his good purpose" (Phil. 2:13). Not only will God be working in you to want to do His will, but He also will be working in you to accomplish it!

The Seven Realities of Experiencing God
Experiencing God (a discipleship course by Henry Blackaby and Claude King) describes a relationship where God invites people to become involved with Him in His redemptive mission. Seven realities describe this relationship to God through which He works to accomplish His purposes in

the world. The following diagram illustrates the seven realities that are stated below it. Take a moment to read the seven realities and see the pattern God works through to invite you to be involved with Him in His work.

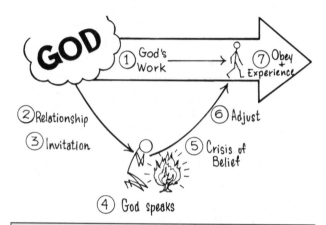

Seven Realities of Experiencing God
1. God is always at work around you.
2. God pursues a continuing love relationship with you that is real and personal.
3. God invites you to become involved with Him in His work.
4. God speaks by the Holy Spirit through the Bible, prayer, circumstances, and the church to reveal Himself, His purposes, and His ways.
5. God's invitation for you to join Him always leads you to a crisis of belief that requires faith and action.
6. You must make major adjustments in your life to join God in what He is doing.
7. You come to know God by experience as you obey Him and He accomplishes His work through you.

[Blackaby, Henry T. and Claude V. King, *Experiencing God: Knowing and Doing the Will of God*, (Nashville: LifeWay Press, 1990), 20. This discipleship study with leader's guide and other audiovisual supplements may be ordered by writing Customer Service, 127 Ninth Avenue, North, Nashville, TN 37234 or by calling 1-800-458-2772. *Used by permission.*]

If you have a saving relationship to God through Jesus Christ, God has called you to be on mission with Him. As you join Him in that mission, you experience Him working through you to accomplish His purposes in His mighty ways. Many people who have studied *Experiencing God* have experienced Him working mightily in church related ministries. Some still have had difficulty making application of these realities in their workplace.

Whether you have studied *Experiencing God* or not, *The Kingdom Agenda* is designed to help you live out your faith in your workplace. God wants to work through you to accomplish His purposes there. I pray that God will use *The Kingdom Agenda* as a tool to help you understand His purposes where you work. Then as you adjust your life to Him, His purposes, and His ways, you will experience God working redemptively through you in your workplace. If you have not studied *Experiencing God,* you may want to consider that discipleship study as a follow-up to *The Kingdom Agenda.*

Overview of The Kingdom Agenda

The Kingdom Agenda is a six-week discipleship course to help you join God in His redemptive mission in your workplace. During these six weeks you will study the following topics:

• **The Kingdom Agenda.** God rules over His kingdom. He has a Kingdom Agenda or plan to accomplish His purposes of world redemption. God has chosen to work through His people to accomplish His kingdom purposes. His Kingdom Agenda includes you and your workplace. He wants to work through you to accomplish His purposes in His ways for His glory.

• **The World's Agenda.** Because of sin-infected human nature, the world has a self-centered agenda or plan to accomplish worldly purposes everywhere. The world's agenda runs contrary to God's purposes for humanity. People who follow the world's agenda reject God's sovereignty, focus upon self, and attempt to satisfy their needs apart from God.

• **The Workplace God Intended.** God created the workplace where He and His workers work together. It is a place where He is present and His workers are aware of His presence. He is Sovereign and the workers are cooperative. God initiates work and His workers respond to God's initiative in obedience. The workplace God intended is a place where all God's purposes are accomplished and His kingdom rule is established.

• **The Workplace Sin Corrupted.** Because of sin, the workplace God intended was corrupted or spoiled. Workers denied God's rule. Their focus was on self. They depended on themselves for direction, resources, and success. Their actions became self-serving. As workers rejected God's involvement, the workplace became stressful, difficult, and less fruitful.

• **The Workplace Christ Restores.** Jesus Christ came to redeem sinful humanity and restore the sovereignty of God in the hearts of people. Jesus calls workers to deny self and follow Him as King. He calls workers to seek His kingdom first and trust Him for all other provisions. He seeks to restore the workplace to God's original intention where work is sacred and fruitful. In cooperation with Jesus, God's work is well fitted for you and the burden is light.

• **The Kingdom Worker.** Not every worker is suitable for Kingdom work. The Kingdom worker finds motivation in the love of Christ. He or she enters, remains in, and functions in a right relationship to the King (God) through faith. The Kingdom worker's character is shaped by God to reflect Christ. God provides everything the Kingdom worker needs.

• **The Kingdom Work.** God does not give jobs just so workers can earn a paycheck. God has a redemptive mission that He intends to accomplish through His workers. Every job has a Kingdom job description that reflects God's purposes in the context of work. The Kingdom worker has the opportunity and the assignment to join God in His work in the workplace. The Kingdom worker develops a prayer strategy to receive assignments and join God in His work. He or she builds redemptive relationships through which God works to reconcile people to Himself. The Kingdom work even brings about change in the social, moral, and ethical fabric of a workplace. The work is accomplished in such a way that God receives glory and His kingdom advances.

Learning Objectives

God is the only One who can accomplish anything of Kingdom value in you and your workplace. Without Him you can do nothing (John 15:4-5). He will be actively at work in you to bring His purposes to pass. He wants to bear fruit through your life. Here are some of the objectives God may have for you during this study:

• To understand the nature of the workplace God originally intended and demonstrate your determination to seek this ideal in your own workplace

• To understand how sin has corrupted the workplace and demonstrate your dissatisfaction with the world's agenda

- To understand how Christ restores the workplace and demonstrate your commitment to the Kingdom Agenda
- To understand the required nature of a kingdom worker and demonstrate your surrender to God's transformation of your own character into Christlikeness
- To understand your role in kingdom work and demonstrate your cooperation by joining God in His work in your workplace

In each of the objectives above you probably noticed the dual focus. The first part of each objective focuses on your understanding. I want you to develop a biblical understanding of work as God intended it. However, I don't want you to settle for understanding alone. God wants to bring about change in your workplace, and He wants to involve you. Consequently, the second part of each objective focuses on ways you can respond to what you are learning. My prayer is that you will join God in seeing His kingdom rule come to pass in your workplace and in your coworkers.

Using This Course

To gain the most from this study, I ask you to do two things:

1. Individual Study. Study the daily lessons for five days each week. Study only one lesson each day and allow God to assist you in applying Kingdom truths to your own work. Each lesson should take about 30 minutes. You may choose, however, to spend more time in personal prayer and meditation on Scripture. In each lesson you will encounter learning activities that begin like this:

➡ **Turn to page 16 and find the first learning activity in lesson 1.**

The learning activities begin with an arrow and indented boldface instructions. <u>Do not skip the learning activities</u>. They are designed to help you learn and apply what you learn. You not only want to know about God's agenda for your workplace, but you also will want to experience Him actively working in your workplace.

Each day you also will be given a Scripture verse for you to meditate on through the day. According to the Psalmist, God's Word *"is a lamp to my feet and a light for my path"* (Ps. 119:105). God's Word is filled with insight that will help you know how to live in a way that pleases Him and is true to His Kingdom Agenda for your work. These verses will give you instruction from God that will orient you to His Kingdom Agenda. You

may want to write out some of these verses on index cards to carry with you for review throughout the day.

At the end of each daily lesson, you will be encouraged to respond to the Lord in some way through prayer. You will find that prayer is not just an activity but a relationship with God. This is one way you stay connected to Jesus—*"the vine."* In the Kingdom Agenda, this kind of prayer relationship needs to become your primary work strategy.

Occasionaly a "For Further Study" section is included at the end of a lesson. This section is optional but may proved to be helpful as you examine the teaching of Scripture for guidance on your lifestyle and your work. As time permits, complete these sections or mark them for study later.

2. Small-Group Sharing. Once each week you should join with one or more believers in a time to share and discuss what God is saying to you about your profession or your workplace. You should try to spend about one hour sharing and praying together each week. This could happen during a lunch hour, before or after work, on a Saturday morning, a Sunday afternoon, or any other time that is most convenient. Your group could be:

❑ coworkers in your immediate workplace
❑ coworkers in your company or larger corporation
❑ Christians from your same line of work (for example: accountants, assembly line workers, lawyers, nurses, school teachers, truck drivers, bankers, salespersons, pastors, missionaries, and so forth)
❑ business persons who meet in a central location like a downtown church or the YMCA
❑ fellow church members
❑ a discipleship training group
❑ a home cell group
❑ or other

Whatever location or grouping you choose, keep the size of your sharing group small (six to eight). This will allow everyone to participate actively. If you do use this study for a larger number, divide into several smaller groups for more personal sharing. You may want to get several small groups together once or twice during the study to report on what God is saying and doing in their workplaces. If several groups are meeting in the same company or workplace, they will want to meet together at some point to share what God has been saying and doing. There also will be great value in praying together with the larger group for

God's agenda in the workplace.

Christian business owners may even want to consider offering this study during regular work hours. Christian managers, team members, committees, boards, and employees could work together to examine their workplace. By seeking God's help, these groups could identify ways their workplace may be functioning on the world's agenda. Under Christ's sovereign leadership, these groups then could join Him in restoring the workers and the workplace to God's original intention. What do you think might happen if whole companies or even multi-national corporations began to seek first the Kingdom Agenda for God's glory? Only God knows the vast potential of such workplaces.

Leadership

Select a leader or facilitator for your sharing time. This could be the same person for the entire study or it could be a different person each week. No separate leader's guide is provided. However, in the back of the book (beginning on p. 156) general suggestions are given for guiding your sharing time.

Following each week's lessons you will find a two-page outline for a "Kingdom Strategy Meeting." The facilitator can lead the discussion, sharing, and praying following the suggestions on these pages. You should feel free to adapt the suggestions to meet the specific work needs of your group. One primary role of the facilitator is to guide the group to seek the Lord and His counsel regarding the Kingdom Agenda for your respective workplaces.

Because members will need to complete the first week's lessons prior to your first strategy meeting, the facilitator will need to conduct an introductory session prior to your first official session. (See p. 158 for suggestions.)

The Role of the Church

The local church is the body of Christ functioning in the world. Christ's commission to the church was to go into all the world. This going is not just for missionaries and Tuesday night visitation. Imagine the impact for the Kingdom if every church member saw his workplace as his personal assignment to make disciples of every coworker. God wants every member functioning where He has placed them so that the whole body will be built up. Think of your church as a diplomatic corps with ambassadors to the high school, the hospital, the manufacturing plant, restaurants, government, the unemployment office, and every other workplace in your community.

- The church can assist by equipping every member to understand the Kingdom Agenda and by encouraging one another to join God in their respective workplaces.
- Pastors can preach sermons about application of Kingdom principles in the workplace.
- Study, discussion, and support groups can provide a forum for problem solving and decision making in Kingdom ways.
- Times of testimony can encourage believers and glorify God as "marketplace ministers" share the results of God's activity in the workplace.
- The church can commission teams of lay missionaries to carry the light of the gospel to the local factory (or any other business). See pages 159-160 for suggestions for a commissioning service.
- The members can function as a house of prayer and undergird lay missionaries in their work.

The ways are almost endless. Christ Himself is Head of your church. He can direct you to join Him in Kingdom purposes that I would never dream of. I challenge you to seek the Lord's directions regarding this course and do everything He desires.

Week 1 The Kingdom Workplace

A few years ago my wife, Debi, and I [Mike] served as missionaries in Caracas, Venezuela. I had to make a trip to the interior of the country. Military check-points were scattered across the country. Normally, I only had to slow down, and the guard would wave me through. Sometimes people were stopped and searched. I had seen whole families standing outside of their cars, helpless to do anything while the guards ransacked their cars.

After two days of travel, I had not been stopped once! Just fifty miles from my destination the guard motioned for me to stop. He checked all of my papers and examined the car. He then went into the gate house and returned with another guard. He "asked" if I would give his friend a ride to my destination. I said yes. You just didn't tell these guards no. I prayed silently as the guard got into the car with his machine gun at his side.

As I pulled away, Pablo asked me why I was in Venezuela. I began to share my testimony. I knew God was at work in this conversation. I glanced at him periodically. His tough military front slowly disappeared as the real person began to emerge.

Pablo said that someone had told him about Jesus Christ years before. He said that he believed Jesus Christ was the Son of God and that he should follow Him. I asked Pablo what was keeping him from giving his life to Christ. He answered, "I can't be a Christian and continue to be a military guard and do the things I have to do. This is all I know how to do. I know it is not right, but I must feed my family. There are no other jobs."

Pablo paused for a moment and with tears in his eyes he said, "I hope God will forgive me, but I can't be one thing and do another. It would not be fair to Christ. I hope one day I can give Him my whole life."

I was shocked by Pablo's honesty and convicted by his struggle to provide for his family. I told him how we must trust the Lord to provide. I explained that we are saved by God's grace through faith. It is not by our good works. But I knew I must not "sell" him a "cheap" gospel. His conviction about being faithful to Christ was from the Holy Spirit. I let him out of the car knowing that God had spoken to both of us. I prayed that one day He would choose to follow Christ.

In the United States Christians often compromise Christ's call to follow Him. They separate their "secular" work life from their faith. When pressured to do things which are out of God's will, they rationalize that it is "just business."

This poorly educated guard knew that to compromise God's call on his life would be to live a lie. He knew that with Christ as his Lord, he could not continue with "business as usual." He knew that he would have to set aside his own personal agenda and take up God's agenda.

OVERVIEW OF WEEK 1

This Week's Scripture-Memory Verse
"Seek first his kingdom and his righteousness, and all these things will be given to you as well" (Matt. 6:33).

This Week's Lessons
Day 1: God Is Sovereign
Day 2: Two Conflicting Agendas
Day 3: Three Workplaces
Day 4: The Kingdom Worker's "Key to Success"
Day 5: Four Facts About Kingdom Work

Summary Statements from Week 1
- God is a worker by nature. God was and is actively involved in the world He has created.
- He is above all in power, rule, and authority. God alone is the Supreme Ruler of the universe.
- The Kingdom of God is the sovereign reign of God in the heart of a believer.
- The world's agenda is man's attempt to live and work apart from the authority of a sovereign God.
- People who follow the world's agenda reject God's sovereignty, focus upon self, and attempt to satisfy their needs apart from God.
- We experience the Kingdom Agenda when we join Christ in a coworker relationship with God, where God is Sovereign and we are cooperative.
- God has a Kingdom Agenda for you and your workplace.
- The workplace God intended is a place where all God's purposes are accomplished and His kingdom rule is established. It is a place where God is the Sovereign Ruler.
- Jesus Christ came to redeem sinful humanity and restore the sovereignty of God in the hearts of people.
- You can do nothing of Kingdom value apart from God's working through you.
- Success in the Kingdom Agenda depends on a right relationship with God. He is the source of all our success and fruitfulness in Kingdom work.

IMPORTANT IDEAS

The workplace God intended is a place where:
1. God and His workers work together.
2. God is present and His workers are aware of His presence. The workers experience an intimate and personal love relationship with God.
3. God is Sovereign and the workers are cooperative.
4. God assigns work and His workers respond to God's initiative in obedience.

The workplace sin corrupted is a place where:
1. Workers reject God's sovereignty.
2. Workers focus upon themselves.
3. Workers attempt to satisfy their needs apart from God.

The workplace Christ restores is a place where :
1. God is Sovereign and His workers are cooperative and obedient.
2. God provides for His workers all that they need.
3. The work is well fitted and fruitful.

Four Facts About the Kingdom Work
Fact 1: God is present and working in your workplace.
Fact 2: God chooses to do His work through people.
Fact 3: God is able to accomplish His purposes.
Fact 4: When you join God and obey Him, you and others experience God in your workplace.

15

DAY 1   God Is Sovereign

Kingdom Agenda
"Seek first his kingdom and his righteousness, and all these things will be given to you as well" (Matt. 6:33).

➡ **Read the "Kingdom Agenda" in the margin. Pause for a moment of prayer. Ask the Lord to help you understand and commit yourself to seeking His Kingdom Agenda first in your life and work.**

As we begin our study of the Kingdom Agenda, I want us to go all the way back to the beginning of all creation. From the account of creation, I want us to understand these truths about God and His creation:
• God Is the Creator
• God's Original Creation Was Very Good
• God Is a Worker
• God Is Sovereign Over All Creation

God Is the Creator
➡ **Read the account of creation in Genesis 1 below and answer the questions that follow.**

In the beginning God created the heavens and the earth. Now the earth was formless and empty, darkness was over the surface of the deep, and the Spirit of God was hovering over the waters. And God said, "Let there be light," and there was light. (Gen. 1:1-3).

Here is a summary of what God created as recorded in Genesis 1:
Day 1: heaven and earth, waters, light, day and night (Gen. 1:1-5)
Day 2: sky (the heavens) above the earth (Gen. 1:6-8)
Day 3: land and seas separated, plants (vegitation) (Gen. 1:9-13)
Day 4: separate lights—sun, moon, stars (Gen. 1:14-19)
Day 5: water animals and birds (Gen. 1:20-23)
Day 6: land animals, man—male and female (Gen. 1:24-31).

"God saw all that he had made, and it was very good. And there was evening, and there was morning—the sixth day" (Gen. 1:31)

➡ **1. Who created the heavens, the earth, and everything in them?**

_____

2. What two words in Genesis 1:31 (above) describe the quality of God's creation? Circle them.

God's Creation Was Very Good
At the beginning of the universe, God was "hovering" above His new work. He carefully contemplated every step before He began. He was preparing to shape the world according to His best intentions. God was preparing the world as a home in which all humanity would live and work. This was truly a "labor of love" of the Creator for His creation. All the creative powers of God brought life and order to what had previously been chaos ("formless") and nothingness. Based on Genesis 1, God created the world and everything in it. When the Creator of the universe examined His creation, He declared that it

was "very good." One characteristic of God's activity in the world is that He always does what is best (most good!) in life. The world God originally created was very good.

God Is a Worker

In the account of creation we learn another very important fact: God is a worker by nature. God was and is actively involved in the world He has created.

➥ **Read Genesis 2:2-3 below and circle the word *work* each time it occurs.**

> *By the seventh day God had finished the work he had been doing; so on the seventh day he rested from all his work. And God blessed the seventh day and made it holy, because on it he rested from all the work of creating that he had done* (Gen. 2:2-3).

God was at work! It is His nature to work! He was and is proactively shaping His creation according to His own original intentions! Because God was the creator, He followed His own plans and purposes. He had a right to. It all belonged to Him.

God Is Sovereign

Creation sets the stage for God's sovereignty over all the world. That God is Sovereign means that He is above all in power, rule, and authority. God alone is the Supreme Ruler of the universe. He has the right to direct it's actions, work in it, and use it as He pleases. This is where the Kingdom comes in. As Sovereign Ruler, God is King.

➥ **3. Who alone has the right to rule over God's creation? Check one.**
❑ a. The person who can whip the others into submission can rule.
❑ b. The person who is most popular can rule.
❑ c. God the Creator has the right to rule.
❑ d. Other_____

What Is the Kingdom of God?

➥ **Read the following definition from W. E. Vine. Underline key words that define God's kingdom.**

> The Kingdom of God is (a) the sphere of God's rule, Ps. 22:28. . . . Since, however, this earth is the scene of universal rebellion against God, e.g., Luke 4:5,6 . . . the Kingdom of God is (b) the sphere in which, at any given time, His rule is acknowledged. God has not relinquished His sovereignty in the face of rebellion, demonic and human, but has declared His purpose to establish it . . . 1 Cor. 15:24,25 . . . God calls upon men everywhere without distinction of race or nationality, to submit voluntarily to His rule . . . When, hereafter, God asserts His rule universally, then the Kingdom will be in glory, that is, it will be manifest to all. (W. E. Vine, "Basileia" in An Expository Dictionary of New Testament Words, nd, p. 624.)

4. Write your own definition of "Kingdom of God:" The Kingdom of God is:

_____

_____

Sidebar

He is above all in power, rule, and authority. God alone is the supreme Ruler of the universe.

Psalm 22:2
"Dominion belongs to the LORD and he rules over the nations."

Luke 4:4,
"Jesus answered, 'It is written: "Man does not live on bread alone." '

"...And he [Satan] said to him, 'I will give you all their authority and splendor, for it has been given to me, and I can give it to anyone I want to.'"

1 Corinthians 15:24-2
"Then the end will come, when he hands over the kingdom to God the Father after he has destroyed all dominion, authority and power. For he must reign until he has put all his enemies under his feet."

The Kingdom of God is not a physical, territorial, political, or social establishment. Jesus said, "My kingdom is not of this world."

> **The Kingdom of God is the sovereign reign of God in the heart of a believer!**

We experience His Kingdom whenever we cooperate with the sovereign will of Almighty God. He is Sovereign in every aspect of our lives whether we acknowledge Him or not. We may work apart from Him and reject His sovereign presence, but God is still at work in our lives. The Kingdom of God is not limited to the church building either. The sovereign Kingdom of God extends to the boardroom, the laboratory, the classroom, the operating room, the waiting room! God is calling on people everywhere to submit to His sovereign rule over their lives—every aspect of their lives.

PRAYER STRATEGY
➡ **Take time to pray about the upcoming study and your relationship to God and His kingdom.**
- Open your heart to God and invite His Holy Spirit be your Teacher.
- Agree with God that He is Sovereign and decide now that you want to follow Him and please Him.
- Ask Him to show you His Kingdom Agenda for your workplace.
- Ask God to begin working in and through your life in such a way that your employer will see God at work—so God will be glorified through your life.
- Express any concerns or fears you have to the Lord. Ask Him to give you peace and direction so that His kingdom will come.

FOR FURTHER STUDY
➡ **Meditate on the following names of God and what they have to say about His sovereignty.**
- God Almighty (Ps. 80:7)
- God Most High (Gen. 14:18)
- KING OF KINGS (Rev. 19:16)
- King of the nations (Jer. 10:7)
- Lord of kings (Dan. 2:47)
- a Master in heaven (Col. 4:1)
- head of the church (Eph. 5:23)
- King of all the earth (Ps. 47:7)
- the only Ruler (1 Tim. 6:15)
- Chief Shepherd (1 Pet. 5:4)
- Great King (Ps. 48:2)
- Lawgiver and Judge (Jas. 4:12)
- our guide (Ps. 48:14)
- Lord of lords (1 Tim. 6:15)
- Lord of all the earth (Josh. 3:13)
- head of every man (1 Cor. 11:3)
- ruler of God's creation (Rev. 3:14)
- the Majesty in heaven (Heb. 1:3)
- Lord of heaven and earth (Matt. 11:25)
- Most High over all the earth (Ps. 83:18)
- ruler of the kings of the earth (Rev. 1:5)
- our only Sovereign and Lord (Jude 1:4)
- great King over all the earth (Ps. 47:2)
- him who sits on the throne (Rev. 5:13)
- the great King above all gods (Ps. 95:3)
- commander of the Lord's army (Josh. 5:15)
- head over every power and authority (Col. 2:10
- leader and commander of the peoples (Isa. 55:4)
- God over all the kingdoms of the earth (2 Kings 19:15)

DAY 2 Two Conflicting Agendas

Kingdom Agenda

"Do not conform any longer to the pattern of this world, but be transformed by the renewing of your mind. Then you will be able to test and approve what God's will is—his good, pleasing and perfect will" (Rom. 12:1-2).

➡ **Read the "Kingdom Agenda" in the margin. Pause for a moment of prayer. Ask the Lord to help you understand and live by that truth today. Ask Him to renew your mind to be like the mind of Christ.**

An *agenda* is a plan to accomplish a certain objective. We live in a world of agendas. There is the Republican agenda, the Democratic agenda, the gay agenda, the environmental agenda, and others. These popular plans reflect the bias of members who want to see their plans bring about change. One consistent attitude can be seen in each group's agenda. It is the idea that "I know what is best for the world I live in!" Shaped by self-interest, all of these agendas and many more, could be gathered together and classified under one simple term: the world's agenda!

The World's Agenda

What is the world's agenda? It is man's attempt to live and work apart from the authority of a sovereign God. It is man's attempt to find answers to his problems within himself rather than seeking to know God's will. The world's agenda is driven by human nature and is focused on fulfilling our needs apart from God.

Because of sin-infected human nature, the world has a self-centered agenda or plan to accomplish worldly purposes everywhere. The world's agenda runs contrary to God's purposes for humanity. People who follow the world's agenda reject God's sovereignty, focus upon self, and attempt to satisfy their needs apart from God.

1 John 2:15-1

"Do not love the world or anything in the world. If anyone loves the world, the love of the Father is not in him. For everything in the world—the cravings of sinful man, the lust of his eyes and the boasting of what he has and does—comes not from the Father but from the world. The world and its desires pass away, but the man who does the will of God lives forever"

➡ **1. Read 1 John 2:15-17 in the margin. Underline three characteristics of the world's agenda that do not come from God.** *"For everything in the world . . . "*

Cravings, lust, and boasting about things and accomplishments—all three of these characteristics of the world's agenda are focused upon self. They also reflect a life that is driven by human nature. In no way do they reflect a heart that is surrendered to a sovereign God! Most people in the workplace operate from the world's agenda. In fact, most of the systems that shape our contemporary marketplace are influenced and dominated by human nature. This was not what God intended when He created us and the world in which we work. In fact the writer of Proverbs says, *"There is a way that seems right to a man, but in the end it leads to death"* (Prov. 14:12). The world's agenda seems right, but it is dead wrong.

➡ **2. Which of the following best describes the world's agenda? Check one.**
   ❑ a. Living for God according to His wishes and depending on His resources.
   ❑ b. Living for self according to my own wishes and depending on my own resources.

The Kingdom Agenda

God rules over His kingdom. He has a Kingdom Agenda or plan to accomplish His purposes of world redemption. God has chosen to work through

His people to accomplish His kingdom purposes. His Kingdom Agenda includes you and your workplace. He wants to work through you to accomplish His purposes in His ways for His glory. The answer to #2 is "b."

God never intended for the workplace to be shaped and dominated by human nature. From the very beginning of time, God created us for a coworker relationship with Him. In this relationship He is Sovereign (has all authority) and we are cooperative or obedient. This agenda is born out of a love relationship with God that is established through our faith in and fellowship with His Son, Jesus Christ. We experience the Kingdom Agenda when we join Christ in a coworker relationship with God, where God is sovereign and we are cooperative.

➡ **3. Which of the following best describes the Kingdom Agenda? Check one.**
  ❑ a. Living for God according to His wishes and depending on His resources.
  ❑ b. Living for self according to my own wishes and depending on my own resources.

The Kingdom Agenda is not about a set of rules or some long list of do's and don'ts. Rather, it is about a relationship with God. When Jesus said: *"I am the way and the truth and the life. No one comes to the Father except through me"* (John 14:6), He was inviting us to trust His leadership in our daily lives as well as all eternity. The answer to #3 is "a."

Romans 12:2
"Do not conform any longer to the pattern of this world, but be transformed by the renewing of your mind. Then you will be able to test and approve what God's will is—his good, pleasing and perfect will."

➡ **Read Romans 12:2 in the margin and answer the following questions.**
  4. What are you NOT to do to the pattern of the world (the world's agenda)?

"Do not _____ any longer to the pattern of this world."
  5. What three words describe God's will (the Kingdom Agenda)?

_____

The Kingdom Agenda is opposite of the world's agenda in many ways. God does not want you to be shaped and guided by or conformed to the world's agenda. Instead He wants you have a renewed mind that knows and follows His Kingdom Agenda that is good, pleasing, and perfect.

Secular and Sacred
Why is the Kingdom of God so important to your life in the workplace? We often have seen the activity and work of God as something that happens only at church or in church-related projects. We have divided the world in which we live into two arenas: *secular* (of the world) and *sacred* (related to God). Christians have been blinded to the reality of God in the secular part of their lives.

Somehow, we have decided that only a select group of called out individuals are truly about "the Father's business." Unless you are a preacher, missionary, denominational worker, or serving on a church staff, you would not be considered by most Christians as a minister or in "the ministry." That God would actually call or assign a person to a position of a brick layer, traffic cop, janitor, lawyer, doctor, or teacher is not our way of thinking. We think and act as though "secular" work is not significant to God. That needs to change. God is very interested in your work—whatever it is. Do you remember that His own Son Jesus probably worked as a carpenter until He was about 30 years old? God has a Kingdom Agenda for you and your workplace!

➥ **6. Would you like to know God's agenda for your workplace?**
❑ YES
❑ NO
❑ I don't think God has an agenda for my workplace.

I hope you checked yes. He does have an agenda for you and your workplace whether you can see it or not. He wants you to move to active duty in the Kingdom. That would please Him.

PRAYER STRATEGY
➥ **Take time now to pray. Let God begin to renew your mind.**
• Ask God to help you begin to see and understand the world's agenda that tries to influence you.
• Give God permission (as needed) to transform your thinking and renew your mind regarding your understanding of your work and workplace.
• Ask God to help you know His will for your work and workplace.

DAY 3   Three Workplaces

Kingdom Agenda

"Jesus began to preach, 'Repent, for the kingdom of heaven is near' " (Matt. 4:17).

➡ **Read the "Kingdom Agenda" in the margin. Pause for a moment of prayer. Ask the Lord to help you understand what repentance might require in your life.**

During the next three weeks we are going to be looking in detail at three workplaces:
- Week 2: The Workplace that God Intended
- Week 3: The Workplace Sin Corrupted
- Week 4: The Workplace Christ Restores

Today, I want us to take a quick overview of these three workplaces. I want you to begin to see from God's viewpoint what your workplace ought to look like. I want you to begin to see how sin may have corrupted your workplace. And finally, I want you to understand how God will involve you with Christ in redeeming and restoring your workplace to God's original intention. That is a challenge that we cannot accomplish alone. Let's turn our hearts to the Lord.

➡ **Stop to pray.**
- Ask God to fill you with His Holy Spirit and give you understanding of spiritual truths related to your work.
- Seeing Christ redeem your workplace through you may seem impossible. Confess to the Lord your concerns and ask Him to enable you to believe Him.
- Ask Him to increase your faith.

The Workplace God Intended

1. God and His workers work together.
2. God is present and His workers are aware of His presence.
3. God is Sovereign and the workers are cooperative.
4. God assigns work and His workers respond to God's initiative in obedience.

The Workplace God Intended

We will look in detail at the workplace God intended in week 2. Right now, let's take a quick look at the original workplace.

When God created the world, everything He created was *very good.* God gave Adam (the first man) work to do in the Garden of Eden: *"The LORD God took the man and put him in the Garden of Eden to work it and take care of it"* (Gen. 2:15). God gave Adam an assignment to be a gardener, a farmer, an agriculturist. We would call that a "secular" job. But it was a holy and sacred assignment because it was a God-given assignment.

From this original workplace we are going to learn that God intended for the workplace to be a place where:
- God and His workers work together.
- God is present and His workers are aware of His presence. The workers experience an intimate and personal love relationship with God.
- God is Sovereign and the workers are cooperative.
- God assigns work and His workers respond to God's initiative in obedience.

The workplace God intended is a place where all God's purposes are accomplished and His kingdom rule is established. It is a place where God is the Sovereign Ruler.

➡ **1. What is one of the workplaces we will study?**

The Workplace _____

2. What characteristics of God are important in the workplace God intended?

The Workplace Sin Corrupted

1. Workers reject God's sovereignty.
2. Workers focus upon themselves.
3. Workers attempt to satisfy their needs apart from God.

The Workplace Sin Corrupted

In the workplace God intended, He is present and He is Sovereign. He has a right to rule over all His creation. God had given Adam and Eve some specific guidelines or rules for living in the garden. He expected obedience.

Because of sin, the workplace God intended was corrupted or spoiled. His workers denied God's rule and followed the suggestions of Satan and their own selfish desires. God judged them and ordered a severe penalty for their disobedience:

> *Cursed is the ground because of you; through painful toil you will eat of it all the days of your life. It will produce thorns and thistles for you, and you will eat the plants of the field. By the sweat of your brow you will eat your food until you return to the ground, since from it you were taken; for dust you are and to dust you will return* (Gen. 3:17-19).

Because of sin, work became difficult, painful, and less fruitful. God promised hardships and resistance throughout one's work life. Because of this penalty, many of the problems you encounter in your workplace are the direct result of sin. The workplace sin corrupted is a place where . . .

1. Workers reject God's sovereignty.
2. Workers focus upon themselves.
3. Workers attempt to satisfy their needs apart from God.

It is a workplace ruled by human nature. Workers focus on self and become self-serving. Workers depend on themselves and human resources rather than on God.

➡ **3. What is a second workplace we will study?**
The Workplace God Intended

The Workplace _____
4. Review the description of this workplace above and write one word or phrase that describes one essential characteristic.

The Workplace Christ Restores

The workplace sin corrupted is human-centered, selfish, difficult, and less fruitful. Jesus Christ came to redeem sinful humanity and restore the sovereignty of God in the hearts of people.

➡ **5. Read again the "Kingdom Agenda" verse at the beginning of today's lesson (p. 22.) What did Jesus call people to do?**

Luke 9:23
"If anyone would come after me, he must deny himself and take up his cross daily and follow me."

Matthew 6:3
"Seek first his kingdom and his righteousness, and all these things will be given to you as well."

Jesus calls people to repent. That means "turn from their self-centered and sinful ways to live under God's rule—His sovereignty, His Kingdom Agenda." Jesus calls workers to deny self and follow Him as King (see Luke 9:23). He calls workers to seek His Kingdom first and trust Him for all other provisions (see Matt. 6:33). Jesus Christ seeks to restore the workplace to

Matthew 11:28-30

"Come to me, all you who are weary and burdened, and I will give you rest. Take my yoke upon you and learn from me, for I am gentle and humble in heart, and you will find rest for your souls. For my yoke is easy and my burden is light."

The Workplace Christ Restores

1. God is sovereign and His workers are cooperative and obedient.
2. God provides for His workers all that they need.
3. The work is well fitted and fruitful!

God's original intention where work is sacred and fruitful. In cooperation with Jesus the work is well fitted and the burden is light (see Matt. 11:29-30).

➥ **6. What is a third workplace we will study?**

The Workplace God Intended

The Workplace Sin Corrupted

The Workplace _____

7. Review the description of this workplace above and write one word or phrase that describes one essential characteristic.

_____

The workplace Christ restores is one where:

1. God is sovereign and His workers are cooperative and obedient.
2. God provides for His workers all that they need.
3. The work is well fitted and fruitful!

Wouldn't you like to work in that kind of setting?

PRAYER STRATEGY

➥ **Take time now to pray. Begin to think about your workplace and what God may want to do there.**

- Ask God to begin showing you ways sin has corrupted your workplace.
- Ask the Holy Spirit to convict you of any sin you are guilty of in your workplace. Confess and seek forgiveness for anything He reveals. [This may require that you also make things right with your employer or a fellow employee.]
- Ask God to begin giving you His vision of what your workplace could look like with Christ in charge. Ask the Lord, "What would Jesus do if He were working in my place?"
- Read again Matthew 11:28-30 in the margin. Are you weary? Tell the Lord about it. Agree to get into the yoke with Jesus. Begin to learn His ways so your work will be well fitted and the burdens light.

DAY 4 The Kingdom Worker's "Key to Success"

Kingdom Agenda
"I tell you the truth, no one can see the Kingdom of God unless he is born again" (John 3:3).

➡ **Read the "Kingdom Agenda" in the margin. Pause for a moment of prayer. Ask the Lord to help you understand what it means to be born again.**

After you have spent time learning about the three workplaces in weeks 2-4, we will turn our focus to the Kingdom worker in week 5. You will find that God has expectations of a Kingdom worker that is pleasing to Him. Today, I want you to look at one special "key to success" in the Kingdom.

Traits for Worldly Success
If you are like many people, you are inspired when you hear success stories about people who have worked their way from the mail room to the boardroom. You may envy the one who didn't even go to college and has now built a multi-million dollar company. Business people buy their books and go to their seminars to learn the secrets of their success. When people tell their success stories about work, they seem to focus primarily upon important habits, personality traits, skills, ideas that motivate, and so forth.

➡ **1. Below is a list of some commonly stated "keys for success" in the workplace. Check those you have heard used to describe how someone achieved success.**

❏ wisdom	❏ proactive	❏ results oriented
❏ courage	❏ good luck	❏ effective planner
❏ empathy	❏ ingenious	❏ ordered priorities
❏ loyalty	❏ initiative	❏ personal integrity
❏ creative	❏ disciplined	❏ skilled negotiator
❏ decisive	❏ intentional	❏ ability to motivate
❏ flexible	❏ trustworthy	❏ focused on excellence
❏ aggressive	❏ common sense	❏ clear mission statement
❏ assertive	❏ perseverance	❏ persuasive communicator
❏ brilliant	❏ clear life goals	❏ knows the right people
❏ energetic	❏ person of vision	❏ good time manager

These are the kinds of traits that the world looks to for success. One most important trait is missing from the list above. Let's look at the story of Joseph to identify that missing trait.

Joseph: From Slave to Ruler
Joseph was a great-grandson of Abraham. His father Jacob favored him far beyond his 11 brothers. Fourteen chapters of the Bible (Gen. 37-50) are devoted to telling Joseph's success story.

Joseph's brothers were very jealous of Joseph because their father (Jacob) gave him special treatment. Joseph made them angry by telling them about two of his dreams. In his dreams the symbols for his father, mother, and brothers all bowed down to him. Before long his "career" was on a "roller-coaster ride."

One day in the desert, Joseph's brothers started to kill him, but instead sold him as a slave to a passing caravan on its way to Egypt. In Egypt he was sold to Potiphar, the captain of Pharoah's guard. From favored son, he hit the bottom as a common slave. However, he didn't stay down long.

➡ **Read the following Scripture and look for the "key" to Joseph's success. Then answer the questions that follow.**

The LORD was with Joseph and he prospered, and he lived in the house of his Egyptian master. When his master saw that the LORD was with him and that the LORD gave him success in everything he did, Joseph found favor in his eyes and became his attendant. Potiphar put him in charge of his household, and he entrusted to his care everything he owned. From the time he put him in charge of his household and of all that he owned, the LORD blessed the household of the Egyptian because of Joseph. The blessing of the LORD was on everything Potiphar had, both in the house and in the field. So he left in Joseph's care everything he had; with Joseph in charge (Gen. 39:2-6)

2. What was the source or the reason for Joseph's success? Check one:
❑ a. his management skills
❑ b. his education
❑ c. his determination and hard work
❑ d. The Lord was with Joseph and gave him success

3. What effect did Joseph's relationship with the Lord have on his boss's home and business? Check one:
❑ a. Potiphar's home and business suffered loss because of Joseph's commitments to the Lord.
❑ b. Potiphar's home and business were greatly blessed because of Joseph's relationship with the Lord.

Joseph's success was not based on anything Joseph had to offer like skills, education, or hard work. His success was based on the fact that God was with Joseph and blessed everything Joseph did. Consequently, Potiphar's home and business were blessed by the Lord (and he was a pagan who did not know the Lord). Joseph's career was on the way up!

God was with Joseph and blessed everything Joseph did.

Then he hit bottom again. Joseph refused to sleep with the boss's wife. He was thrown into prison when the rejected wife falsely accused him of rape. From a human perspective, Joseph's integrity didn't count for much. Had God let him down? No. God used every turn of events for Kingdom purposes. Even though he was in prison for 13 years, he didn't stay on the bottom.

God used every turn of events for Kingdom purposes.

➡ **Read the following Scripture and look for the next "key" to Joseph's success. Then answer the questions that follow.**

While Joseph was there in the prison, the LORD was with him; he showed him kindness and granted him favor in the eyes of the prison warden. So the warden put Joseph in charge of all those held in the prison, and he was made responsible for all that was done there. The warden paid no attention to anything under Joseph's care, because the LORD was with Joseph and gave him success in whatever he did (Gen. 39:20-23).

4. How did Joseph gain the favor of his prison "boss" (warden)? Check one:
❑ a. The Lord gave Joseph favor in the eyes of the warden.
❑ b. Joseph's good behavior finally got him a break.
❑ c. Potiphar gave him a good reference and recommended Joseph's promotion.

5. Was the prison better off or worse off because of Joseph's faithfulness to the Lord? ❏ better off ❏ worse off

Joseph's favor with the warden and success in prison was due to God's involvement in his life. God blessed Joseph and gave him success in everything he did. Because God blessed Joseph's work, the prison was a much better place. Joseph's final rise to the top came as he interpreted some dreams correctly—first for two prisoners and then for Pharoah himself.

Even in the greatest promotion of his career, Joseph still realized God was his source of success. To the two prisoners Joseph said, *"Do not interpretations belong to God?"* (Gen. 40:8). Joseph interpreted their dreams, and both dreams came true just as he said they would.

When Pharoah had a dream, no one could interpret it for him. Then one of these former prisoners remembered Joseph and recommended his skill to Pharoah. Pharoah sent for Joseph and said, *"I had a dream, and no one can interpret it. But I have heard it said of you that when you hear a dream you can interpret it"* (Gen. 41:15).

➡ **6. How do you think you would have responded if you were Joseph? I would say . . . (check one)**
❏ a. "Yes, I can do that."
❏ b. "No, I can't do that. Only God can do that."

Most of us have too much pride to tell someone important that we can't do something, especially if we have been successful in that way in the past. Joseph was brutally honest about his abilities. He said, *"I cannot do it, . . . but God will give Pharaoh the answer he desires"* (Gen. 41:16). When God did give Pharoah an interpretation through Joseph, Joseph got the promotion of a lifetime. Pharoah said:

> *"Can we find anyone like this man, one in whom is the spirit of God?"*
> *Then Pharaoh said to Joseph, "Since God has made all this known to you, there is no one so discerning and wise as you. You shall be in charge of my palace, and all my people are to submit to your orders. Only with respect to the throne will I be greater than you."*
> *So Pharaoh said to Joseph, "I hereby put you in charge of the whole land of Egypt"* (Gen. 41:38-41).

Did you notice that even this pagan Pharoah recognized the reason for Joseph's skill, wisdom, and discernment? He realized that God was with Joseph and was the source of Joseph's success.

The "Key to Success"

No one would deny that Joseph was successful. But before our study is over, you will understand that success in God's kingdom may be defined very differently than it is by the world's standards. The important lesson for today is that success in the Kingdom Agenda depends on a right relationship with God. He is the source of all our success and fruitfulness in Kingdom work. This is how Jesus describes the "key to success" in the Kingdom:

Success in the Kingdom Agenda depends on a right relationship with God.

> *"Remain in me, and I will remain in you. No branch can bear fruit by itself; it must remain in the vine. Neither can you bear fruit unless you remain in me.*

"I am the vine; you are the branches. If a man remains in me and I in him, he will bear much fruit; apart from me you can do nothing" (John 15:4-5).

You can do nothing of Kingdom value apart from God's work through you.

When you are connected to God, He makes your life fruitful—very fruitful.

An important lesson in the Kingdom Agenda is that you can do nothing of Kingdom value apart from God's work through you. God wants a personal love relationship with you. When you are connected to Him, He makes your life fruitful—very fruitful.

PRAYER STRATEGY

➡ **Take time now to pray. Remember God is King of His kingdom. You may want to address Him as "King."**
- Agree with God that you can do nothing of Kingdom value apart from Him.
- Ask Him to help you develop a close and personal love relationship with Him so that He can bear fruit through your life.
- Give God permission to mold and shape your life so He can work through you for Kingdom purposes in your workplace.

FOR FURTHER STUDY

➡ **In the column on the left are some Scriptures describing the natural human nature that is bent toward sin. In the right column are Scriptures describing the traits of a person who has been born again by the Spirit of God. As you read the Scriptures, see which side best describes you. Talk to the Lord about your findings.**

World's Ways

"The acts of the sinful nature are obvious: sexual immorality, impurity and debauchery; idolatry and witchcraft; hatred, discord, jealousy, fits of rage, selfish ambition, dissensions, factions and envy; drunkenness, orgies, and the like. I warn you, as I did before, that those who live like this will not inherit the kingdom of God" (Gal. 5:19-21).

"Those who live according to the sinful nature have their minds set on what that nature desires. . . The mind of sinful man is death. . . the sinful mind is hostile to God. It does not submit to God's law, nor can it do so. Those controlled by the sinful nature cannot please God. . . . And if anyone does not have the Spirit of Christ, he does not belong to Christ" (Rom. 8:5-9).

Kingdom's Ways

"The fruit of the Spirit is love, joy, peace, patience, kindness, goodness, faithfulness, gentleness and self-control. Against such things there is no law. Those who belong to Christ Jesus have crucified the sinful nature with its passions and desires" (Gal. 5:22-24).

"Those who live in accordance with the Spirit have their minds set on what the Spirit desires. . . . the mind controlled by the Spirit is life and peace. . . . You, however, are controlled not by the sinful nature but by the Spirit, if the Spirit of God lives in you. . . . But if Christ is in you, your body is dead because of sin, yet your spirit is alive because of righteousness" (Rom. 8:5-6,9-10).

DAY 5 Four Facts About Kingdom Work

Kingdom Agenda

"I tell you the truth, the Son can do nothing by himself; he can do only what he sees his Father doing, because whatever the Father does the Son also does. For the Father loves the Son and shows him all he does" (John 5:19-20).

➡ **Read the "Kingdom Agenda" in the margin. Pause for a moment of prayer. Ask the Lord to help you understand how Jesus came to know the will of His Father and joined Him in His work.**

Yesterday we took a look at the up-and-down career of Joseph. He went from being a slave to ruling over all Egypt. Today we turn our focus from Kingdom worker to Kingdom work. First let's review briefly.

➡ **1. Which of the following best describes the "key to success" for a Kingdom worker? Check one.**
  ❏ a. Living by the right principles and practicing right habits for success.
  ❏ b. Living in a right relationship with God who is present and working through me.
  ❏ c. Having a vision and doing whatever it takes to reach my personal goals.

Principles and habits can be important in a workplace. A vision, personal goals, and hard work may also help you "get ahead." In fact you may be able to achieve great success in the world's eyes by working this way. Principles, habits, visions, and goals can be valuable in the Kingdom if they are God-given and God-directed. But if God Himself is not present and actively involved, they will not accomplish anything that is of value to God. The "key to success" in God's kingdom is a right relationship with God—the King. Remember that apart from Him you can do nothing of Kingdom value. (See John 15:5.)

Joseph's life is a good example of living by the Kingdom Agenda. Joseph had principles and healthy and productive work habits. He even had two God-given dreams to let him know he would one day be a ruler—what a vision! But none of those alone would have meant much without God's active involvement.

John 15:5

"I am the vine; you are the branches. If a man remains in me and I in him, he will bear much fruit; apart from me you can do nothing."

Jesus' Kingdom Work

In week 6 we are going to look in more detail at the Kingdom work. You will seek God's guidance as you develop a Kingdom job description for your work. First, I want you to see how Jesus went about His kingdom work.

➡ **Read John 5:17,19-20 and answer the following questions:**

2. Who is always at His work? _____

3. How much can the Son do by Himself? _____

4. The Son can only do what?

_____

5. Why does the Father show the Son what He is doing?

_____

John 5:17,19-20

"My Father is always at his work to this very day, and I, too, am working. . . .

I tell you the truth, the Son can do nothing by himself; he can do only what he sees his Father doing, because whatever the Father does the Son also does. For the Father loves the Son and shows him all he does."

In Scripture God reveals Himself as Father, Son, and Holy Spirit; yet, He is One. God is so great, He is beyond our understanding. Rather than trying to figure out the Trinity (three in one), just focus on what Jesus had to say about His work. God the Father is always at work in His world (Jn. 5:17). The Father sent His Son Jesus into the world with an assignment for redeeming a lost world.

Jesus described His approach to Kingdom work in John 5:19-20. Jesus realized that He did not take the initiative. He could not accomplish the work by Himself. He watched to see where the Father was working, and that is what He did also. Because of love, the Father showed Jesus where He was working so Jesus could be involved! As a Christian, you have been adopted into God's family. You, too, are children (sons and daughters) of God. Because of love, God will reveal where He is working when He wants you involved.

Today, I want you to understand four facts about the Kingdom work. Once more, we will look at the story of Joseph to see how each fact is illustrated in his work experience. Here are the facts we will examine today:

> **God will reveal where He is working when He wants you involved.**

Four Facts About the Kingdom Work
Fact 1: God is present and working in your workplace.
Fact 2: God chooses to do His work through people.
Fact 3: God is able to accomplish His purposes.
Fact 4: When you join God and obey Him, you and others experience God in your workplace.

Fact 1: God Is Present and Working in Your Workplace.
Throughout the Bible we see God actively working in and around people. God is actively working in His world. You may tend to think of God's activity only when "good" things happen such as a financial windfall, a promotion, or a physical healing. The Bible also reveals God at work in people's lives building character, training and disciplining their lives, guiding their destiny, influencing the world through them, and shaping history. God is always present, and He is actively working whether you recognize His work or not.

> **God is actively working whether you recognize His work or not.**

Joseph was aware of God's presence early in life when he received two dreams from God about his future. When Joseph was sold as a slave and followed along behind some stinking camels in a caravan to Egypt, he had no idea that God was sending him to Egypt so that his family could be saved. He became more aware of God's presence and activity in his work for Potiphar and in the jail. Though he didn't always understand, Joseph was willing to be a coworker with God in every up and down in his career. Joseph trusted God even when he didn't understand. God knew that, in just a few years, there would be a life-threatening drought and famine that could cause His people to perish. Joseph was destined to become a coworker with God as "Prime Minister" of Egypt.

> **Joseph trusted God even when he didn't understand.**

You will face times in your life and work where you may not see or understand how God is at work. In those times you must trust in the fact that God is present and He is at work.

➤ **6. What is one fact about Kingdom work?**

1. _____
2. God chooses to do His work through people.
3. God is able to accomplish His purposes.
4. When you join God and obey Him, you and others experience God.

Fact 2: God Chooses to Do His Work Through People.
Though we cannot understand why He does it, God chooses to do His work through people. Some have very prominent roles like the Apostle Paul who started churches and wrote much of the New Testament. Others, like Aquila and Priscilla, seem much less prominent. They were tentmakers who worked with Paul and helped train Apollos.

We do not choose our own assignments.

Who God chooses for any given job is solely His decision. We do not choose our own assignments. He is Sovereign Ruler, and He takes the initiative to accomplish His work. As God's coworkers (servants), we follow His initiative and join in His work. Of the twelve sons of Jacob, God chose Joseph to send on assignment to Egypt.

➡ **7. What is the second fact about Kingdom work?**
1. God is present and working.

2. _____
3. God is able to accomplish His purposes.
4. When you join God and obey Him, you and others experience God.

Fact 3: God Is Able to Accomplish His Purposes
God is Sovereign, and He is all powerful. He can accomplish what He purposes to do, regardless of the opposition of people or our enemy, Satan. Here is how Isaiah described His power:

This is the plan determined for the whole world; this is the hand stretched out over all nations. For the LORD Almighty has purposed, and who can thwart him? His hand is stretched out, and who can turn it back? (Isa. 14:26-27).

Joseph's brothers decided to sell him as a slave, but God used that to get him to Egypt. Potiphar's wife tried to seduce Joseph. When he refused, she got him thrown into prison. But God used the prison experience to connect Joseph with Pharaoh's butler. God then worked through the butler to get Joseph an audience with the Pharaoh. God accomplished His purposes in spite of the actions and opposition of others. Here is how Joseph stated it to his brothers:

God accomplished His purposes in spite of the actions and opposition of others.

"God sent me ahead of you to preserve for you a remnant on earth and to save your lives by a great deliverance.
"So then, it was not you who sent me here, but God" (Gen. 45:7-8)
"You intended to harm me, but God intended it for good to accomplish what is now being done, the saving of many lives" (Gen. 50:20).

Joseph accepted God's sovereignty over His life and was faithful even in difficult circumstances. He later understood that God was able to accomplish His purposes, even when people seem to oppose His work.

Being a Christian in the "real world" is not easy. You will run into situations that call you to respond differently than most people in the world would respond. When your value system, priorities, and motives are shaped by Christ, you may find yourself at odds with the world's agenda where you work. Remember that God is the one who can accomplish His work where you are. *"In all things God works for the good of those who love him, who have been called according to his purpose"* (Rom. 8:28).

➡ **8. What is the third fact about Kingdom work?**
1. God is present and working.
2. God chooses to do His work through people.

3. _____

4. When you join God and obey Him, you and others experience God.

Fact 4: When You Join God and Obey Him, You and Others Experience God in Your Workplace.

One final fact that you can always count on in kingdom work is: When you join God and obey Him, He reveals Himself to you and those around you. God wants to reveal Himself to a watching world. He often chooses the little and the weak things of the world, so His power and presence is seen clearly (see 1 Cor. 1:27-29). You cannot boast about what you have done. You can merely testify to what you have seen and experienced God do—and those watching will know it is God's work.

Sometimes the ones who are closest to us are the ones who hurt us the deepest. Joseph had a very good reason to seek revenge on his brothers, but he didn't! Why not? He knew that God had another agenda in mind for his life. Joseph, all Egypt, and even his own family experienced God working to save many. Joseph so experienced God's power that he had the capacity to forgive his brothers. All the way through Joseph's experience people were experiencing God. Potiphar, the jailer, the butler, and Pharaoh all saw God at work in and through Joseph.

➡ **9. What is the fourth fact about Kingdom work?**
1. God is present and working.
2. God chooses to do His work through people.
3. God is able to accomplish His purposes.

4. _____

_____

1 Corinthians 1:27-29
"God chose the foolish things of the world to shame the wise; God chose the weak things of the world to shame the strong. He chose the lowly things of this world and the despised things — and the things that are not — to nullify the things that are, so that no one may boast before him."

PRAYER STRATEGY
➡ **Take time now to pray and seek to know God's activity around your life.**
- Ask God to open your spiritual eyes to see where He is at work around you.
- Ask God to give you understanding about past experiences that reveal what God has been doing in and around your life.
- If you are facing difficulties, opposition, or hardships at work, ask God to give you understanding about what He wants to do through those experiences.
- If people have hurt you, begin asking God for grace to forgive them. Ask God to use the experience for your good.

Notes

FOR FURTHER STUDY

➡ **Meditate on the following Scriptures and ask the Lord how these may apply to your workplace. Make notes to yourself in the margin.**

Proverbs 2:3-6 • *If you call out for insight and cry aloud for understanding, and if you look for it as for silver and search for it as for hidden treasure, then you will understand the fear of the LORD and find the knowledge of God. For the LORD gives wisdom, and from his mouth come knowledge and understanding.*

Proverbs 3:9-10 • *Honor the LORD with your wealth, with the firstfruits of all your crops; then your barns will be filled to overflowing, and your vats will brim over with new wine.*

Proverbs 3:27-28 • *Do not withhold good from those who deserve it, when it is in your power to act. Do not say to your neighbor, "Come back later; I'll give it tomorrow" —when you now have it with you.*

Proverbs 11:24-25 • *One man gives freely, yet gains even more; another withholds unduly, but comes to poverty. A generous man will prosper; he who refreshes others will himself be refreshed.*

Proverbs 11:28 • *Whoever trusts in his riches will fall, but the righteous will thrive like a green leaf.*

Proverbs 14:23 • *All hard work brings a profit, but mere talk leads only to poverty.*

Proverbs 14:31 • *He who oppresses the poor shows contempt for their Maker, but whoever is kind to the needy honors God.*

Proverbs 15:16-17 • *Better a little with the fear of the LORD than great wealth with turmoil. Better a meal of vegetables where there is love than a fattened calf with hatred.*

Proverbs 16:3-4 • *Commit to the LORD whatever you do, and your plans will succeed. The LORD works out everything for his own ends.*

Proverbs 20:24 • *A man's steps are directed by the LORD. How then can anyone understand his own way?*

Proverbs 21:2 • *All a man's ways seem right to him, but the LORD weighs the heart.*

Proverbs 22:29 • *Do you see a man skilled in his work? He will serve before kings; he will not serve before obscure men.*

Proverbs 26:12 • *Do you see a man wise in his own eyes? There is more hope for a fool than for him.*

Proverbs 29:25 • *Fear of man will prove to be a snare, but whoever trusts in the LORD is kept safe.*

KINGDOM STRATEGY
MEETING 1

*U*se the following suggestions to guide a one-hour small-group discussion of *The Kingdom Agenda* covering the lessons in this week's study. For general instructions for the group facilitator, see page 156.

Prior to this first session, you should have already conducted an introductory session. If members have already completed the lessons for week 1, go ahead with this session. Review, however, the suggestions for the introductory session on page 158 and complete those that you think will be helpful for the group.

This Week's Learning Objective
You will understand the Kingdom Agenda as God's sovereign rule and you will demonstrate your desire to seek the Lord's will for your workplace.

Opening Prayer (2 minutes)
• Begin with prayer acknowledging God's presence.
• Ask the Holy Spirit to be your Teacher.
• Tell the Lord that you want to understand His Kingdom Agenda and follow Him faithfully in your workplaces.

Getting Better Acquainted (8 minutes)
Ask members to explain briefly how they came to choose their current type of work or employer. Encourage them to be brief.

Content Review (10 minutes)
Ask members to turn in their books to the Overview of Week 1 on page 15. Using the time suggested, review the following items of content from this week's lessons:
• Ask members to recite this week's Scripture-memory verse together— Matthew 6:33.
• Ask: Which one of the summary statements from week 1 was most meaningful to you and why?
• Ask: What are some of the characteristics of the workplace God intended?
• Ask: What are some of the characteristics of the workplace sin corrupted?
• Ask: What are some of the characteristics of the workplace Christ restores?

• Ask members to turn to the diagram of the Seven Realities of Experiencing God on page 10. Read one of the "Four Facts About the Kingdom Work" (p. 15) and ask members to identify one of the seven realities that corresponds to that fact. Do the same with the other three facts. (Answer: fact 1 = reality1; fact 2 = reality 3; facts 3 & 4 = reality 7)

Discussion Questions (25 minutes)
Look over the following list of questions and lead the group to discuss those that you think would be most meaningful or helpful to your group. Watch your time (invite members to help you), so that you will allow adequate time for prayer at the end of the session.

1. What statement or idea that you read this week seems to be the most meaningful or significant for your workplace?
2. What questions have been raised in your own mind about living by the Kingdom Agenda?
3. What do you think is the most important fact you studied this week about who God is?
4. How would you define "kingdom of God"? (See p. 17.)
5. Which name of God listed on page 18 seems to you to be the most significant, powerful, or meaningful to you?
6. Why is prayer such an important part of the Kingdom Agenda? What does it mean that prayer should be a primary work strategy?
7. How would you define "Kingdom Agenda"?
8. How would you define "World's Agenda"?
9. What are some evidences from your own work life that you and/or your company functions by the world's agenda rather than the Kingdom agenda?
10. What evidences do you see in your own workplace or profession that sin has corrupted your workplace?
11. On page 24 read Matthew 11:28-30 and ask: What do you feel or experience in your work life that causes you to want to respond to Jesus' invitation?
12. Based on your experience, what are the traits that the world says are most important for success? (See p. 25.)

13. In your opinion, what is the most interesting thing you learned about Joseph's career path? Explain.
14. What are some of the times or ways that Joseph could have turned away from the Lord and missed the Kingdom Agenda for his life?
15. Which of the four facts about kingdom work (pp. 29-32) is most meaningful or enlightening for you?
16. Can you think of a time or way that 1 Corinthians 1:27-29 (p. 32) would describe what God did in your life or work? Tell us about it.

Priority Praying (15 minutes)
Conclude the session by spending time as a group praying for each other.
- Ask each person to share with the group one concern they have about their work life, job, or workplace.
- Invite members to pray for these specific needs. You may use sentence prayers, conversational prayer, or pray in any other way you feel led. Give members permission to pray as many times as they choose or as time permits. Remind them that they do not have to pray aloud if they choose not to.
- Invite members to use the space in the right column to record work-related prayer requests for group members so they can pray about them during the coming week.

WORK-RELATED PRAYER REQUESTS

Week 2 The Workplace God Intended

Jim was struggling to decide which applicant he should select as the new operations manager for his heating and air conditioning company. He had worked hard, and the business had grown to be the largest privately owned company of its type in the state. Jim knew that God had been at work in his life and his company. He was careful to give God the credit when people would compliment him on his success.

Not everything in his business had gone smoothly. Jim had been through some tough problems and had survived times of economic slowdown. The operations manager was the most critical position in the company. He had responsibility over the repair and new installation sides of the business. Whoever filled this position had to be a good administrator and be able to build cooperation between the different crews. The future success of the business could rest on the effectiveness of this person's work.

Jim had received many resumes and had interviewed several applicants. Still, he could not decide on the "right" person. He took the file of applicants home with him and spent the evening searching through the resumes one more time. After looking through each one, Jim suddenly realized that he had not been praying about this decision. Jim prayed and then fell asleep in his easy chair.

Later that evening, his wife woke him up to come to bed. As he was walking upstairs to his bedroom, Steve's name came to his mind. Steve was a long-time friend. Jim thought that he ought to consider Steve, but he argued with himself, "That's ridiculous, Steve has a great job and probably wouldn't be interested." The more he thought about it, the more he realized that Steve would be ideal. He could hardly go to sleep.

The next morning Jim called Steve. He was surprised when Steve said he was unhappy with his current position and felt like he should start looking around. Jim offered Steve the job and he turned out to be just the right person.

Jim told Steve that he believed God had led him to make that phone call. Steve was moved by Jim's testimony of how God was working in this situation. Before long Steve also began to see God at work in the company. Steve eventually surrendered his life to Christ as a result of his seeing Jim's daily walk with the Lord.

You can have no greater influence in your life than God's presence and activity. Christians often make the mistake of thinking that they have to change the world. You don't have to carry that load alone. God is the One who brings about lasting change in the lives of people. You must focus on your relationship with God and trust God to work through you to touch the lives of others. God is on mission to change the world, and He invites you to join Him in that work!

OVERVIEW OF WEEK 2

This Week's Scripture-Memory Verse
"We are God's workmanship, created in Christ Jesus to do good works, which God prepared in advance for us to do" (Eph. 2:10).

This Week's Lessons
Day 1: The Original Workplace
Day 2: Adam's Coworker Relationship with God
Day 3: God's Influence in the Workplace He Intended
Day 4: God's Influence in the Workplace (cont.)
Day 5: Characteristics of a Coworker Relationship

Summary Statements from Week 2
- God's desire for the Kingdom Agenda is that His rule would be complete in every heart and life.
- Submitting to His sovereign rule is a pleasure that leads to purpose and fulfillment in life.
- His commands are to be obeyed if we are to experience the fullness of life God intended.
- In the original workplace, work was an opportunity for Adam to experience God.
- A job is holy when God assigns it, and He is present and actively involved in the work.
- Everything good comes from God who reveals truth.
- We need to give God the glory due Him and not take credit for what He does.
- He is Sovereign whether we recognize Him as Ruler or not.
- God will not call you to an assignment without also providing the necessities to see it accomplished.
- God wants a love relationship with you also. He wants you to spend time with Him, to show your dependence on Him, and to express your love and praise to Him.
- As you remain in close relationship to the Lord, He provides the life giving resources through you that bear fruit.
- Jesus works through you to produce fruitfulness.
- God will be seeking what is best and right for you.
- God wants you to learn to trust Him and follow His instructions without debating whether He is right.
- In the original workplace God intended, work was to be a pleasant and fulfilling experience.

IMPORTANT IDEAS

Adam's Coworker Relationship with God
1. God was present...
   Adam was aware of God's presence.
2. God provided for Adam's needs...
   Adam depended on God's provision.
3. God revealed His will...
   Adam obeyed God's will.
4. God initiated work...
   Adam followed God's lead.
5. God worked... Adam worked with God.
6. God was Sovereign... Adam was cooperative.

God's Influence in the Original Workplace
1. God was the Creator of everything new and good.
2. God always took the initiative.
3. God was the Sovereign Ruler, and He made the rules.
4. God was present and involved in the work.
5. God provided all that His worker needed.
6. God had a personal love relationship with His worker.

Characteristics of a Coworker Relationship with God
1. Relationship Based on Love
2. Proper Order of Authority
3. Mutual Respect and Trust
4. Clear Division of Labor
5. Atmosphere of Peace and Harmony
6. Clearly Defined Guidelines
7. Regular Evaluation and Communication

DAY 1 The Original Workplace

Kingdom Agenda
"We are God's workman-ship, created in Christ Jesus to do good works, which God prepared in advance for us to do" (Eph. 2:10).

➡ **Read the "Kingdom Agenda" in the margin. Pause for a moment of prayer. Ask the Lord to help you understand and live by that truth today.**

We must consider several important insights about God's original intention for our work life before we can fully understand the Kingdom Agenda. In order to prepare you to see what may be wrong in your workplace, we need to understand what God wanted from the very beginning. The clear picture of God's original intention for the workplace is found in the workplace God created before the "fall of man" in the Garden of Eden.

Already we have studied some truths about God's nature and position. Let's review.

➡ **1. Turn to pages 16-18 and find three facts about who God is. List them below.**

a. God is _____

b. God is _____

c. God is _____

Read the following description of God's creation of humanity and answer the questions that follow.

> *Then God said, "Let us make man in our image, in our likeness . . . " So God created man in his own image, in the image of God he created him* (Gen. 1:26-27).
>
> *The LORD God said, "It is not good for the man to be alone. I will make a helper suitable for him"* (Gen. 2:18).
>
> *Then the LORD God made a woman . . . and he brought her to the man.* (Gen. 2:22,25).

2. In whose likeness was man created? _____

3. Which of the following is true based on the text above?
❑ a. God had no concern for man and treated him like a machine.
❑ b. God loved and cared for man and worked to meet man's needs.

God Is Creator

God is Creator. He created humanity in His own likeness. Human beings are not God, but in some ways we are like God. Because of our similarities, we can have an intimate love relationship with God. From the very beginning God loved and cared for man and worked to meet his needs. Here are other ways God cared for the needs of Adam and Eve.

> *Now the LORD God had planted a garden in the east, in Eden; and there he put the man he had formed. And the LORD God made all kinds of trees grow out of the ground — trees that were pleasing to the eye and good for food. In the middle of the garden were the tree of life and the tree of the knowledge of good and evil.* (Gen. 2:7-9).
>
> *Then God said, "I give you every seed-bearing plant on the face of*

the whole earth and every tree that has fruit with seed in it. They will be yours for food" (Gen. 1:26-29).

God Is a Worker
Last week you also learned that God is a worker by nature. God took great pleasure in His work. He was proud of the quality of His work—it was very good! In the workplace God intended, work was a fulfilling and meaningful part of life. It was something that brought pleasure and satisfaction. Because work added meaning and purpose to life, God gave Adam some work assignments.

➡️ **4. Read the verses from Genesis 1 and 2 in the margin and underline key words that describe the work God assigned to Adam and Eve. I have underlined one example for you.**

God created us. He knows how we need to live so we can get the most out of the life He has given. Because all the earth and all humanity belongs to God, He is Sovereign. That means He is the King of all. He has the right to rule and do as He pleases. His will and purposes don't need to be questioned. They are to be obeyed. God's desire for the Kingdom Agenda is that His rule would be complete in every heart and life.

Now if God were a brutal dictator, His rule would be miserable. If He were evil or had bad motives, we would have no desire to submit to His rule. But God is not like that. God is perfect love. He always wants what is best and good for our lives. Submitting to His sovereign rule is a pleasure that leads to purpose and fulfillment in life.

➡️ **5. In your opinion, which of the following is the best reason for submitting to God's sovereign rule? Check one you think is best.**
❑ a. God created me and He knows what is in my best interest.
❑ b. God loves me and cares about me. He will lead me to do what is best and right.
❑ c. The world and everyone in it belongs to God. He has a sovereign right to direct my life and work.
❑ d. God has done so much for me, He deserves my loyalty and obedience.
6. Why did you choose the one you did?

_____

_____

God Is Sovereign
All of these are good reasons to obey God's sovereign rule. No matter which one you selected, God is your Sovereign Ruler and He expects obedience. Because He is Sovereign, He has a right to set boundaries. He is the One who decides what is right and what is wrong. His commands are to be obeyed if we are to experience the fullness of life God intended from the very beginning. As Sovereign Ruler, God gave one rule to Adam:

> The LORD God commanded the man, "You are free to eat from any tree in the garden; but you must not eat from the tree of the knowledge of good and evil, for when you eat of it you will surely die" (Gen. 2:16-17).

Genesis 1—2
"The LORD God took the man and put him in the Garden of Eden to <u>work it</u> and take care of it" (Gen. 1:15).

"God blessed them and said to them, 'Be fruitful and increase in number; fill the earth and subdue it. Rule over the fish of the sea and the birds of the air and over every living creature that moves on the ground' " (Gen. 1:28).

"Now the LORD God had formed out of the ground all the beasts of the field and all the birds of the air. He brought them to the man to see what he would name them; and whatever the man called each living creature, that was its name. So the man gave names to all the livestock, the birds of the air and all the beasts of the field" (Gen. 2:19-20).

In His sovereignty God gave Adam the choice to obey or disobey. Adam was free to obey God because of the love relationship they had together. Adam also was free to disobey, but disobedience had severe consequences. In week 3 we will see the consequences of sin on Adam's workplace.

➡ **7. Are you willing to submit to God's sovereign rule of your life and work? Check your response or write your own.**
❑ a. Yes. I love the Lord and will obey Him no matter what He asks of me.
❑ b. I don't want to, but I know it is the right thing to do. Yes, I am willing to obey Him.
❑ c. Don't push me. I'm afraid to submit until I know what He wants. I want to wait.
❑ d. No. I can run my own life just fine. Thank you.

❑ e. Other: _____

_____

He wants you to love Him and come to the place that you surrender to His rule unconditionally —no reservations.

How you responded to this question, may reveal what is really in your heart toward God. He wants you to love Him and come to the place that you surrender to His rule unconditionally —no reservations. If you were not able to answer "a" above, do not despair or quit this study. God pursues a love relationship with you. He will meet you right where you are and help you move to where you need to be.

PRAYER STRATEGY
➡ **Take time now to pray about God's sovereign rule in and around your life. As time permits, pray about the following matters.**
• Think about some of your good, fulfilling, or meaningful work experiences. Thank God for them.
• Take a few moments thanking God for all the ways He has provided for you (food, clothing, home, health, family, job, etc.).
• Talk to God about His sovereign rule. Tell Him what you are thinking. Discuss any concerns you have with Him. If you are ready, tell Him about your willingness to obey.
• If you are struggling with absolute surrender, ask God to reveal His love and goodness to you. Ask Him for the faith to trust Him with your life.
• If you have been hurt by an earthly father (or other significant person), you may keep your distance from your heavenly Father. Ask God to heal the hurt. Ask Him to reveal His safe and trustworthy love to you in such a way that you know you are loved unconditionally. Take some time alone to walk and talk with your heavenly Father.

FOR FURTHER STUDY

Deuteronomy 11:13-15

"If you faithfully obey the commands I am giving you today — to love the LORD your God and to serve him with all your heart and with all your soul — then I will send rain on your land in its season, both autumn and spring rains, so that you may gather in your grain, new wine and oil. I will provide grass in the fields for your cattle, and you will eat and be satisfied."

Deuteronomy 13:3-4

"The LORD your God is testing you to find out whether you love him with all your heart and with all your soul. It is the LORD your God you must follow, and him you must revere. Keep his commands and obey him; serve him and hold fast to him."

1 Samuel 12:14-15

"If you fear the LORD and serve and obey him and do not rebel against his commands, and if both you and the king who reigns over you follow the LORD your God — good! But if you do not obey the LORD, and if you rebel against his commands, his hand will be against you, as it was against your fathers."

➡ **Read Deuteronomy 11:13-15 and answer these questions:**
1. What is the condition for God's blessings?
2. What are the commands to be obeyed?
3. What blessings does God promise for obedience?
4. If God were making this statement to you and your workplace what do you think the blessings might be? Ask the Lord.

➡ **Read Deuteronomy 13:3-4 and answer these questions:**
5. Has God ever tested your obedience to see what was in your heart? How? When?
6. What verbs in this passage describe what you must do?
7. If you were to follow, revere, obey, serve, and hold fast to the Lord in your workplace, what would it look like? What would you do?

➡ **Read 1 Samuel 12:14-15 and answer these questions:**
8. What is the consequence of rebelling against God and His commands?
9. How important do you think it is that your employer and boss submit to and obey God's sovereign rule? Does it matter?
10. Who are the key people in your workplace for whom you should pray that they will obey and not rebel against the Lord?

NOTES

_____

_____

_____

_____

_____

_____

_____

_____

_____

_____

_____

_____

DAY 2 — Adam's Coworker Relationship with God

Kingdom Agenda
"Neither he who plants nor he who waters is anything, but only God, who makes things grow. The man who plants and the man who waters have one purpose, and each will be rewarded according to his own labor. For we are God's fellow workers" (1 Cor. 3:7-9).

In the original workplace, work was an opportunity for Adam to experience God.

➡ **Read the "Kingdom Agenda" in the margin. Pause for a moment of prayer. Ask the Lord to help you understand what part of His Kingdom work He wants you to do as His coworker.**

God was not the only worker in the original workplace. Adam cooperated with God as a coworker. By "coworker" we do not mean they were peers. God is far above all human authority and ability. But Adam did work together with God.

When God created man, it was for a purpose. He was created to live and work in "fellowship" with God. This meant that his destiny on earth was defined in terms of a living, dynamic, and daily relationship with God. In the original workplace, work was an opportunity for Adam to experience God. Let's take a look at the coworker relationship. Here is Adam's role at work in terms of God's activity in the following ways:

> **Adam's Coworker Relationship with God**
> God was present—Adam was aware of God's presence.
> God provided Adam's needs—Adam depended on God's provision.
> God revealed His will—Adam obeyed God's will.
> God initiated work—Adam followed God's lead.
> God worked—Adam worked with God.
> God was Sovereign—Adam was cooperative

This is the way God intended the workplace to be. It was never a question of whether Adam was doing a "sacred" job rather than a "secular" job. Isn't it ironic that the first job God ever gave man would be classified by the church today as a "secular" assignment. The nature of the work we do is NOT what makes it holy. A job is holy if God assigned it. It is holy when God is present and involved in the work and we are rightly related to Him.

A job is holy if God assigned it

➡ **1. What makes a job holy? Check ALL the correct responses.**
❏ a. Working for a church or other religious group.
❏ b. God is present and involved in the work.
❏ c. God assigned the work.

> **A job is holy when God assigns it, and He is present and actively involved in the work.**

If a job is immoral, unethical, or contrary to the will of God, then it would be secular (or separated from God). In the workplace that God originally intended, work was sacred and holy. Work was a time where man experienced God! Work becomes an opportunity for you to experience God!

Work becomes an opportunity for you to experience God!

Do you have a coworker relationship with God in your work life? Let's see how your experience measures up against Adam's coworker relationship with God.

➡ **2. Read the following statements and check A for "Always," S for "Sometimes," or N for "Never" to indicate how frequently that statement is true of your work life.**

A S N

❑ ❑ ❑ a. I am aware of God's presence while I am working.

❑ ❑ ❑ b. I pray and ask God to provide those things I need.

❑ ❑ ❑ c. I find myself waiting on God and trusting in Him to meet my needs.

❑ ❑ ❑ d. I sense God guides me to know what to do and how He would have me do it.

❑ ❑ ❑ e. I seek God's directions and watch to see where He is already working so I know the Kingdom work I am to do.

❑ ❑ ❑ f. Once I know what God wants me to do at my place of work, I obey Him.

❑ ❑ ❑ g. I realize that God is involving me in Kingdom work.

❑ ❑ ❑ h. I acknowledge that God is Sovereign and I cooperate with Him in His kingdom work.

3. This last activity may have raised other questions about what the Kingdom Agenda would look like in your workplace. If you could sit down and ask the Lord some questions about the Kingdom Agenda in your workplace, what would you ask? Write your questions. If you need more space, use the margin or a separate sheet of paper.

_____

_____

_____

_____

_____

_____

_____

_____

_____

PRAYER STRATEGY

➡ **Take time now to pray. Spend some extra time today seeking God's directions for your work.**

• Begin your prayer time by asking God the questions you wrote in question 3 above.

• Ask God to examine the quality of your relationship with Him.

• Ask Him to show you how to live in a right coworker relationship with Him, where God is Sovereign and you are cooperative.

DAY 3   God's Influence in the Workplace He Intended

Kingdom Agenda
"Every good and perfect gift is from above, coming down from the Father of the heavenly lights, who does not change" (Jas. 1:17).

➡ **Read the "Kingdom Agenda" in the margin. Pause for a moment of prayer. Thank God for the good things He has done for your. Meditate about the fact that God is unchanging and faithful.**

As we study the workplace God intended, we see that God had a profound influence on everything that took place. Today, I want us to look at the influence God had in the original workplace. Then we will try to understand how He wants to influence our workplace. Here is an overview of some of the ways God influenced the original workplace.

God's Influence in the Original Workplace
1. God was the Creator of everything new and good.
2. God always took the initiative.
3. God was the Sovereign Ruler, and He made the rules.
4. God was present and involved in the work.
5. God provided all that His worker needed.
6. God had a personal love relationship with His worker.

Today, we will look at the first three ways God influences the workplace and tomorrow we will look at the last three.

God Is Creator
God is the Creator of everything new and good. Adam created nothing. God created everything—even Adam. God worked as the Creator of that which was new and the Author of that which was good! May I test your memory from school days?

➡ **1. On the right is a list of inventions or discoveries. On the left are the ones who invented or discovered those items. Draw a line from one name to the thing they discovered or invented.**

1. Alexander Graham Bell   a. incandescent light bulb
2. Jonas Salk   b. motorized airplane
3. Thomas Edison   c. polio vaccine
4. Wright Brothers   d. telephone

Based on our history books the answers are 1-d, 2-c, 3-a, and 4-b. Now let me ask another question:

➡ **2. Did God have anything to do with these inventions or discoveries?**
❏ Yes ❏ Some of them ❏ No ❏ I don't know

James 1:17
"Every good and perfect gift is from above, coming down from the Father of the heavenly lights, who does not change."

The truth is that man creates nothing. God alone creates. Everything good comes from God who reveals truth (see Jas. 1:17). We only cooperate with God's revelation. The vanity of mankind takes credit for creating, inventing, and discovering. It is true that these men listed above were involved. They hold a place in history because of their involvement. But God is the Author of everything good.

I know what you may be thinking: "This can't be true. I know of people who are not Christians who have made great discoveries."

Let me remind you that Almighty God is a sovereign God over all the earth and humanity. God *"causes his sun to rise on the evil and the good, and sends rain on the righteous and the unrighteous"* (Matt. 5:45). God does good things for all His creation. We cannot understand God's ways. We don't think like He does (Isa. 55:8-9).

Isaiah 55:8-9

" 'For my thoughts are not your thoughts, neither are your ways my ways,' declares the LORD. 'As the heavens are higher than the earth, so are my ways higher than your ways and my thoughts than your thoughts.'"

We need to recognize the role God has chosen to play in our work life and return to a right understanding of God. We should have an attitude of awe and wonder at the inspiration and creativity of God. We need to give God the glory due Him and not take credit for what He does. Remember, Joseph was careful to explain that he couldn't interpret dreams but that God was able. Only sin drives us to see ourselves as the authors of innovation or the creators of good.

➡ **3. Suppose that you were working to discover a cure for AIDS. With this understanding of God as Creator, how would you begin your search? Check an answer or write your own.**

❏ a. I would begin studying the virus and patients with AIDS.

❏ b. I would enlist people to pray with me that God would reveal the cure as I conduct the research.

❏ c. Other: _____

God Is Initiator

God always takes the initiative. God started everything "in the beginning." God never asked Adam what he wanted to do for God. God took the initiative and told Adam what to do.

God wants to lead you in your workplace, not follow you. We have a tendency to make our own plans and then ask God to come in and help us accomplish them. That is directly backwards to what God wants. He wants to show you what He is wanting to do and ask you to join Him. He can initiate things you never would have dreamed possible. He can order circumstances and create opportunities you would not think to ask.

This was Jesus' pattern for doing His Father's will. He watched to see where His Father was working and joined Him. He followed the Father's initiative (John 5:19-20).

A prayer relationship is where God will give you directions for your work life.

This is why you need to make prayer a primary work strategy. Prayer is a relationship with God where you talk to Him and He talks to you. A prayer relationship is where God will give you directions for your work life. He will instruct you about right and wrong. In prayer God may give you answers to problems or reveal the ways that will accomplish the desired result.

➡ **4. Knowing that God wants to take the initiative, how would you begin a new day in prayer? Check an answer or write your own.**

❏ a. "God, here is what I am going to do today. Would you please bless my work."

❏ b. "Lord, You know the demands I will face at work today. Please guide me to know what to do and how to do it in a way that would bring glory and honor to You."

❏ c. Other: _____

If, for some reason, you would not choose to seek God's directions, that may indicate that you really do not believe God is able to show you, cares about your work, or knows what to do. Or this may indicate that you do not want to follow God's initiative in your work—and that is rebellion.

God Is Sovereign Ruler

God is the Sovereign Ruler, and He makes the rules. God was the King, Master, Lord, Boss in the original workplace. Adam was not given the authority to decide what was right and wrong or what he was to do and not do. He did, however, have the freedom to rebel against God's sovereign rule. You have the freedom to rebel against God's rule, but there are consequences for your rebellion.

➥ **5. If I were to ask you "Is God the Sovereign Ruler in your workplace?" how would you respond?**

❑ a. "You must be kidding, nobody pays attention to God there."

❑ b. "Mike, you obviously don't know what the workplace is like. It's a pagan world out there."

❑ c. "Yes, I have a wonderful workplace where God is seen as Ruler of all."

❑ d. "I believe He is Sovereign, but we do not acknowledge His rule like we should."

Was "a" or "b" your truthful response? That is the sad truth about our world. We have forgotten God. Whether we recognize God's sovereign right to rule in our work lives or not, God still has that right. He is Sovereign whether we recognize Him as Ruler or not. The problem is not whether God is Sovereign, but rather whether men and women accept His sovereign rule.

He is Sovereign whether we recognize Him as Ruler or not.

We are not finished looking at God's influences in the workplace. We will finish this study tomorrow. For now, turn your mind and heart to the Lord in prayer.

PRAYER STRATEGY

➥ **Take time now to pray.**

• Thank God for some of the good things He has permitted people to invent or discover that have been meaningful or helpful to you.

• Agree with God that He should lead and you should follow. Let Him be the Initiator. Ask Him to begin showing you what He is doing or wanting to do in your workplace. Volunteer to join Him when He shows you.

• Pray that God will begin to work in the people you work with in such a way that He becomes Sovereign Ruler of your workplace.

DAY 4 — God's Influence in the Workplace (continued)

Kingdom Agenda
"I have been crucified with Christ and I no longer live, but Christ lives in me. The life I live in the body, I live by faith in the Son of God, who loved me and gave himself for me" (Gal. 2:20).

➡️ **Read the "Kingdom Agenda" in the margin. Pause for a moment of prayer. Ask the Lord to help you understand and live by that truth that Christ lives in you. Thank God for loving you so much.**

Yesterday, we looked at three ways God influences the workplace. Today, we want to look at three more of those ways:
4. God was present and involved in the work.
5. God provided all that His worker needed.
6. God had a personal love relationship with His worker.

Matthew 28:20
"Surely I [Jesus] am with you always, to the very end of the age."

God Is Present

God is present and involved in your work. In the original workplace, God was not an "absentee owner" as many think He is today. God didn't leave Adam alone. God was present and actively involved with Adam in the workplace. God created animals and brought them to Adam to name them. They had a coworker relationship. Now this doesn't mean that Adam was on an equal level with God, but Adam did work together with God.

Colossians 1:27
"God has chosen to make known among the Gentiles the glorious riches of this mystery, which is Christ in you, the hope of glory."

If you have not done so, you need to recognize that God is present with you throughout the day. You need to see Him as an active participant in your work. You do not have to do your work alone.

➡️ **Read the Scriptures in the margin including "Kingdom Agenda" and underline the words that describe where God is. Remember He is Father, Son, and Holy Spirit. I have underlined one for you.**

1 Corinthians 6:19
"Do you not know that your body is a temple of the Holy Spirit, who is in you, whom you have received from God?"

1. Where is God? _____

2. Is God with you when you go to work? _____

Yes, God is with you when you go to work. He is present and He is ready to be involved in your work as you allow Him to guide you.

➡️ **3. Try an experiment the next time you go to work. Pray and ask God to help you be aware of His presence throughout the day. Take times to pray silently and talk to Him since He is present with you. Seek His guidance, counsel, or help. You may even want to begin keeping a spiritual journal about your experiences of God in your workplace. Be prepared to share your experience with your small group.**

God Provides for Needs

God will provide all that you need. God is the One who created the first workplace (the Garden of Eden). He placed in it everything the man and woman needed. God also is able to provide for your needs: *"My God will meet all your needs according to his glorious riches in Christ Jesus"* (Phil. 4:19).

Philippians 2:13
"It is God who works in you to will and to act according to his good purpose."

Keep in mind, however, that the word is "needs" not "wants." God is going to be working on what you need. For instance: if you need to develop patience, God will take you through circumstances that will test the limits of your patience so you will grow in that area. God also has a condition on His provision. Jesus said:

"Do not worry about your life, what you will eat or drink; or about your body, what you will wear. . . . But seek first his kingdom and his righteousness, and all these things will be given to you as well" (Matt. 6:25,33).

➥ **4. Based on Matthew 6:25 and 33 above, what is the condition for God's provision?**

_____

When you seek God's kingdom rule as your first priority, God will take care of things like food and clothes. Another way God will provide is with resources to accomplish any assignment He calls you to. God will not call you to an assignment without also providing the necessities to see it accomplished. Trusting in God's provisions, however, will call you to walk by faith in God and not by sight.

> God will not call you to an assignment without also providing the necessities to see it accomplished.

God Seeks a Personal Love Relationship

God wants a personal love relationship with you. God created man in His own image so man could have a relationship with God. God pursued that relationship Himself. He didn't wait on Adam's initiative. Adam had the privilege of working together with God. Evidently, God made a habit of "walking in the Garden in the cool of the day" with Adam and Eve (Gen. 3:8). This is a beautiful picture of an intimate relationship between humanity and their Creator and Sovereign Lord.

God wants a love relationship with you also. He wants you to spend time with Him, to show your dependence on Him, and to express your love and praise to Him. Jesus used two visual images to describe a working relationship with Him. In one case He invites you to get into the yoke with Him (Matt. 11:28-30). A yoke is a wooden block that holds two animals together as they work. Jesus wants you to join His work by working along side Him in close fellowship.

The other visual image is that of a branch and a [grape-] vine (John 15:5). As you remain in close relationship to the Lord, He provides the life giving resources that bear fruit. Jesus works through you to produce fruitfulness.

➥ **5. In the boxes in the margin with Matthew 11:28-30 and John 15:5, draw a picture for each that illustrates the working relationship Jesus invites you to experience. Draw a yoke for two animals and a grape vine with its branches and fruit.** [Don't worry, I will not ask you to show these to anyone else!]

Matthew 11:28-30

"Come to me, all you who are weary and burdened, and I will give you rest. Take my yoke upon you and learn from me, for I am gentle and humble in heart, and you will find rest for your souls. For my yoke is easy and my burden is light."

John 15:5

"I am the vine; you are the branches. If a man remains in me and I in him, he will bear much fruit; apart from me you can do nothing."

PRAYER STRATEGY

➥ **Take time now to pray. Focus your prayers on your relationship to God.**

- Thank Jesus for living in you. Ask Him to help you die to self so that He may live through you.
- Thank God for the ways He has provided for your needs. If you sense some need in your personal or work life, talk to the Lord about it and ask Him to provide.
- Perhaps, you may have reached this point in our study; and you realize that you don't have a personal love relationship with God. If you want to surrender your life to Jesus Christ and trust Him as your personal Savior, turn to page 153 for some help on how to respond to God.

DAY 5 Characteristics of a Coworker Relationship

Kingdom Agenda
"There is no fear in love. But perfect love drives out fear, because fear has to do with punishment. The one who fears is not made perfect in love" (1 John 4:18).

➡ **Read the "Kingdom Agenda" in the margin. Pause for a moment of prayer. Ask the Lord to help you understand and live by that truth today.**

The workplace God originally intended had some awesome qualities to consider. These are characteristics God intends for any work experience where God is Sovereign and man is cooperative. Let's examine these characteristics of a relationship between God and His coworker:

> **Characteristics of a Coworker Relationship with God**
> 1. Relationship Based on Love
> 2. Proper Order of Authority
> 3. Mutual Respect and Trust
> 4. Clear Division of Labor
> 5. Atmosphere of Peace and Harmony
> 6. Clearly Defined Guidelines
> 7. Regular Evaluation and Communication

Relationship Based on Love

God's very nature is love. Love is seeking the very best for another. God created Adam for a love relationship with his Creator. God showed His love for Adam by inviting Adam to work with Him, providing for Adam's needs, and providing Adam with his wife Eve. The picture we see in Genesis 1—2 is one of a loving relationship between God and His creation. God intends for your work relationship with Him to be based on love. In that relationship God will be seeking what is best and right for you.

God will be seeking what is best and right for you.

➡ **1. What is one characteristic of the workplace God intended?**

_____

Mutual Trust

"Perfect love drives out fear."

The Scripture says, *"There is no fear in love. But perfect love drives out fear, because fear has to do with punishment. The one who fears is not made perfect in love"* (1 John 4:18). Because this work relationship is based on love, God and Adam had mutual trust for each othe —no contracts, no courts of law, no audits, just trust. Before sin entered the scene, God trusted Adam to carry out His assignments. Adam trusted God to provide for his needs, and Adam also trusted God's instructions and followed them without question. Adam trusted God to do the right things. God wants you to learn to trust Him and follow His instructions without debating whether He is right.

God wants you to learn to trust Him and follow His instructions without debating whether He is right.

➡ **2. What is a second characteristic of the workplace God intended?**

_____

Proper Order of Authority

From the very beginning Adam knew that God was in charge. When Adam acknowledged God as Sovereign, their work relationship was beautiful, wholesome, and productive. God intends to be your Sovereign Ruler and for you to be cooperative and obedient.

➡ **3. What is a third characteristic of the workplace God intended?**

_____

Clear Division of Labor

What an incredible concept: God and man working alongside of each other! Adam didn't try and take over God's responsibilities. And God gave Adam his own assignments. God works as the Creator and Initiator, and Adam joins God by following God's directions. In a sense there were two job descriptions: one God's and the other Adam's.

In your workplace, there are some things that only God has the right to do. These are the items on God's job description. There are some things only God is able to do.

You need to understand what God wants you to do and how He wants you to do it. These are the items on your Kingdom job description (more about this in week 6). Once you understand and desire what God wants, God enables you to do the work He desires from you. In the Kingdom work is clearly divided between God and His workers.

God enables you to do the work He desires from you.

➡ **4. What is a fourth characteristic of the workplace God intended?**

_____

Atmosphere of Peace and Harmony

When Adam was in a proper working relationship described in the previous characteristics, he worked in peace and harmony. He and God had no fights or arguments. Adam was submissive to God's place of authority so there was no spirit of competition—just cooperation. Expectations were realistic and Adam's needs were met, so there was no unhealthy stress.

Can you even imagine such a work environment? In the original workplace God intended, work was to be a pleasant and fulfilling experience. He didn't intend for man to get sick from stress and conflict in the workplace!

God didn't intend for man to get sick from stress and conflict in the workplace!

➡ **5. What is a fifth characteristic of the workplace God intended?**

_____

Clearly Defined Guidelines

Adam knew what he was to do and what he was not to do. Clear understanding of God's will was evident before the fall of man. God wants you to know what to do and how to do it. He wants you to understand what not to do—those things that would be wrong or harmful to you or others. God is the One who establishes the guidelines for right and wrong.

➡ **6. What is a sixth characteristic of the workplace God intended?**

_____

Regular Evaluation and Communication

When God went about His six days of creation, He stopped at the end of each day to evaluate His work. Each day the work completed was "good," and in the end it was "very good." God's original intention was for work to be productive and fruitful. Only after Adam and Eve sinned was fruitfulness difficult to come by. God evidently spent time with Adam and Eve daily. After they sinned, He came to meet with them in the "cool of the day" and they were not in their expected place. Prior to their sin, communication kept their relationship alive and meaningful.

God wants you to be fruitful and He wants your fruit to last (John 15:1-5). But that fruitfulness comes from the close relationship to Him and the instruction from His Word.

➡ **7. What is a seventh characteristic of the workplace God intended?**

_____

8. Try to evaluate your own work relationship with God. On a scale between 10 (God's Ideal) and 0 (Man's Failure) how would you rate on these characteristics? Write a number beside each of the characteristics. Remember this is measuring your relationship with God and His standards not your human coworkers and their standards.

God's Ideal — 10 - 9 - 8 - 7 - 6 - 5 - 4 - 3 - 2 - 1 - 0 — Man's Failure

___ A. Relationship of Love—No Relationship
___ B. Proper Order of Authority—My "Self" is Boss
___ C. Mutual Respect and Trust—Disrespect and Fear
___ D. Clear Division of Labor—Don't Know God's Will
___ E. Peace and Harmony—Stress and Strife
___ F. Clearly Defined Guidelines—Don't Know Right from Wrong
___ G. Evaluation and Communication—Don't Talk with God

These characteristics of the workplace God originally created provide us with a better understanding of God's original intention for Kingdom work. This means that a janitor can be on divine assignment just as much as his brother in Christ who serves as a missionary to Bangladesh. God plans to work redemptively in both places through His servants. Understanding the workplace God intended should open your eyes to the way things ought to be.

Next week you will study about the workplace that sin has corrupted. You will probably encounter some familiar situations, because most of our workplaces are corrupted by sin in some way—even churches and religious organizations. Keep in your mind the image about how things ought to be—how God designed them to be. Later, we are going to learn how Christ can restore your workplace as you live out the Kingdom Agenda.

PRAYER STRATEGY
➡ **Take time now to pray. Review what God has been teaching you this week.**
- Ask God to reveal to you those areas of your life where you must make adjustments to live and work in harmony with His intentions.
- Ask God to give you experiences where He can teach you how to work with Him under the Kingdom Agenda.
- Confess any doubts and fears you may have to the Lord. Ask Him to bring you to such a love and understanding of Him and His ways that you can trust Him with no fear.
- Pray for each one of the members of your small group. Ask the Lord to prepare each of you for your time of sharing this week. If you know of specific needs members may have, pray for those needs.

John 15:1-5
"I am the true vine, and my Father is the gardener. He cuts off every branch in me that bears no fruit, while every branch that does bear fruit he prunes so that it will be even more fruitful. You are already clean because of the word I have spoken to you. Remain in me, and I will remain in you. No branch can bear fruit by itself; it must remain in the vine. Neither can you bear fruit unless you remain in me.

"I am the vine; you are the branches. If a man remains in me and I in him, he will bear much fruit; apart from me you can do nothing."

KINGDOM STRATEGY
MEETING 2

*U*se the following suggestions to guide a one-hour small-group discussion of *The Kingdom Agenda* covering the lessons in this week's study. For general instructions for the group facilitator, see page 156.

This Week's Learning Objective
You will understand the nature of the workplace God originally intended and demonstrate your determination to seek this ideal in your own workplace.

Opening Prayer (2 minutes)
- Begin with prayer acknowledging God's presence.
- Ask the Holy Spirit to be your Teacher.
- Ask the Lord to help you all come to a clear understanding of what work and the workplace ought to be like.
- Thank Him for creating a wonderful workplace and ask Him to restore it through Christ for His glory!

Getting Better Acquainted (8 minutes)
Ask volunteers to share briefly one experience they have had this week at work that has caused them to realize that the workplace is not what God intended it to be. If anyone has a testimony of how God has worked through them or in their workplace this week invite them to share it with the group.

Content Review (10 minutes)
Ask members to turn in their books to the Overview of Week 2 on page 37. Using the time suggested, review the following items of content from this week's lessons:
- Ask members to recite this week's Scripture-memory verse together—Ephesians 2:10.
- Ask: Which one of the summary statements from week 2 was most meaningful to you and why?
- Ask: How did Adam experience God in his coworker relationship with God?
- Ask: What are the ways God influenced the original workplace and how does He want to influence our workplaces?
- Ask: What are the characteristics of a coworker relationship with God?

Discussion Questions (25 minutes)
Look over the following list of questions and lead the group to discuss those that you think would be most meaningful or helpful to your group. Watch your time (invite members to help you), so that you will allow adequate time for prayer at the end of the session. You may want to ask members to help you select the most helpful questions for discussion.

1. What does our Scripture-memory verse in Ephesians 2:20 have to say about who we are in Christ? What difference should that make?
2. What are some of the ways God has provided for you and demonstrated His love for you? (You may want to spend a few moments in thanksgiving for what God has done.)
3. In your opinion, what is the best reason for submitting to God's sovereign rule? Why? (See #5 on p. 39.)
4. How did you respond to #7 on page 40 and how did that make you feel about your relationship with the Lord?
5. [Consider reviewing and/or discussing questions listed under "For Further Study" on page 41.]
6. Which way did Adam respond in relationship to God in the original workplace that is least evident in your workplace? Why do you think this is true? (See #2 on p. 43.)
7. Have you ever considered your job to be holy? Why? or Why not?
8. What questions would you most like to ask the Lord about the Kingdom Agenda in your workplace? (See #3 on p. 43)
9. Based on your response to #3 on page 45, what success in your work may be waiting on God's involvement and will be impossible without it?
10. How important is prayer to the Kingdom Agenda? Why? or So what? What difference should this make in your own prayer life?
11. What evidence do you see in your workplace that God is or is not treated as Sovereign Ruler?
12. How have you experienced God's presence at work this week? When and how?

13. What do you think you could change in your relationship to God that would allow Matthew 11:28-30 and John 15:5 to become a reality for you? (Scriptures are on p. 48.)

14. If you could pick one characteristic of a coworker relationship with God (p. 49) that you would like to see become reality in your work, which one would it be and why?

15. If God were to evaluate the quality of your work from His kingdom perspective how do you think He would rate your work and why?
    ❑ Very Good; ❑ Good; ❑ Fair; or ❑ Poor

Priority Praying (15 minutes)
Conclude the session by spending time as a group praying for each other.

• Ask members to share with the group the one area they would like to see God work to bring change in their workplace or profession.

• Invite members to pray for these specific areas. You may use sentence prayers, conversational prayer, or pray in any other way you feel led. Give members permission to pray as many times as they choose. Remind them that they do not have to pray aloud if they choose not to.

• Invite members to use the space in the right column to record work-related prayer requests for group members so they can pray about them during the coming week.

WORK-RELATED PRAYER REQUESTS

Week 3 The Workplace Sin Corrupted

*T*his was Jennifer's big day, her high school graduation! My wife's cousin was a bright, bubbly teenager who would later become a doctor. She was graduating from an excellent Christian high school. I sat beside her father as we listened to the commencement address. The speaker told the graduates how they should go out into the world and live their lives according to such Christian principles as honesty, fairness, justice, love, and kindness. I caught myself becoming irritated and even confused by the speaker's words. He was talking about God as if He had something to do with everyday life.

Leaning over, I whispered to Jennifer's dad, "This guy is selling these kids a false bill of goods. He's living in a fantasy world. This isn't reality. If they do what he's telling them, they'll get eaten alive out there! I've got news for him, God doesn't have any part of the workplace."

My thoughts drifted from the speaker's words to focus on my own life. I couldn't remember when I had worked a mere 40-hour week. I was constantly driven by my desire to succeed. I was working for a demanding but incompetent boss. He was under investigation by the corporation's security department for violation of company regulations.

Several coworkers were involved in affairs with other coworkers. Our days were filled with gossip and political maneuvering, just trying to look good at the right times! My personal life was way out of control, and my family was beginning to disintegrate. It seemed as if the more successful I became, the more empty I felt on the inside. There was nothing to satisfy the growing frustration I was feeling.

You see, I didn't know the Lord Jesus Christ! I was baptized into church membership as a child, but I didn't have a personal relationship with the Lord. I couldn't recognize God's activity in my life, because I really didn't know Him. During this time of working in Florida, I surrendered my life to Jesus Christ, and He became my Lord and Savior.

Looking back on this time, I realize that even the Christians I knew in the workplace didn't handle their work life any differently than I did. As I looked around the corporation, I couldn't find anyone who seemed to be following Christ. Many went to church on Sunday, but handled their work life like everybody else. I came to the conclusion that the only way I could truly follow Christ was to become a preacher, pastor, deacon, Sunday School teacher, or missionary. I felt as though my world was being split in half! There was a secular world that God seemed to avoid and the sacred world of the church where God was at work.

Now I realize that what I was seeing was a workplace corrupted by sin.

OVERVIEW OF WEEK 3

This Week's Scripture-Memory Verse
"Do not love the world or anything in the world. If anyone loves the world, the love of the Father is not in him" (1 John 2:15).

This Week's Lessons
Day 1: Sin Corrupted the Original Workplace
Day 2: The World's Agenda
Day 3: When Self Rules Your "Kingdom"
Day 4: Influences of the World's Agenda
Day 5: Sin's Corruption in Your Workplace

Summary Statements from Week
- The sinful nature is hostile to God, does not submit to God's law, and cannot please God.
- At the very heart of the world's agenda is an attitude that rejects God's rule.
- Our refusal to accept God as our Sovereign Authority in no way cancels His rightful position on the "throne" of life.
- You must die to self daily and follow His agenda if you are to know real life.
- God doesn't have to provide for anything that you are not trusting Him for.
- When we are driven by our human nature, our daily behavior on the job draws us away from God and His Kingdom Agenda.
- With our emphasis on self, we cannot possibly live and work in a proper coworker relationship where God is Sovereign and we are cooperative.
- God wants us to learn and practice absolute dependence on Him.
- When you surrender to Him and receive His saving grace, He adopts you into His family. That is where you find your true value.
- Our job is to serve God for His Kingdom purposes.
- Ultimately we must all give account of our actions to God who knows the truth
- Loving things puts you at odds with God.

IMPORTANT IDEAS

The World's Agenda Corrupts the Workplace
1. The world's agenda rejects the sovereignty of God.
2. The world's agenda is focused upon self.
3. The world's agenda seeks to satisfy needs apart from God.

Ways the World's Agenda May Influence You
1. You can do anything.
2. Find value in yourself.
3. Serve yourself.
4. Blame others for your problems.
5. Love things and use people.

Human Nature May Influence the Workplace
1. Quality may be sacrificed for quantity.
2. Pricing may be deceiving.
3. Immoral, illegal, or unethical practices may be common.
4. Welfare of people and nature may be overlooked for the sake of profit.
5. Taking responsibility for actions may not be important.

DAY 1 Sin Corrupted the Original Workplace

Kingdom Agenda

"Do not love the world or anything in the world. If anyone loves the world, the love of the Father is not in him. For everything in the world—the cravings of sinful man, the lust of his eyes and the boasting of what he has and does—comes not from the Father but from the world" (1 John 2:15-16).

➡ **Read the "Kingdom Agenda" in the margin. Pause for a moment of prayer. Ask the Lord to help you understand the nature of the world's agenda and how you can avoid it.**

The "Kingdom Agenda" verses you just read command you not to love the world. *World* refers to earthly things like possessions, riches, systems, and pleasures. It refers to "the present condition of human affairs, in alienation from and opposition to God." [1] This week we will be studying the *world's* agenda and the workplace sin corrupted.

➡ **1. First, I want you to do a quick review. Turn to pages 15 and 37 and read through the two lists of "Important Ideas." As you look through the lists, select one idea that seems to be most important to you and your work as a servant of God—wherever you work. After you have selected an idea, write it below.**

_____

_____

_____

The Original Sin

When God first created the world and placed Adam and Eve in the Garden of Eden, everything was very good. No sin was present in the original workplace. God gave Adam and Eve one rule that set a boundary for their lives. One fateful day they chose to disobey God.

➡ **2. Read Genesis 1:1-6 below and underline the reasons Eve chose to disobey God and eat fruit from the tree of knowledge.**

Now the serpent was more crafty than any of the wild animals the LORD God had made. He said to the woman, "Did God really say, 'You must not eat from any tree in the garden'?"

The woman said to the serpent, "We may eat fruit from the trees in the garden, but God did say, 'You must not eat fruit from the tree that is in the middle of the garden, and you must not touch it, or you will die.'"

"You will not surely die," the serpent said to the woman. "For God knows that when you eat of it your eyes will be opened, and you will be like God, knowing good and evil."

When the woman saw that the fruit of the tree was good for food and pleasing to the eye, and also desirable for gaining wisdom, she took some and ate it. She also gave some to her husband, who was with her, and he ate it. (Gen. 3:1-6).

Eve was attracted to the forbidden fruit. It looked good for food, and it was *"pleasing to the eye."* She also wanted wisdom to be *"like God, know-*

Genesis 3:7-13

⁷*Then the eyes of both of them were opened, and they realized they were naked; so they sewed fig leaves together and made coverings for themselves.*

⁸*Then the man and his wife heard the sound of the LORD God as he was walking in the garden in the cool of the day, and they hid from the LORD God . . .* ⁹*But the LORD God called to the man, "Where are you?"*

¹⁰*He answered, "I heard you in the garden, and I was afraid because I was naked; so I hid."*

¹¹*And he said, "Who told you that you were naked? Have you eaten from the tree that I commanded you not to eat from?"*

¹²*The man said, "The woman you put here with me —she gave me some fruit from the tree, and I ate it."*

¹³*Then the LORD God said to the woman, "What is this you have done?"*

The woman said, "The serpent deceived me, and I ate."

The Serpent

Eve

Adam

ing good and evil." Adam, *"who was with her"* also chose to sin by disobeying God. In this act of rebellion against God, sin entered the world and corrupted or ruined the first workplace.

➥ **3. Below is a list of some of the ways sin began to affect Adam and Eve as described in Genesis 3:7-13 in the margin. Beside each item below write the number of a verse in the margin that shows that affect of sin.**

v.___ a. Adam blamed Eve for leading him to sin.

v.___ b. Adam blamed God for putting Eve in the garden with him.

v.___ c. Eve blamed the serpent for deceiving her.

v.___ d. They felt shame because they were naked.

v.___ e. They ran away from God. Their intimate fellowship with God was broken.

v.___ f. They experienced fear instead of love.

Are you amazed at how quickly life can become miserable because of sin? Because of one sin fear, shame, blame, and separation from God appeared in the original workplace. (Answers: a-12, b-12, c-13, d-7 & 10, e-8, f-10). Sin also brought some harsh consequences.

➥ **4. What were the consequences of sin for each one listed below? Read the verses and write a brief description (or key words) of the penalty each received from God.**

So the LORD God said to the serpent, "Because you have done this, "Cursed are you above all the livestock and all the wild animals! You will crawl on your belly and you will eat dust all the days of your life. And I will put enmity between you and the woman, and between your offspring and hers; he will crush your head, and you will strike his heel" (Gen. 3:14-15).

Sin's Penalty for the Serpent: _____

_____

_____

To the woman he said, "I will greatly increase your pains in childbearing; with pain you will give birth to children. Your desire will be for your husband, and he will rule over you" (Gen. 3:16).

Sin's Penalty for Eve _____

_____

_____

To Adam he said, "Because you listened to your wife and ate from the tree about which I commanded you, 'You must not eat of it,' "Cursed is the ground because of you; through painful toil you will eat of it all the days of your life. It will produce thorns and thistles for you, and you will eat the plants of the field. By the sweat of your brow you will eat your food until you return to the ground, since from it you were taken; for dust you are and to dust you will return" (Gen. 3:17-19)

Sin's Penalty for Adam _____

_____

_____

Hebrews 12:5-6

"My son, do not make light of the Lord's discipline, and do not lose heart when he rebukes you, because the Lord disciplines those he loves, and he punishes everyone he accepts as a son."

God disciplines those He loves (see Heb. 12:5-6). Even though He also forgives, forgiveness does not remove all the consequences of sin. The penalties you just described continue for all humanity:

- enmity between serpents and humanity (Gen. 3:15)
- pain in childbearing for women (Gen. 3:16)
- wife's desires for her husband (Gen. 3:16)
- husband's rule over his wife (Gen. 3:16)
- painful and difficult work life for men (Gen. 3:17-19)
- death (Gen. 3:19)

➡ **5. What are some ways that your work life reflects these working conditions? Write one or more ways for each one that applies to your workplace.**

"painful toil" _____

_____

"thorns and thistles" (things that hinder or make work difficult)

_____

_____

"sweat of your brow" _____

_____

God not only punished Adam and Eve, but He also showed His mercy: *"The LORD God made garments of skin for Adam and his wife and clothed them"* (Gen. 3:21). God reached out to Adam and Eve in love. By providing clothes, He began to invite them back into the love relationship with Himself. He sought to remove their fear and shame. In this action we see the first step God took to restore the workplace as He intended it. Next week we will look carefully at the workplace that Christ restores.

PRAYER STRATEGY

➡ **Take time now to pray about the conditions you face at work that reflect the consequences of sin. Pray that God would:**

- work to bring people into a right relationship with God
- work at removal of sin, fear, and shame
- provide strength to stand up under difficult times
- remove the obstacles that hinder your effectiveness

---

[1]W. E. Vine, "kosmos" in *An Expository Dictionary of New Testament Words*, nd, p. 1245.

DAY 2 The World's Agenda

Kingdom Agenda
"Those who live according to the sinful nature have their minds set on what that nature desires... The mind of sinful man is death, but the mind controlled by the Spirit is life and peace; the sinful mind is hostile to God. It does not submit to God's law, nor can it do so. Those controlled by the sinful nature cannot please God" (Rom. 8:5-8).

➡ **Read the "Kingdom Agenda" in the margin. Pause for a moment of prayer. Ask the Lord to help you understand how the sinful nature resists His Kingdom Agenda. Ask the Holy Spirit to control your mind and grant life and peace.**

The "Kingdom Agenda" verse for today describes the corruption that a sinful nature can bring. The sinful nature is hostile to God, does not submit to God's law, and cannot please God. The mind of this nature leads to death and separation from God.

➡ **1. Match the results on the left with the sinful mind and the Spirit-controlled mind on the right. Write the letter beside the number.**
a. leads to life and peace with God   __ 1. sinful mind
b. leads to death and cannot please God   __ 2. Spirit-controlled mind

When people give their minds over to the sinful nature they cannot please God and they continually experience spiritual death around them (1-b). Those who have surrendered to the lordship of Jesus Christ have His Spirit in them. Their Spirit-controlled mind experiences life and peace with God (2-a).

The world's agenda is man's attempt to live and work apart from the authority of a sovereign God. It is hostile to God and does not submit to His sovereign rule. It is man's attempt to find answers to his problems within himself rather than seeking to know God and follow Him. The world's agenda is driven by sinful human nature and is focused on fulfilling our needs apart from God.

Sin corrupts the workplace when the world's agenda is followed.

Today, I want us to look more carefully at the world's agenda. Sin corrupts the workplace when the world's agenda is followed. Let's look at three reasons the world's agenda corrupts the workplace.

> **Reasons the World's Agenda Corrupts the Workplace**
> 1. The world's agenda rejects the sovereignty of God.
> 2. The world's agenda is focused upon self.
> 3. The world's agenda seeks to satisfy needs apart from God.

The World's Agenda Rejects the Sovereignty of God.
The world's agenda was born on that day when Eve and Adam rebelled against God's instructions and ate the forbidden fruit. At the very heart of the world's agenda is an attitude that rejects God's rule. Self, rather than God, becomes ruler of life.

When we ignore the will of God and write our own agenda, we sin and often cause others to sin. We live and work each day with little or no sense of God's presence. We may even assume that God has nothing to do with our work. We conveniently forget that God is our Creator and that He has authority, dominion, and sovereignty over all creation. Our refusal to accept God as our Sovereign Authority in no way cancels His rightful position on the "throne" of life. God truly is King over all. The real question you must face is this: Will you let God rule on the throne of your life? God cre-

Will you let God rule on the throne of your life?

ated us, and He knows what is best to experience fullness of life. Rejecting His ways causes us to miss life's best. One way sin corrupts our workplace is that we reject God's sovereign rule over our work.

➡ **2. What is one reason the world's agenda corrupts the workplace?**

_____

_____

3. Why does rejecting God's rule corrupt the workplace?
❑ a. God just wants to be boss and makes our work miserable if He does not get His way.
❑ b. Rejecting His rule rejects what is best and right.

The World's Agenda Is Focused upon Self.

When you reject God's rule in your work life, you reject what is best and right. When the serpent tempted Eve to eat from the tree in the middle of the garden, he encouraged her to think about what would be best for herself. In reality her selfish focus was the worst thing she could have done. The serpent wanted her to think about her desires and needs above every other consideration. The serpent was tempting Eve to love herself above God. He was encouraging her to think only of satisfying her own need for significance. This is when people began to seek importance by looking to self for the answers.

In our society "self" often becomes more important than anything else. Society tells us to raise the battle cry for complete freedom—not realizing that it leads us into the bondage of sin. When we become selfish, we will make wrong choices in God's kingdom. This is why Jesus said, *"If anyone would come after me, he must deny himself and take up his cross daily and follow me"* (Luke 9:23). You must die to self daily and follow His agenda if you are to know real life.

> You must die to self daily and follow His agenda if you are to know real life.

➡ **4. What is a second reason the world's agenda corrupts the workplace?**

_____

_____

5. In which of the following ways have you seen or heard the world encourage you to focus on self instead of God and others? Check all that apply.
❑ "Look out for number one."
❑ "Have it your way."
❑ "Take care of yourself."
❑ "Be all you can be..."
❑ "Get all the gusto you can get."
❑ "Don't let anyone walk over you."
❑ "You deserve the very best."
❑ "If you want anything done right, you must do it yourself."
❑ "You can do anything you set your mind to."
6. Can you think of others? Write them in the margin.

The World's Agenda Seeks to Satisfy Needs Apart from God.

When Adam and Eve decided to eat the forbidden fruit, they stopped trusting God's provision. They decided to try meeting their needs apart from Him. They yielded to the "lust of the eyes" and the "pride of life." They wanted to be like God and, therefore, independent of Him.

Soon, they would discover how difficult life could be when they would try to satisfy their own needs apart from God. They were seeking to satisfy their need for significance apart from their relationship with God. God had not created them to live and work apart from Him. They were created to trust in His provisions. A deep sense of alienation, fear, and guilt would be a part of life as humans tried to satisfy their deepest needs apart from God.

➡ **7. What is a third reason the world's agenda corrupts the workplace?**

_____

_____

8. Mark the following statement true (T) or false (F). Circle one.
T   F   "I can do a better job of providing for my needs than God can."

You probably marked the statement false. That is correct. Don't we have a tendency, however, to live as though we can do it better than God. Or perhaps we don't trust God to come through, so we work out our own way to provide for our needs. God doesn't have to provide for anything that you are not trusting Him for.

> God doesn't have to provide for anything that you are not trusting Him for.

PRAYER STRATEGY
Take time now to pray.
- Ask God to examine your life and reveal how you may have allowed the world's agenda to affect your life.
- Agree with God about the truth of anything He may reveal to you.
- Ask God to forgive and cleanse you from guilt of self-centered living.
- Agree to take up your cross for daily death to self so you may follow the Kingdom Agenda.
- Ask God to empower and enable you to follow Him obediently and in faith.

DAY 3 When Self Rules Your Kingdom

Kingdom Agenda
"The acts of the sinful nature are obvious: sexual immorality, impurity and debauchery; idolatry and witchcraft; hatred, discord, jealousy, fits of rage, selfish ambition, dissensions, factions and envy; drunkenness, orgies, and the like. I warn you, as I did before, that those who live like this will not inherit the kingdom of God" (Gal. 5:19-21).

James 1:14-15
"Each one is tempted when, by his own evil desire, he is dragged away and enticed. Then after desire has conceived, it gives birth to sin; and sin, when it is full-grown, gives birth to death."

A Rich Young Ruler

➡ **Read the "Kingdom Agenda" in the margin. Pause for a moment of prayer. Circle words that describe the acts of the sinful nature. Ask the Lord to enable you to live by your Spirit-controlled nature.**

The Hostile Takeover

When we are driven by our human nature, our daily behavior on the job draws us away from God and His Kingdom Agenda. We begin to believe that we control our own destiny. God is relegated to a convenient corner of our lives, and we put self in His place. I call this a "hostile takeover" of the soul (see Jas. 1:14-15). We see everything in the light of "self-interest". With our emphasis on self, we cannot possibly live and work in a proper coworker relationship where God is Sovereign and we are cooperative. We've got it all upside-down! We consider ourselves "sovereign", and expect God to "cooperate" with us. Remember, when we choose to live by the world's agenda, we do three things.

➡ **1. See if you can fill in the blanks below as a review of yesterday's lesson. If you need help, you may peek.**

1. The world's agenda rejects the _____ of God.

2. The world's agenda is focused upon _____.

3. The world's agenda seeks to satisfy _____ apart from God.
Look at yesterday's lesson to check your work.

Read the following story of a rich young ruler who came to Jesus with an important question. Underline the question and see what kept him from following Jesus.

A certain ruler asked him, "Good teacher, what must I do to inherit eternal life?"

"Why do you call me good?" Jesus answered. "No one is good—except God alone. You know the commandments: `Do not commit adultery, do not murder, do not steal, do not give false testimony, honor your father and mother.'"

"All these I have kept since I was a boy," he said.

When Jesus heard this, he said to him, "You still lack one thing. Sell everything you have and give to the poor, and you will have treasure in heaven. Then come, follow me."

When he heard this, he became very sad, because he was a man of great wealth. Jesus looked at him and said, "How hard it is for the rich to enter the kingdom of God! Indeed, it is easier for a camel to go through the eye of a needle than for a rich man to enter the kingdom of God" (Luke 18:18-25).

➡ **2. What kept the young man from following Jesus?**

_____

When the rich young ruler approached Jesus, he was looking for a way to satisfy some aspect of his human nature that controlled his life. Some have suggested that he was driven by his need to feel "safe and secure". Others think that he was driven by his need to "self-actualize" and reach his ultimate potential in life. One thing is for sure, he didn't have a clue that he was working and living on the "world's agenda." He was missing the agenda of the Kingdom of God!

He stood in the presence of the King of Kings and could not recognize the King or the Kingdom! When Jesus offered him an opportunity to follow Him and experience the power and presence of the Kingdom, the young man could not trust in God to meet his own needs. He had always trusted in himself. He was in love with his wealth. This would have required a radical change in his life. A change from what he perceived to be safe and secure. He would have to put his trust in the provision of God. He couldn't do it. So the young man turned away from the greatest opportunity ever offered to him. He would miss God's invitation to live and experience the awesome power and presence of His Kingdom—an invitation to live and learn from the King, Himself!

What is so incredible about this experience is that Jesus actually was offering to invest His own life into this young man. Jesus wanted to teach and disciple him, personally! He was willing to pour out His life for this person. Yet, the young man chose to walk away from this awesome opportunity, because he was dominated by his own need for safety and security! In the workplace corrupted by sin, man continuously rejects the sovereignty of God and chooses to try to meet his own needs apart from God!

➡ **3. If you were to come before Jesus today, what do you think He would point to in your life that needed to be put away in order for you to follow Him? Ask Him what He sees in your life that may get in the way of your love relationship with God. Pray through the list in the margin to see if any of these may get in your way. Circle any that apply.**

It is vitally important that we understand how our own human nature can dominate our lives and lead us to sin. Let's look at human nature and then we will examine how it corrupts the marketplace.

Driven by Needs

Psychologists broadly accept the fact that humans are driven and motivated by their needs. A person needs food to live. If he gets hungry enough, he will do almost anything to get food. Once his needs for food are met, he can focus on other needs that he has. One of the most widely accepted descriptions of human nature was developed by Abraham Maslow and is known as the "Hierarchy of Needs." According to Maslow, we are driven to satisfy our human needs. His descriptions are insightful, but they describe a human nature that is totally self-centered.

Self usually takes priority over other concerns. When we allow ourselves to give first priority to meeting our own needs, we cannot seek God's kingdom first. When your human needs take first priority in your life, you are being dominated by your human nature which is corrupted by sin. That, in turn, is one way sin can corrupt the workplace.

We do have human needs, and some of them must be met if we are to live. We can choose, however, to obey God or seek His Kingdom's Agenda first and trust Him to meet our needs. Let's look at some of the human needs that you could desire in such a way that you would not follow the Kingdom

- love of wealth and money
- depending on others instead of God
- desire to run my own life
- fear of losing family or friends
- fear of what God might ask me to do
- fear of what people might say
- love for the things of the world
- love for traditions, even religious tradition
- love of a sinful relationship
- love of position or power
- love of self-centered "freedom"
- love the praise of people
- trusting in self to provide needs
- others:

_____

_____

_____

_____

Agenda.

Physical Needs. These are the strongest and most basic of human needs. They include hunger, thirst, the need for air, and so forth

The Need for a Safe Environment. People do not function well when they live in fear for their safety. They need freedom from the threat of danger in order to focus on other matters.

The Need to Be Loved and Accepted. These needs include the need for acceptance, affection, affiliation, and belonging to a group. The focus of these needs is on meaningful relationships with others. The desire to see these needs met can cause people to do "whatever it takes" to see the needs met. They sometimes will do wrong, sinful, illegal, and even evil things just to find acceptance and love.

The Desire for Recognition and Esteem. These include the desire to be respected by others and the desire for achievement, reputation, status, and prestige. The driving motivation at this level is to "be somebody." Many people base their identity on what others think about them. That is a very fragile position to take, because it can be shattered in a moment. It also has a tendency to be very self-centered.

The Desire to Be All You Can Be. Many people have a strong desire to achieve. They want to reach the top. They want realize their full potential. Psychologists suggest that a person cannot function at this level unless most or all of the lower level needs have been met.

These needs are not bad in themselves. God created us with needs. We cannot live without some of these needs being met. The problem comes when the desire to meet these needs takes priority over obedience to God's will and purposes. Problems also come when we try to meet these needs in ways other than ways God intended. Being driven by your human needs is one way sin corrupts the workplace.

➡ **4. See if you can think of an experience in your work life where you were motivated, pressured, or chose to do something because of each of these needs. I have given you an example for each. Write a brief note to yourself regarding an experience in your own work life. If you have trouble thinking of a personal example leave the line blank.**
A. Physical Needs (example: *You changed jobs because you didn't make enough money to buy groceries. Your family was hungry.*)

Your experience: _____

_____

B. The Need for a Safe Environment. (example: *You chose not to volunteer for an assignment because it was dangerous or had high risk.*)

Your experience: _____

_____

C. The Need for Love and Acceptance. (example: *You took up golf in order to relate to peers in company management.*)

Your experience: _____

_____

> The problem comes when the desire to meet these needs takes priority over obedience to God's will and purposes.
>
> Being driven by your human needs is one way sin corrupts the workplace

D. The Desire for Recognition and Esteem. *(example: You worked long hours and weekends in order to "wow" your supervisor with your presentation.)*

Your experience: _____

_____

E. The Desire to Be All You Can Be. *(example: You went far beyond what is expected for the personal satisfaction of knowing you did your very best.)*

Your experience: _____

_____

The Heart of Sin: Self-Centeredness

This way of describing human nature and motivation is widely accepted as the way we are. It is fairly accurate when you are only looking at the human dimension of life. When we are driven to try and meet the needs of our human nature, apart from God, we become self-focused and self-centered rather than God-centered. This is the very heart of sin. Following Christ calls us to move beyond self and meeting our needs to obedience to Christ—regardless of the cost. A life driven to satisfy only human needs is one lived in bondage to sin.

> Following Christ calls us to move beyond self and meeting our needs to obedience to Christ—regardless of the cost.

➡ **5. Take a few moments to reflect on the following questions. You do not have to write answers, but you may jot notes to yourself on the lines provided.**
   a. Have you ever "missed God's agenda" for your life, because you chose to satisfy a human need instead of obey God?

   _____

   b. Have you gotten caught up in trying to satisfy your own needs apart from God?

   _____

   c. What aspect (level of needs) of your human nature seems to be the strongest or most pressing in your life?

   _____

   d. How has your human nature affected your work and your decisions?

   _____

> When we allow some aspect of human nature to dominate our lives, it always leads to sin and leads us away from God.

When we allow some aspect of human nature to dominate our lives, it always leads to sin and leads us away from God. This is the primary reason that the workplace in which we work today is corrupted. The world needs:
- people who have been delivered from the domination of their own self-centered human nature
- people who have been redeemed from the old "self" and are living under the influence of God's divine nature
- people who are working according to the Kingdom Agenda!
   The Bible is full of examples of how man's sinful nature impacts the

world around us. Every time we reject the sovereignty of God and try to "take charge" of our own lives, we refuse to abide by God's agenda. We willingly select the agenda of this world, including all of the consequences that such a choice brings.

When human nature (rather than God) reigns in a person's life, he or she will experience certain consequences that are readily predictable. The person may experience sin, immoral or unethical behavior, broken relationships with others and God, prejudice, emotional distress, loneliness, fear, lack of financial responsibility or even loss of life just to mention a few. The consequences can be devastating! In the optional "For Further Study" at the end of today's lesson you can examine the dominating human nature in the lives of some biblical characters and how their lives were affected.

PRAYER STRATEGY
Take time now to pray.
• Thank God for ways in which He has provided for your human needs.
• Pray for strength to obey Him and trust Him even when you don't know how your human needs will be met.
• Ask the Lord to reveal any area of your life where your human nature is so strong that you are missing His Kingdom Agenda for your life and work.

FOR FURTHER STUDY
➡ **Read each scripture passage listed on the following page. Identify an aspect of human nature that seemed to be dominating the person's life. Then describe the consequences when human nature was in control.**

Human Nature
1. Physical Needs
2. Need for Safe Environment
3. Need for Love and Acceptance
4. Desire for Recognition and Esteem
5. Desire to Be All You Can Be

Genesis 4:1-16—Cain
Human Nature: _____

Consequences: _____
1 Samuel 18:6-9—Saul
Human Nature: _____

Consequences: _____
Genesis 25:29-34—Esau
Human Nature: _____

Consequences: _____
2 Samuel 11:1-5 and 12:7-14—David
Human Nature: _____

Consequences: _____
Matthew 2:1-16—Herod
Human Nature: _____

Consequences: _____
Luke 22:55-62—Peter
Human Nature: _____

Consequences: _____
Acts 5:1-10—Ananias and Sapphira
Human Nature: _____

Consequences: _____

DAY 4 Influences of the World's Agenda

Kingdom Agenda

"Each one is tempted when, by his own evil desire, he is dragged away and enticed. Then, after desire has conceived, it gives birth to sin; and sin, when it is full-grown, gives birth to death" (Jas. 1:14-15).

➡ **Read the "Kingdom Agenda" in the margin. Pause for a moment of prayer. Ask the Lord to help you understand the nature of temptation, evil desires and sin. Ask Him for help in overcoming temptation to live victoriously in Christ.**

Ways the World's Agenda May Influence You
1. You can do anything.
2. Find value in yourself.
3. Serve yourself.
4. Blame others for your problems.
5. Love things and use people.

"You Can Do Anything"

Today, I want us to look at five ways the world's agenda may influence the way you work. The mindset of most people in the world reflects their attempt to believe in themselves and their accomplishments. At first glance, this seems to be good. The problem with this way of thinking is that it leads us away from God. Instead of placing our trust in God, we are taught to believe in ourselves. God wants us to learn and practice absolute dependence on Him.

God wants us to learn and practice absolute dependence on Him.

You can do many things as a human being that may receive the praise of others. However, even your life and breath are dependent on God's provision. As for the Kingdom, Jesus said you can do nothing of Kingdom value apart from Him. (See John 15:5.) With Him, you can do all things. (See Phil. 4:13.)

John 15:5

"I am the vine; you are the branches. If a man remains in me and I in him, he will bear much fruit; apart from me you can do nothing."

➡ **1. Write the statement below in a way that makes it true instead of false.** "I can do anything."

_____

Philippians 4:13

"I can do all things through Christ which strengtheneth me." (KJV)

One important lesson to learn as a disciple is to agree with God. To agree with God you might have said, "I can do nothing apart from Christ," or "I can do all things through Christ who gives me strength."

"Find Value in Yourself"

The world teaches us to find a sense of meaning and worth in ourselves. It's not that each of us does not have value; we most certainly do! But we were not created to satisfy this deep need within ourselves and apart from God. Your relationship to God gives you the greatest value. Don't forget that God valued you so highly and His love for you was so great that He gave His only Son to die for you. When you surrender to Him and receive His saving grace, He adopts you into His family. That is where you find your true value.

When you surrender to Him and receive His saving grace, He adopts you into His family. That is where you find your true value.

➡ **2. Rewrite the following statement in a way that correctly identifies the source of your value.** "Find value in myself."

_____

Matthew 6:33

"Seek first his kingdom and his righteousness."

John 12:25-26

"The man who loves his life will lose it, while the man who hates his life in this world will keep it for eternal life. Whoever serves me must follow me; and where I am, my servant also will be. My Father will honor the one who serves me."

Romans 14:12

"Each of us will give an account of himself to God."

1 John 2:15

"Do not love the world or anything in the world. If anyone loves the world, the love of the Father is not in him."

John 15:12

"My command is this: Love each other as I have loved you."

"Serve Yourself"

The world's agenda is driven by our self-focused view of the world around us. We see every decision and situation we face in light of what will most benefit ourselves. We may sell our ideas to others disguised in a more noble image, but deep down inside we consider everything according to what would be best for ourselves. There are times when we step outside of this agenda and unselfishly do what is best for others. Rarely, do we truly realize that our job is to serve God for His Kingdom purposes. (See Matt. 6:33 and John 12:25-26.) This can only be accomplished when we abandon self and trust God.

➡ **3. Rewrite the following statement in a way that gives it a right focus instead of a wrong focus.** "Serve myself."

_____

"Blame Others for Your Problems"

Accepting responsibility for our own actions is rare. If everything goes well, we want the credit. But if things go wrong or problems develop we immediately try to blame the problems on others. We may blame our past, circumstances, or other people; but we seldom want to accept responsibility for our own actions. Isn't that what Adam and Eve did in the garden? We try to protect ourselves from the hurt, the failure, or the consequences of our actions. Ultimately we must all give account of our actions to God who knows the truth. (See Rom. 14:12.)

➡ **4. Rewrite the following statement in a way that describes the right way to respond to problems.** "Blame others for my problems."

_____

"Love Things and Use People"

Living in a world of materialism, our thinking is saturated with the empty concept that "things" will bring happiness. People are constantly trying to satisfy the deepest needs of their human nature by acquiring things. In order to do that, we may do whatever it takes—including taking advantage of others for personal gain. Things provide only a temporary "fix" for what really ails us. In fact, loving things places you at odds with God. (See 1 John 2:15.)

No matter how much a person has, the deepest needs of life can only be satisfied by God. Unfortunately, we often tend to love things and use people in the world today. We need to learn to truly love people and simply use things. That is the Kingdom way. (See John 15:12.)

➡ **5. Rewrite the following statement in a way that describes the proper way to relate to things and people.** "Love things and use people."

_____

Here is the way I would rewrite these statements:
1. I can do nothing of Kingdom value apart from Christ working through me.
2. Find value in my love relationship with God.
3. Serve God and His Kingdom Agenda.
4. Accept responsibility for my own actions.
5. Love people and use things.

There are many other ways the world's agenda shapes our actions. One way to recognize the world's ways is to ask yourself the following questions:
- Does this action violate God's sovereign rule in my life?
- Is this action "self-centered" or "God-centered"?
- When I act this way, am I drawn closer to God or do I find myself further away from Him?

PRAYER STRATEGY

➡ **Take time now to pray. Review the five ways the world's agenda may influence your work.**
- Ask God to reveal to you any ways in which you have been influenced wrongly by the world's agenda.
- Confess that you need His Spirit to straighten out your thinking.
- Ask the Lord to give you opportunities to demonstrate a different way of living and working in these five areas.

For Further Study

➡ **Read the following Scriptures. Let God speak to you about sin and things in life that you should avoid. You may want to write notes to yourself in the margin.**

Colossians 3:5-9 • *Put to death, therefore, whatever belongs to your earthly nature: sexual immorality, impurity, lust, evil desires and greed, which is idolatry. Because of these, the wrath of God is coming. You used to walk in these ways, in the life you once lived. But now you must rid yourselves of all such things as these: anger, rage, malice, slander, and filthy language from your lips. Do not lie to each other, since you have taken off your old self with its practices*

1 Peter 2:11-12 • *Dear friends, I urge you, as aliens and strangers in the world, to abstain from sinful desires, which war against your soul. Live such good lives among the pagans that, though they accuse you of doing wrong, they may see your good deeds and glorify God on the day he visits us.*

1 Thessalonians 4:3 • *It is God's will that you should be sanctified: that you should avoid sexual immorality;*

1 Timothy 6:10-12 • *For the love of money is a root of all kinds of evil. Some people, eager for money, have wandered from the faith and pierced themselves with many griefs.*

2 Chronicles 26:16 • *But after Uzziah became powerful, his pride led to his downfall. He was unfaithful to the LORD his God.*

Galatians 6:7-9 • *Do not be deceived: God cannot be mocked. A man reaps what he sows. 8 The one who sows to please his sinful nature, from that nature will reap destruction; the one who sows to please the Spirit, from the Spirit will reap eternal life. 9 Let us not become weary in doing good, for at the proper time we will reap a harvest if we do not give up.*

Ways the World's Agenda May Influence You

1. You can do anything.
2. Find value in yourself.
3. Serve yourself.
4. Blame others for your problems.
5. Love things and use people.

DAY 5 Sin's Corruption in Your Workplace

Kingdom Agenda

"What causes fights and quarrels among you? Don't they come from your desires that battle within you? You want something but don't get it. You kill and covet . . . You quarrel and fight. You do not have, because you do not ask God. When you ask, you do not receive, because you ask with wrong motives, that you may spend what you get on your pleasures . . .

Don't you know that friendship with the world is hatred toward God? Anyone who chooses to be a friend of the world becomes an enemy of God" (Jas. 4:1-4).

➡ **Read the "Kingdom Agenda" in the margin. Pause for a moment of prayer. Ask the Lord to help you identify ways your workplace has been corrupted by sin and the world's agenda. Circle the ways listed in James 4:1-4.**

We are so familiar with the world's agenda that we often have difficulty recognizing just how much our own human nature controls us. It is very subtle in its influence, guiding us to do something "good" in place of "God's best." Our "salt-like" influence on the world is hindered by this subtle shift from God's Agenda to the world's! There are many ways that human nature and sin influence our workplace. Let's examine a few:

Human Nature May Influence the Workplace
1. Quality may be sacrificed for quantity.
2. Pricing may be deceiving.
3. Immoral, illegal, or unethical practices may be common.
4. Welfare of people and nature may be overlooked for the sake of profit.
5. Taking responsibility for actions may not be important.

Quality May Be Sacrificed for Quality

Recently a teenager became very sick after she returned home from summer camp. Her mom took her to the doctor, waiting quite a while before they were able to finally see him. She was quickly diagnosed, given a prescription for antibiotics, and sent home. Her parents carefully followed the doctor's orders, but their daughter did not seem to get any better. Her mom called the doctor once again, to report to him that her daughter had not improved. She was told that she should give her daughter a higher dose of the antibiotic. After two more days, the teenager was so lethargic that she had to be carried to the bathroom. Her parents rushed her back to the doctor, again waiting a considerable amount of time. The doctor seemed to hurry through the appointment. The mother insisted that something was very wrong. She asked the doctor to run some tests. Though he was sure of his diagnosis, the doctor reluctantly agreed to run a few basic tests. The tests revealed a very serious disease.

Now you and I know that doctors do make mistakes. Some conditions are difficult to diagnose. Yet, the "assembly line" approach to medical care can leave a doctor little time to really give adequate attention to a patient. Why must one doctor treat such a large quantity of patients? Have some chosen to sacrifice quality for quantity?

Before we start pointing our finger at doctors, insurance companies, or lawyers, we need to recognize the influence of human nature over the entire system. If you reduce all the factors down to their lowest common denominator, you will discover people who are driven to satisfy some aspect of their human nature—greed for example. Too many people are working off the world's agenda. Compromising quality for quantity is evident in almost every area of the workplace. Even churches can focus on numbers and not give adequate attention to helping disciples mature in Christ. Corporations may let profit dictate their actions. Whenever quality is com-

Even churches can focus on numbers and not give adequate attention to helping disciples mature in Christ.

promised for quantity you know the world's agenda is at work.

➥ **1. If your company or employer were to sacrifice quality for quantity, what would it look like? How would they do it?**

_____

_____

2. Can you think of a time or a way in which they have sacrificed quality for quantity? When? or How?

_____

_____

Pricing May Be Deceiving

Recently I spoke with a young college student who had been employed part-time in a clothing store. He told me how they priced their clothing. In this particular store they mark the regular price up before showing a 20-50% "discount." So the actual sale price is not a true 20-50% savings. Many consider it good business or marketing savvy.

Deceiving a potential customer can happen in other ways as well. Direct mail may be "disguised" in envelopes to look like government checks in order to get special attention. A time-share company may offer a "free vacation" to lure potential buyers. But they may end up charging "fees" and "taxes" that wind up more than paying for the vacation expenses.

➥ **3. If your company or employer were to use deceiving practices to increase business, what would they do?**

_____

_____

4. Can you think of a time or a way in which they have deceived customers for the sake of business? When? or How?

_____

_____

Immoral, Illegal, or Unethical Practices May Be Common

In some businesses providing sexual favors may be an expected "fringe benefit" for clients that are decision makers. Other industries are known for the practice of giving bribes or kick-backs to secure favorable decisions. Less obvious practices might include overlooking unfavorable research data that indicates potential harm. Accounting practices may fix the books to keep from revealing sources of income or expenditures to stockholders or directors.

➥ **5. If your company or employer were to engage in immoral, illegal, or unethical practices, what is one practice that might occur?**

_____

_____

6. Can you think of a time or a way in which they have engaged in a practice that was immoral, illegal, or unethical?

❏ YES ❏ NO [You do not have to write down a specific instance.]

Welfare of People and Nature May Be Overlooked for the Sake of Profit

A friend of mine recently had a heart attack. He had worked for twenty-nine years for a well-known national grocery chain. While he was in the hospital, he received notice that he had been terminated. He was just one year away from retirement. Here was a man who had given twenty-nine years of his life to a company and yet, their main concern was that he might not be able to continue to do his job effectively. There were also financial considerations. He threatened legal action, and they reluctantly gave him his job back. Now he faces subtle harassment for not going along with the company decision.

Other companies have polluted soil and water with toxic waste because the cost for disposal is high. Some industries (like alcohol and tobacco) conduct their legal business knowing that their products are directly related to the deaths of thousands and even hundreds of thousands of users each year. The agenda which places "profits" above the welfare of people and nature is one in which people are driven by some aspect of their own human nature.

➡ **7. If your company or employer were to sacrifice the welfare of people or nature for the sake of profit, how could they do it in your line of work?**

_____

8. Can you think of a time or a way in which they have sacrificed the welfare of people or nature for the sake of profit? When? or How?

_____

Taking Responsibility for Actions May Not Be Important

Human nature prefers the "path of least resistance." We prefer to blame someone else rather than face the consequences of our own actions. That is exactly what Adam and Eve did in the original workplace. Displacement of responsibility has become the norm rather than the exception. With the threat of lawsuits over practically anything, people constantly use this self-preservation strategy in the midst of conflict.

A young man kills his parents and then seeks to blame them for their own deaths. A husband has an affair and blames his wife for not satisfying his needs. A country singer gets arrested for drug abuse, and sympathetic fans blame the fast-paced lifestyle of show business. The national debt continues to grow as politicians look for others to blame. There is a long list of irresponsibility, and we all are on it somewhere.

➡ **9. If your company or employer were to avoid taking responsibility for its actions, what kind of circumstance might arise that would tempt them to do so?**

_____

10. Can you think of a time or a way in which they denied responsibility for their actions to avoid adverse consequences? When? or How?

_____

The ways human nature and sin can corrupt your workplace are almost limitless.

The ways human nature and sin can corrupt your workplace are almost limitless. Many of us have gotten so used to a sinful workplace, that we

If you, however, want to join God in His redemptive work in the world, you need to see from God's perspective how sin has corrupted the workplace.

don't stop to think about how very sinful it is. If, however, you want to join God in His redemptive work in the world, you need to see from God's perspective how sin has corrupted the workplace. Another tendency of many companies or employers is to justify sinful practices as their only alternative. They may not be willing to make a major or costly adjustment to do things in a way pleasing to God.

➡ 11. **Read through the lists below. Check any item that is present in your workplace that may be an evidence of sin or sin's corruption in your workplace. Check all that you personally know about in your workplace. Then list any others you can think of that are not on this list. Write them in the margin.**

❑ oppression	❑ pornography	❑ prejudice
❑ prostitution	❑ quarreling	❑ racism
❑ rage	❑ revenge	❑ robbery
❑ rudeness	❑ selfish ambition	❑ selfishness
❑ sexual misconduct	❑ shame	❑ slander
❑ stingy	❑ swearing oaths	❑ theft
❑ unfair wages	❑ unjust gain	❑ workaholism
❑ addictions	❑ anger	❑ arrogance
❑ belittling	❑ bribery	❑ carelessness
❑ cheating	❑ cursing	❑ deceit
❑ demeaning	❑ dirty jokes	❑ dishonesty
❑ disobedience	❑ dissension	❑ drug abuse
❑ drunkenness	❑ envy	❑ exploitation
❑ extortion	❑ false witness	❑ favoritism
❑ fighting	❑ fraud	❑ gambling
❑ gossip	❑ greed	❑ harassment
❑ harsh words	❑ hatred	❑ hot temper
❑ hoarding wealth	❑ hypocrisy	❑ immorality
❑ illegal activity	❑ injustice	❑ insults
❑ laziness	❑ lying	❑ murder

❑ concealing sin (cover-up)	❑ deceitful advertising
❑ failure to pay debts	❑ insensitivity to human need
❑ unethical practices	❑ unforgiveness/bitterness
❑ preventable pollution	❑ violating Sabbath commands
❑ waste of resources	❑ withholding wages earned

❑ broken relationships between coworkers
❑ broken relationships between employer and employee
❑ broken relationships between union and management
❑ harming families for the sake of gain
❑ manipulation for personal gain
❑ not giving an honest day's work
❑ witchcraft and occult practices

PRAYER STRATEGY

➡ **Take time now to pray.**
- Share with the Lord burdens or concerns you have about your workplace.
- Begin praying now that God will show you how He wants to work redemptively in your workplace or through you.
- Confess and repent of any sin of which the Holy Spirit may have revealed that you are guilty.

KINGDOM STRATEGY
MEETING 3

U se the following suggestions to guide a one-hour small-group discussion of *The Kingdom Agenda* covering the lessons in this week's study. For general instructions for the group facilitator, see page 156.

This Week's Learning Objective
You will understand the nature of the workplace sin corrupted and demonstrate your dissatisfaction with the world's agenda.

Opening Prayer (2 minutes)
• Begin with prayer acknowledging God's presence.
• Ask the Holy Spirit to be your teacher.
• Ask the Lord to help you all come to a clear understanding of how desperately sin has tarnished our workplaces.
• Ask the Lord to reveal the specific ways sin has corrupted your own workplaces.

Getting Better Acquainted (8 minutes)
Ask volunteers to share briefly one experience they have had this week at work that indicated sin has corrupted their workplace or profession in some way.

Content Review (10 minutes)
Ask members to turn in their books to the Overview of Week 3 on page 55. Using the time suggested, review the following items of content from this week's lessons:
• Ask members to recite this week's Scripture-memory verse together—1 John 2:15.
• Ask: Which one of the summary statements from week 3 was most meaningful to you and why?
• Ask: What are three primary ways the world's agenda corrupts the workplace?
• Ask: What are some ways the world's agenda may influence you?
• Ask: What are some ways human nature may influence the workplace?

Discussion Questions (25 minutes)
Look over the following list of questions and lead the group to discuss those that you think would be most meaningful or helpful to your group. Watch your time (invite members to help you), so that you will allow adequate time for prayer at the end of the session.
1. On page 56, which idea did you write down for #1 and why?
2. How did Adam and Eve's sin corrupt the original workplace?
3. What are some of the consequences of Adam's sin that still affect us today?
4. On page 58, what are some of the ways your work life reflects these working conditions (#5)?
5. What difference does it make in a workplace when God is no longer treated as Sovereign?
6. What does Mike mean by "Hostile Takeover" on page 62 (see Jas. 1:14-15)?
7. If you were standing before Jesus, what do you think He would ask you to change in order to follow Him? Have you asked Him? What, if anything did He say? (See #3 on p. 63.)
8. What are some ways you have been motivated, pressured, or chosen to do something because of the needs of your human nature? (#4, pp. 64-65)
9. [Turn to page 65 and discuss responses to the questions in #5. Invite members to relate experiences.]
10. Which of the five "Ways the World's Agenda May Influence You" (p. 67) has been the most difficult for you to overcome?
11. In pairs or groups of three, ask members to review their responses to questions 1-10 (pp. 71-72) What are some of the ways you have seen the evidence of sin's corruption in your workplace?
12. Which one or two sins on page 73 seem(s) to be most damaging to your workplace?

Priority Praying (15 minutes)

Conclude the session by spending time as a group praying for each other.

- Ask members to share with the group the one greatest burden they have regarding their workplace, profession, or work relationships.
- Invite members to pray for these specific areas. You may use sentence prayers, conversational prayer, or pray in any other way you feel led. Encourage members to focus on one subject at a time and pray until they sense they have covered the subject adequately. Give members permission to pray as many times as they choose.
- Encourage members to confess sins to one another and pray for one another as the Holy Spirit may lead. See James 5:16:

    "Confess your sins to each other and pray for each other so that you may be healed. The prayer of a righteous man is powerful and effective."

- Invite members to use the space below to record prayer requests so they can pray about them during the coming week. Encourage them to pray about specific individuals or situations that need God's redemptive work.

WORK-RELATED PRAYER REQUESTS

Week 4 The Workplace Christ Restores

*L*isa was shocked by her two-year-old Elliot's comment: "I'm the boss, and you are the baby!" It was all she could do to keep from laughing at her son's attempt to establish some new ground rules for their relationship. Here this little man was attempting to exert his authority over his mom. Debi and I were watching a family "mutiny."

We might giggle to ourselves and say, "It's all part of going through the terrible two's!" However, these words give us an insight into our sinful human condition. Elliot said what most of us would not admit. He revealed his desire to be in charge of his life. He was creating his own agenda, where self was in charge. This self-centeredness is at the heart of life that is shaped by sinful human nature. Elliot's parents will have to teach him that he is not "the boss" in their family. On a larger scale they will need to help Elliot understand that God is the boss and we are all "babies" throughout life.

This God-centeredness is a central issue in the Gospel of the Kingdom that Jesus preached. It is a radical new agenda, unlike one shaped by human hearts. This God-centeredness requires a complete change in our perspective on life. That is why Jesus preached, "Repent, for the kingdom of heaven is near" (Matt. 4:17).

Lisa gave some thought to Elliot's attempt at "mutiny" and then said, "You wait until your Father gets home. He is going to straighten you out about this."

Jesus came to straighten us out about "who the boss is." Christians often confess that Jesus Christ is Lord, but their daily lives often reveal a different reality. We prefer to live and work according to our own agenda where self is the boss. Jesus wants us to turn away from that selfish life and follow Him as Lord. He seeks to restore the workplace God intended where He is Sovereign, and we are cooperative and obedient.

OVERVIEW OF WEEK 4

This Week's Scripture-Memory Verse

"God was in Christ, reconciling the world unto himself. . . and hath committed unto us the word of reconciliation. Now then we are ambassadors for Christ" (2 Cor. 5:19-20, KJV).

This Week's Lessons

Day 1: Christ Restores the Workplace
Day 2: Christ Overcomes the World
Day 3: Christ Changes Lives
Day 4: Christ Changes Relationships
Day 5: Christ Changes Conduct and Productivity

Summary Statements from Week 4

• He changes lives and then works through them to restore what has been corrupted by sin and the consequences of sin.
• Repent means "to change your mind."
• When you repent, you have the opportunity to experience the abundant life Christ came to give
• You will be aware of God's presence, depend on His provision, obey His will, follow His lead, join God in His work, and cooperate under His sovereignty.
• Jesus was the Second Adam. He came to reestablish the Kingdom rule of God over His creation.
• There is a condition: Jesus must be "Lord."
• You do not have to be driven by your human needs for things like food, drink, and clothes. . . . You can choose to seek God's kingdom as your first priority.
• Jesus did not allow human needs to get in the way of the Kingdom Agenda—obedience to His assignment from His Father.
• Jesus chose to obey His Father even when it meant suffering and death.
• It is in a love relationship with God the Father that your need for love and acceptance is most completely fulfilled.
• God also meets our need to belong to a group by placing us in a church that functions like a body.
• Jesus saw His role as that of a Servant. . . . He set an example for us to be willing to assume the lowly role of servanthood also.
• Each day and in every way, Jesus chose to live and work with the understanding that His Father was Sovereign. He intentionally chose to live according to His divine nature and reject the temptations of sinful human nature.
• Jesus begins to restore the workplace by restoring people to a right relationship with God, their

King. Once they are right with God, they begin to live differently.
• You can trust completely in God's provision, His protection, His power, and His promises! This is a life and work strategy that is born out of a daily intimate relationship with God.
• As Christ begins living out His life through more and more people in a workplace, that workplace will look more and more like the original workplace God intended.
• Christ changes a life, and He also changes the person's relationship with God and relationships with others.
• The world's agenda will encourage you to take assignments from God's job description rather than your own.
• When you repent, you quit working off God's job description and begin working off your own in a proper relationship with God.
• We sin when we try to take over God's job description instead of attend to our own.
• A believer must function by revelation (God's revealed will) rather than by human reasoning.
• When the love of Christ shows in your life, people will know you are His disciple.
• God wants to put you on public display to show what a difference Christ makes in a life.
• God has eternity in view. At times, circumstances will appear negative and unproductive.

IMPORTANT IDEAS

Christ Restores the Workplace
1. Christ Changes Lives
2. Christ Changes Relationships
3. Christ Changes Conduct
4. Christ Changes Productivity

Returning to the Kingdom Agenda
1. Surrender to God's sovereignty.
2. Deny self and follow Christ.
3. Depend on God to satisfy needs.

A Restored Coworker Relationship
1. God is present. I acknowledge His presence.
2. God provides for His worker's needs. I depend on God's provision.
3. God reveals His will. I obey God's will.
4. God initiates work. I follow God's lead.
5. God works. I join God in His work.
6. God is Sovereign. I cooperate under God's sovereignty.

DAY 1   Christis Restores the Workplace

Kingdom Agenda
"God was in Christ, reconciling the world unto himself. . . and hath committed unto us the word of reconciliation. Now then we are ambassadors for Christ" (2 Cor. 5:19-20, KJV).

➡ **Read the "Kingdom Agenda" in the margin. Pause for a moment of prayer. Thank God for bringing you into a right relationship with Him. Meditate on what it means for you to be an ambassador for the King!**

In the workplace God intended, God invited Adam to join Him in a coworker relationship. Because of sin, the workplace was corrupted and Adam and Eve had to live with the consequences of their sin. Because of sin, death entered the world. Work became difficult, stressful, and less fruitful. Ever since then, people have been working in a workplace sin has corrupted.

➡ **1. What are the first two workplaces we have studied? Fill in the blanks.**

1. The Workplace God _____ (Week 2)

2. The Workplace Sin _____ (Week 3)

Since Adam and Eve, every generation has been working on the world's agenda because of our sinful human nature. But:

> *God so loved the world that he gave his one and only Son, that whoever believes in him shall not perish but have eternal life. For God did not send his Son into the world to condemn the world, but to save the world through him* (John 3:16).

Jesus Christ came to redeem sinful humanity and restore the sovereignty of God in the hearts of people. He wants to bring men and women back into a right relationship with God in every aspect of their lives—including their work lives. Jesus wants to restore the workplace to God's original intention where work is sacred, meaningful, and fruitful. He wants to restore people to the coworker relationship with God that He intended from the beginning. This week we are going to study "The Workplace Christ Restores."

Christ's Ministry Agenda

Isaiah 61:1-4
"The Spirit of the Sovereign LORD is on me, because the LORD has anointed me to preach good news to the poor. He has sent me to bind up the brokenhearted, to proclaim freedom for the captives and release from darkness for the prisoners, to proclaim the year of the LORD's favor and the day of vengeance of our God, to comfort all who mourn, and provide for those who grieve in Zion—to bestow on them a crown of beauty instead of ashes, the oil of gladness instead of mourning, and a garment of praise instead of a spirit of despair. They will be called oaks of righteousness, a planting of the LORD for the display of his splendor. They will rebuild the ancient ruins and restore the places long devastated; they will renew the ruined cities that have been devastated for generations."

Early in Jesus' earthly ministry, He stood in the synagogue and read a passage from Isaiah 61. Then He simply stated: *"Today this scripture is fulfilled in your hearing"* (Luke 4:21). Jesus Christ had a Kingdom Agenda given Him by His Father. Here is a summary from Isaiah 61:1-4 describing the work of Christ. He came to:

- preach good news to the poor
- bind up the brokenhearted
- proclaim freedom for the captives
- proclaim release from darkness for the prisoners
- proclaim the year of the Lord's favor
- proclaim the day of vengeance of our God
- comfort all who mourn
- provide for those who grieve . . .
    - a crown of beauty instead of ashes
    - the oil of gladness instead of mourning
    - a garment of praise instead of a spirit of despair

As a result of His earthly ministry, Christ will have prepared a people who will . . .

- be called oaks of righteousness for the display of the Lord's splendor
- rebuild the ancient ruins
- restore the places long devastated
- renew the ruined cities

This passage reveals one of the primary ways Christ restores a workplace. He begins by meeting the needs of an individual and preparing him or her as an instrument of righteousness. Then He works through that person to rebuild, restore, and renew *"for the display of the Lord's splendor."*

➥ **2. What is one way that Christ restores the workplace God intended? Check one.**

❏ a. He kills everybody that doesn't obey Him and starts over again.

❏ b. He changes lives and then works through them to restore the things that have been corrupted.

> He changes lives and then works through them to restore what has been corrupted by sin and the consequences of sin.

If you checked the second response (b), you are correct. He changes lives and then works through them to restore what has been corrupted by sin and the consequences of sin. Christ changes lives and then orients them to work according to the Kingdom Agenda rather than the world's agenda. This week we will study the following ways Christ restores the workplace:

Christ Restores the Workplace
1. Christ Changes Lives
2. Christ Changes Relationships
3. Christ Changes Conduct
4. Christ Changes Productivity

Repentance Required

Where does this process begin? Jesus Christ began His preaching ministry by saying, *"Repent, for the kingdom of heaven is near"* (Matt. 4:17). Christ calls us to repent. That is where He begins to restore lives. Repent means "to change your mind." But it is more than that. He wants you to change your whole way of living. Let's illustrate repentance. Because of sin you are following the world's agenda:

> Repent means "to change your mind."

When you repent, you turn to follow the Kingdom Agenda. You surrender to God's sovereignty in your life. You choose to live your life to please Him rather than self. When you repent, you have the opportunity to experience the abundant life Christ came to give—the full dimensions of the kingdom of heaven (John 10:10).

In order to prepare for the coming of the Lord, John the Baptist preached

> **John 10:10**
> *"I have come that they may have life, and have it to the full"*

a baptism of repentance. He said that a repentant person would produce the fruit (evidence) of repentance.

Fruit of Repentance

➡ **3. As you read the following Scripture, underline the things repentant people would do as fruit of repentance.**

> John said to the crowds coming out to be baptized by him, ". . . Produce fruit in keeping with repentance. . . ."
> "What should we do then?" the crowd asked.
> John answered, "The man with two tunics should share with him who has none, and the one who has food should do the same."
> Tax collectors also came to be baptized. "Teacher," they asked, "what should we do?"
> "Don't collect any more than you are required to," he told them.
> Then some soldiers asked him, "And what should we do?"
> He replied, "Don't extort money and don't accuse people falsely— be content with your pay." (Luke 3:7-14).

Did you notice that a repentant person acts differently? He will share what he has with others who have needs. Tax collectors will be honest and fair in their tax collecting. Military men will not use their authority for unjust gain. They, too, will be honest and content with their pay. Do any of those things affect the workplace? Yes, they do! When a person repents and turns to follow God's agenda, life will change in the workplace.

When a person repents and turns to follow God's agenda, life will change in the workplace.

➡ **4. To see if you understand repentance, read the list of sinful things below. Then pretend that you are John the Baptist. What would you tell a person to do to show he or she had repented of this action. Write a statement that would be the fruit of repentance.**

a. Being lazy and not giving a full day's work for a full day's pay

_____

b. Taking things belonging to your company for personal use

_____

c. Slandering a coworker in order to make yourself look good

_____

d. Falsifying an expense report to pocket a little extra money

_____

A repentant person would turn from sinful ways and act uprightly. He would work hard and give a faithful day's work for his pay. She would not steal company resources. She would be truthful in all speech about others. He would be honest "to the penny" on expense reports. If you repent to follow the Kingdom Agenda, your life will reflect it in the way you do your work.

Reasons the World's Agenda Corrupts the Workplace

1. The world's agenda rejects the sovereignty of God.
2. The world's agenda is focused upon self.
3. The world's agenda seeks to satisfy needs apart from God.

➡ **5. The list in the left margin reviews the reasons the world's agenda corrupts the workplace (from p. 59). For each of those statements write a statement of what you would expect Christ to do in us to restore the Kingdom Agenda.**

a. Since the world's agenda rejects the sovereignty of God, Christ will lead us to:

_____

b. Since the world's agenda is focused on self, Christ will lead us to:

_____

c. Since the world's agenda seeks to satisfy needs apart from God, Christ will lead us to:

_____

Returning to the Kingdom Agenda
1. Surrender to God's sovereignty.
2. Deny self and follow Christ.
3. Depend on God to satisfy needs.

To counter what the world's agenda has done to corrupt the workplace, Christ will lead us to surrender to God's leadership and sovereignty in our lives. He will lead us to deny self and follow His Lordship, and He will guide us to turn to Him and depend on Him to satisfy our needs.

➥ **6. Turn to the overview of "The Workplace God Intended" on page 37 and review the three lists under "Important Ideas." Check here after you have done so: ❏**

You will be aware of God's presence, depend on His provision, obey His will, follow His lead, join God in His work, and cooperate under His sovereignty.

When Christ begins to restore the workplace, it will begin to look like the workplace God intended. Your coworker relationship with God will begin to look like Adam's relationship with God. You will be aware of God's presence, depend on His provision, obey His will, follow His lead, join God in His work, and cooperate under His sovereignty. When you acknowledge God's sovereignty, God will begin to influence the workplace in such a way that the results will be *"very good."*

PRAYER STRATEGY

➥ **Take time to pray that Christ will begin to restore the workplace in which you work.**

• Ask the Lord to give you the faith to believe Him and what He can do to change your world.

• Ask Christ to begin His deeper work in you that you will be rightly related to God in a coworker relationship.

• Ask the Lord to reveal to you this week things you need to do differently to reflect repentance in your own life and in your work.

DAY 2
Christ Overcomes the World

Kingdom Agenda

"His divine power has given us everything we need for life and godliness through our knowledge of him who called us by his own glory and goodness. Through these he has given us his very great and precious promises, so that through them you may participate in the divine nature and escape the corruption in the world caused by evil desires" (2 Pet. 1:3-4).

➡ **Read the "Kingdom Agenda" in the margin. Pause for a moment of prayer. Carefully pray through each phrase of the Scripture. Thank God for His provisions. Claim His promises. Thank the Lord that you can have His divine nature and overcome the corruption in the world.**

Adam and Eve were tempted to sin in the garden. When they followed the suggestions of the serpent, they dethroned God in their lives and placed self and the world's agenda in charge. Sin entered the world and corrupted the original workplace. Humanity no longer gave God His rightful place as Sovereign Ruler of the universe. Jesus was the Second Adam. He came to reestablish the Kingdom rule of God over His creation.

➡ **Read the following passage to see what Christ has done for you. Circle the word that describes what Christ gives you.**

> It is written: *"The first man Adam became a living being"; the last Adam, a life-giving spirit. The spiritual did not come first, but the natural, and after that the spiritual. The first man was of the dust of the earth, the second man from heaven. As was the earthly man, so are those who are of the earth; and as is the man from heaven, so also are those who are of heaven. And just as we have borne the likeness of the earthly man, so shall we bear the likeness of the man from heaven . . . . then the saying that is written will come true: "Death has been swallowed up in victory."*
>
> *"Where, O death, is your victory?*
>   *Where, O death, is your sting?"*
> *The sting of death is sin, and the power of sin is the law. But thanks be to God! He gives us the victory through our Lord Jesus Christ.*
>
> *Therefore, my dear brothers, stand firm. Let nothing move you. Always give yourselves fully to the work of the Lord, because you know that your labor in the Lord is not in vain* (1 Cor. 15:45-49,54-58).

➡ **1. What has Christ given you? What can you do because of Christ?**
❑ a. I can know and experience victory over sin and death.
❑ b. I can stand firm in the Lord.
❑ c. I can know that my work is not in vain in the Lord.
❑ d. All of the above.

Victory!
You should have circled the word *victory*. That is what Christ has given you! Jesus did not allow Himself to be dominated by the natural man even though He was fully human. He chose to follow His spiritual nature and He won a victory over sin and death. Because of Him, you, too, can know that kind of victory. You can stand firm, and you can know that your work is not in vain.

Notice, however, that there is a condition: Jesus must be "Lord." That is not just a part of His name. Calling Him "Lord" means you have denied self and surrendered to Him as your Master. He must be Sovereign in your life, including your work life. But when He has that position of authority,

There is a condition: Jesus must be "Lord."

Matthew 6:25-33

"Therefore I tell you, do not worry about your life, what you will eat or drink; or about your body, what you will wear. Is not life more important than food, and the body more important than clothes? Look at the birds of the air; they do not sow or reap or store away in barns, and yet your heavenly Father feeds them. Are you not much more valuable than they? Who of you by worrying can add a single hour to his life?

"And why do you worry about clothes? See how the lilies of the field grow. They do not labor or spin. Yet I tell you that not even Solomon in all his splendor was dressed like one of these. If that is how God clothes the grass of the field, which is here today and tomorrow is thrown into the fire, will he not much more clothe you, O you of little faith? So do not worry, saying, `What shall we eat?' or `What shall we drink?' or `What shall we wear?' For the pagans run after all these things, and your heavenly Father knows that you need them. But seek first his kingdom and his righteousness, and all these things will be given to you as well."

you can know victory over sin's corruption!

Last week we saw how human nature has a tendency to be driven by human needs. We are selfish and self-centered. We do have those needs. After all, you cannot live without food. The problem with human nature is that it seeks to dominate your life. When you are always making choices and taking actions based on fulfilling your human needs you may miss God's agenda. Jesus dealt with this problem in the Sermon on the Mount.

➡ **2. Read Matthew 6:25-33 in the margin. Circle the words describing the things you do not have to worry about. Then answer the following questions.**

3. What are some things Jesus said not to worry about?

_____

4. Who can you depend on to provide those things?

_____

5. In the last sentence (v. 33), what does Jesus command you to do?

_____

According to Jesus' teaching, you do not have to be driven by your human needs for things like food, drink, and clothes. God the Father knows you have need for those things. You can choose to seek God's kingdom as your first priority. Then you can depend on your Heavenly Father to provide for your needs. It is one thing for Jesus to say that you can live this way. It is another thing to do it. Let's look to see if Jesus lived consistently with His teaching.

Jesus Did Not Live by the World's Agenda.

Jesus did not allow human needs to get in the way of the Kingdom Agenda—obedience to His assignment from His Father. He was not dominated by His human needs. He chose to seek the Kingdom first.

Physical Needs. Though Jesus got hungry and thirsty, He did not let those needs be the driving force in His life. When He had been fasting and praying in the desert for 40 days, He was hungry. The devil came and tempted Him to eat by turning stones into bread. Jesus said: *"It is written: 'Man does not live on bread alone, but on every word that comes from the mouth of God'"* (Matt. 4:4). Jesus was more concerned about what His Father was saying during this time of prayer and fasting.

On another occasion, the disciples went into a village to buy food because they were hungry. Jesus stayed outside the village at the well and encountered a Samaritan woman. He led her to understand that He was the Christ and that He was *"living water."* Later, she brought the whole town out to encounter Christ—the promised Messiah. When the disciples spoke to Jesus about eating, He responded: *"'I have food to eat that you know nothing about. . . . My food,' said Jesus, 'is to do the will of him who sent me and to finish his work'"* (John 4:32,34).

➡ **6. When Jesus had to choose between satisfying physical needs and following the Kingdom Agenda, what did He choose to care about most?**
  ❏ a. He chose to satisfy His needs for food and water.
  ❏ b. He chose to listen to the words of His Father and do His will.

Need for a Safe Environment. Humans are influenced by their need for safety and security, for shelter, and the like. Did Jesus let these needs take first place over the will of His Father? No. Jesus said to those who wanted to follow Him and be a disciple: *"Foxes have holes and birds of the air have nests, but the Son of Man has no place to lay his head"* (Matt. 8:20). Jesus followed His Father's agenda for His ministry even though it meant not having a home to live in.

We see His commitment to the Kingdom Agenda even more clearly as Jesus faced the ultimate purpose for His earthly ministry—the cross. Jesus chose to obey His Father even when it meant suffering and death—not just any death but a very cruel and agonizing death on a cross. Here are ways Jesus responded to His Father's agenda:

> *"Now my heart is troubled, and what shall I say? 'Father, save me from this hour'? No, it was for this very reason I came to this hour. Father, glorify your name!"* (John 12:27-28).

> *Your attitude should be the same as that of Christ Jesus: Who, being in very nature God, did not consider equality with God something to be grasped, but made himself nothing, taking the very nature of a servant, being made in human likeness. And being found in appearance as a man, he humbled himself and became obedient to death—even death on a cross!* (Phil. 2:5-8).

Jesus obeyed His Father and went to the cross. He refused to allow His human need for safety to keep Him from obedience.

➡ **7. What are some ways that you may be tempted to allow your need for safety and security to overshadow obeying God's will in your workplace?**
❑ disobey God's commands to please my employer and keep my job
❑ lie to avoid punishment
❑ steal to provide better living conditions for my family

❑ others? _____

Need to Be Loved and Accepted. Human nature strives to be loved by other humans and to belong to a group—to be accepted. This human need drives us to want to be a part of some group, organization, clique, or a team. For many people this need can be so great that they will choose to do things that are not right, just to "fit-in." Jesus did not let these needs influence Him when service to the Kingdom was at stake. On many occasions He chose not to belong to the "religious leadership group" because they were doing wrong.
• He drove money changers out of the temple with a whip.
• He healed people on the Sabbath even when He knew the Pharisees would begin plotting His death because of it.
• He publicly condemned the actions of the religious leaders.
• He associated with "sinners" and "tax collectors" when the "in" crowd would not.
• After feeding the 5,000 they wanted to make Him king. But Jesus rejected their offer and sent them home.

Like the other needs of our human nature, these needs cannot be satisfied by man alone. It is in a love relationship with God the Father that your need for love and acceptance is most completely fulfilled. Listen to Jesus describe the love He experiences with His Father and with us: *"As the Father has loved me, so have I loved you. Now remain in my love"* (John 15:9) and

God also meets our need to belong to a group by placing us in a church that functions like a body.

"If anyone loves me, he will obey my teaching. My Father will love him, and we will come to him and make our home with him" (John 14:23). God also meets our need to belong to a group by placing us in a church that functions like a body (1 Cor. 12). In the body of Christ we are needed and loved. The greatest fulfillment of love and acceptance comes through a love relationship with God and belonging to the body of Christ.

➡ **5. You have a choice to live by the world's agenda or the Kingdom Agenda. Which of the following seems most important to you? Check your response.**

❑ a. I want to be loved by God and have a right relationship with Him. I want to experience the love and importance of belonging to His family—the church.

❑ b. I want to please the people around me even when I have to do things I know are wrong. I know God will understand and forgive me so I don't mind offending Him.

Desire for Recognition and Esteem. In his temptations of Jesus, the devil appealed to Jesus' human desire for recognition and esteem. He took Jesus to the temple. *"'If you are the Son of God,' he said, 'throw yourself down'"* (Matt. 4:6). It was as if the devil were trying to make Jesus validate His favored position with God, and impress the crowds in the temple area. Jesus once again chose another way. His desire for esteem did not drive Him to put His Father to the test.

We also have a tendency to want the high positions of respect and honor. We want to prove ourselves and be recognized for our accomplishments. Look at what Jesus—the Son of God, the Teacher, the Master—did: He took a towel and stooped to wash His disciple's feet like a lowly servant. Then He said:

> *"Do you understand what I have done for you?" he asked them. "You call me 'Teacher' and 'Lord,' and rightly so, for that is what I am. Now that I, your Lord and Teacher, have washed your feet, you also should wash one another's feet. I have set you an example that you should do as I have done for you. I tell you the truth, no servant is greater than his master, nor is a messenger greater than the one who sent him. Now that you know these things, you will be blessed if you do them"* (John 13:12-17).

Jesus saw His role as that of a Servant. . . . He set an example for us to be willing to assume the lowly role of servanthood also.

Jesus saw His role as that of a Servant. He was serving His Father, but in doing so He served others. He set an example for us to be willing to assume the lowly role of servanthood also. Jesus found His esteem in pleasing His Father: *"a voice from heaven said, 'This is my Son, whom I love; with him I am well pleased'"* (Matt. 3:17). We don't need self-esteem when we have God's esteem and love! Self is supposed to die! We are delivered from serving the appetite for esteem when we have the assurance that God is pleased with us!

➡ **6. Which of the following is MOST important to you?**

❑ a. I want to be respected and esteemed by my employer for my personal achievements.

❑ b. I want to be esteemed by my peers for my abilities.

❑ c. I want to be esteemed by my family for my hard work.

❑ d. I want to be esteemed by my church for my dedication and sacrifice.

❑ e. I want to know and experience God's love, acceptance, and pleasure.

❑ f. Other: _____

Overcomers

"You, dear children, are from God and have overcome them, because the one who is in you is greater than the one who is in the world" (1 John 4:4).

"This is love for God: to obey his commands. And his commands are not burdensome, for everyone born of God overcomes the world. This is the victory that has overcome the world, even our faith" (1 John 5:3-4).

"No, in all these things we are more than conquerors through him who loved us" (Rom. 8:37).

"His divine power has given us everything we need for life and godliness through our knowledge of him who called us by his own glory and goodness. Through these he has given us his very great and precious promises, so that through them you may participate in the divine nature and escape the corruption in the world caused by evil desires" (2 Pet. 1:3-4)

Desire to Be All You Can Be. The devil tried to appeal to Jesus's desire to reach his greatest potential as a ruler—quickly. If Satan could have convinced Jesus to choose all the *"kingdoms of the world"* by just bowing down to him, then Jesus would have rejected the sovereignty of God! Jesus knew that God, and only God is Sovereign over *"all the Kingdoms of the world."* Jesus' need to reach His royal potential as a King did not determine His actions. Once again, Jesus submitted His will, His needs, His desires to the perfect, sovereign will of His Father. Even at the cross, Jesus chose to be a suffering Servant rather than follow the exalted path of being a military ruler like many desired.

Jesus operated from a different agenda. Jesus was not dominated by His human nature, because he was also full of the divine nature of God. Jesus did have a choice to live according to His human nature or according to His divine nature. Each day and in every way, Jesus chose to live and work with the understanding that His Father was Sovereign. He intentionally chose to live according to His divine nature and reject the temptations of sinful human nature. Jesus said: *"In this world you will have trouble. But take heart! I have overcome the world"* (John 16:33).

➥ **Read the Scriptures in the margin about the fact that you, too, can be an overcomer and a conqueror. Then move to a time of prayer.**

PRAYER STRATEGY

➥ **Take time now to pray about overcoming the world's agenda in your own life and workplace.**
- Confess to the Lord any ways you realize you have allowed your sinful human nature to control your actions contrary to God's will.
- Agree with God that the Spirit of Christ in you *"is greater than the one who is in the world."*
- Thank God that He makes you an overcomer. If necessary, ask Him to increase your faith to trust in Him and to experience the reality of overcoming the world's agenda.
- Claim the Lord's promise to give you His divine nature so that you can escape the corruption of the world.

DAY 3 Christ Changes Lives

Kingdom Agenda

"If anyone is in Christ, he is a new creation; the old has gone, the new has come!" (2 Cor. 5:17).

Zacchaeus

Jesus begins to restore the workplace by restoring people to a right relationship with God, their King. Once they are right with God, they begin to live differently.

➡ **Read the "Kingdom Agenda" in the margin. Pause for a moment of prayer. Ask the Lord to help you understand the difference Christ makes in a life that He has redeemed.**

Jesus Restored Zacchaeus

Jesus begins to restore the workplace by restoring people to a right relationship with God, their King. Once they are right with God, they begin to live differently. They treat other people differently, and they work differently. While walking through Jericho one day, Jesus encountered Zacchaeus and a life was forever changed.

➡ **1. Read the story of Jesus and Zacchaeus and look to see what a difference Jesus made in Zacchaeus and his work life. <u>Underline</u> what Zacchaeus decided to do differently after his encounter with Jesus.**

> *Jesus entered Jericho and was passing through. A man was there by the name of Zacchaeus; he was a chief tax collector and was wealthy. He wanted to see who Jesus was, but being a short man he could not, because of the crowd. So he ran ahead and climbed a sycamore-fig tree to see him, since Jesus was coming that way.*
>
> *When Jesus reached the spot, he looked up and said to him, "Zacchaeus, come down immediately. I must stay at your house today." So he came down at once and welcomed him gladly.*
>
> *All the people saw this and began to mutter, "He has gone to be the guest of a 'sinner.'"*
>
> *But Zacchaeus stood up and said to the Lord, "Look, Lord! Here and now I give half of my possessions to the poor, and if I have cheated anybody out of anything, I will pay back four times the amount."*
>
> *Jesus said to him, "Today salvation has come to this house"* (Luke 19:1-9).

After his encounter with Jesus, Zacchaeus, the despised tax collector, was born again—salvation came to his house. Forgiven and restored to a right relationship to God, he decided to give half his wealth to the poor and pay back those he had cheated four times the amount he had taken unjustly.

➡ **2. What do you think? Did Zacchaeus' response follow the world's selfish agenda or the pattern of God's Kingdom Agenda?**
❑ a. The world's agenda
❑ b. The Kingdom Agenda

Jesus' first message about the Kingdom was *"Repent, for the kingdom of heaven is near"* (Matt. 4:17). This initial call was a call to salvation. Jesus begins to restore the workplace by redeeming and changing lives. As individual lives begin to change, everything around them begins to change. Sin no longer has dominion (control) over them because: *"If anyone is in Christ, he is a new creation; the old has gone, the new has come!"* (2 Cor. 5:17). When a person repents and is born again, Christ forgives sin, cleanses away guilt, heals, and gives life. The old sinful nature passes away and a new nature—Christ's nature takes its place. That is what happened to Zacchaeus.

2 Corinthians 5:17
"If anyone is in Christ, he is a new creation; the old has gone, the new has come!"

Zacchaeus began to show the fruit of repentance by the way he did his work.

➡ **3. Second Corinthians 5:17 (in the margin) is your memory verse for this week. Take a few moments to read it through several times and begin committing it to memory.**

Now write it below (from memory if possible).

_____

_____

_____

4. If God were to evaluate your life based on that verse, what would He conclude? Pray right now and ask Him.
❑ a. I am in Christ because I have a new nature. My old sinful nature is past. Christ and His nature now live in me.
❑ b. Nothing much has changed since I decided to become a Christian and joined the church. My old sinful nature is still very strong. I may not be *"in Christ"* like I thought.
❑ c. I've always had this "old" sinful nature, and I realize I am a sinner. I have never repented of my sin and turned to Christ to be born again.
❑ d. Other: _____

Dying to Self

The beginning of the Kingdom Agenda is for a person to be born again. Jesus begins to restore the workplace God intended by changing people. He wants you to have a new nature. If you had to check "b" or "c" above, now is the time Jesus wants to invite you to enter into a genuine love relationship with Him. Jesus, however, has described what being a disciple (a follower) would cost:

"If anyone would come after me, he must deny himself and take up his cross daily and follow me. For whoever wants to save his life will lose it, but whoever loses his life for me will save it" (Luke 9:23-24).

➡ **5. Based on Luke 9:23-24 above, what are three things Jesus demands of those who want to be His followers? Write one of the following words in the blanks below: lose, cross, deny, follow**

a. _____ himself

b. take up his _____

c. _____ me [Jesus]

To be a follower of Christ the King, you first must deny self. Actually you must die to self—that is what a cross is all about: death. This means a daily death to a "self-focused" life and a turning to a "God-focused" life. Taking up the cross calls for a daily obedience to God's will for your life. To be in Christ's kingdom you must surrender to Christ as Lord and Master. He wants to rule in your life. He wants to guide your choices. If you want to hold on to your self-centered life and rule your own direction in life, you will lose your life—that is, you will miss out on the abundant and fulfill-

To be in Christ's kingdom you must surrender to Christ as Lord and Master.

ing life God intended. If you die to self, you will experience life as God intended.

In this new life God is Sovereign over every aspect of your life. Since He is Sovereign and He is love, you can trust completely in God's provision, His protection, His power, and His promises! This is a life and work strategy that is born out of a daily intimate relationship with God. You will experience the Kingdom of God when you join Christ in a coworker relationship with God, where God is Sovereign and you are cooperative.

You can trust completely in God's provision, His protection, His power, and His promises!

➡ **6. If you have not already done so, would you be willing to die to self right now, so that Christ can give you a new nature?**
❑ a. I have already repented, been forgiven, and been changed by Christ. [Move to the next paragraph below.]
❑ b. Yes, I want to become a follower of Christ. [If you are willing, talk to the Lord. Repent by turning from your old self-centered life. Turn to Christ and surrender unconditionally to His sovereign rule in your life. Ask Him to forgive you, cleanse you, and give you a new nature.]
❑ c. No, I'm not ready to do that. [Would you at least give God permission to continue working in your life to bring you to the place you will one day be willing? Tell Him what you are thinking.]

Christ In You

We believe so strongly in our human potential that often we develop our own programs and plans for "improvement" to change our circumstances at work and in our lives. We believe that when we practice certain principles, we can direct our own destiny. But we need to understand that principles alone cannot change and empower people the way God can. Only a vital, authentic relationship with the living God can truly empower a person to live and work as a citizen of His Kingdom. When Jesus Christ restores people, He doesn't expect them to live the Christian life alone. He takes up residence in them!

In his letter to the church at Colosse, Paul explained that God had called him to present the Word of God to them so they might know this great mystery *"which is Christ in you, the hope of glory"* (Col. 1:27). When you die to self, Christ becomes your life. Here is how Paul described his new life in Christ:

Christ becomes your life.

"I have been crucified with Christ and I no longer live, but Christ lives in me. The life I live in the body, I live by faith in the Son of God, who loved me and gave himself for me" (Gal. 2:20).

➡ **7. When a person dies (is crucified) to self, who comes to live in place of self?** _____

8. Pause for a moment of prayer. Pray through Galatians 2:20 (in the margin) and ask Christ to work in you in such a way that you could say this about your life.

Galatians 2:20
"I have been crucified with Christ and I no longer live, but Christ lives in me. The life I live in the body, I live by faith in the Son of God, who loved me and gave himself for me."

As Christ restores your workplace, he begins by changing people through a personal relationship with Himself. When people die to self, Christ lives through them. When Christ is living and working through people, sin's corruption will no longer dominate the workplace. Can you imagine what work would be like if you kept seeing Jesus Christ live through those around you?

➡ **Read the following Scripture and answer the questions that follow by filling in the blanks.**

Just as you received Christ Jesus as Lord, continue to live in him, rooted and built up in him, strengthened in the faith as you were taught, and overflowing with thankfulness.

See to it that no one takes you captive through hollow and deceptive philosophy, which depends on human tradition and the basic principles of this world rather than on Christ.

For in Christ all the fullness of the Deity lives in bodily form, and you have been given fullness in Christ, who is the head over every power and authority (Col. 2:6-10).

➡ **9. How might others try to take us captive to the world's agenda?**

through hollow and _____ _____

10. On what does this philosophy depend? what is the basis of it?

human _____ and the basic _____

of this _____ rather than on _____.

11. How much of God [Deity] was in Christ? _____ the fullness . . .

12. How much of Christ has been given to you as a believer?

you have been given _____ in Christ.

As Christ begins living out His life through more and more people in a workplace, that workplace will look more and more like the original workplace God intended.

Human traditions and principles of this world form a hollow and deceptive philosophy. The kind of philosophy for life you need is one based on Christ Himself. In Christ all of God dwells. Jesus Christ is God. When you surrender your life to Christ, all of Christ is present to begin living and working through your life. As Christ begins living out His life through more and more people in a workplace, that workplace will look more and more like the original workplace God intended.

PRAYER STRATEGY

Changed Lives

_____

_____

_____

_____

People Who Need Christ

_____

_____

_____

_____

➡ **Take time to pray about your own relationship to Jesus Christ and begin to pray for others in your workplace who may need to experience the salvation only Christ can give.**

- Reflect on the things God may have been saying to you through this lesson. Talk to Him about your own relationship. Thank Him for every spiritual blessing He has given you.
- Ask the Lord to begin revealing to you others in your workplace who are followers of His. Begin making a list in the margin of other Christians you know in your workplace because they have the nature of Christ. Pray for those who may be Christians but may not be living out of their new nature as God intends.
- Ask the Lord to impress you to pray for individuals in your workplace who need to be born again—those who need new life in Christ. Begin making a list in the margin of those for whom God impresses you to pray.
- Ask Christ to begin restoring your workplace by saving and changing lost people. Give God permission to work through you in any way He chooses to be part of their coming to Christ.
- Ask Christ to continue restoring your workplace by bringing Christians to faithful obedience to His will. Pray that they will reveal the new nature of Christ to all who see their lives in action.

DAY 4 Christ Changes Relationships

Kingdom Agenda
"'Love the Lord your God with all your heart and with all your soul and with all your mind.' This is the first and greatest commandment. And the second is like it: 'Love your neighbor as yourself'" (Matt. 22:37-39).

Christ changes a life, and He also changes the person's relationship with God and relationships with others.

➥ **Read the "Kingdom Agenda" in the margin. Pause for a moment of prayer. Ask the Lord to help you learn to love Him with all your being. Then ask Him to enable you to demonstrate love for others. Invite Him to love others through you.**

When Adam and Eve sinned against God in the garden, they hid from Him because they were afraid of Him and ashamed of their nakedness. The intimate love relationship they had with God had been broken and corrupted by sin. Disobedience broke the relationship and ushered fear and shame into existence.

Because of sin, people are separated from God; and they may experience fear and shame. When they surrender their lives to Christ, He reconciles them to God—He restores a right love relationship. *"There is no fear in love. But perfect love drives out fear, because fear has to do with punishment. The one who fears is not made perfect in love"* (1 John 4:18).

When Christ restores a workplace, He begins by reconciling people to God. He changes the relationship between God and those who are born again. When a person loves God with all his or her being, that person will also have a different kind of relationship with others. Christ changes a life, and He also changes the person's relationship with God and relationships with others.

➥ **1. Christ changes lives. What is a second change Christ brings about in restoring a workplace?**
• Christ changes lives.
• Christ changes _____

2. What are two relationships Christ changes?

• Relationship with _____

• Relationships with _____

Christ changes lives. He also changes relationships between an individual and God and between that individual and other people. These changed relationships will affect your workplace.

Christ Restores the Coworker Relationship
As Christ works to restore the workplace God intended, He is also seeking to restore you to a coworker relationship with God like the one Adam had.

➥ **3. Turn to page 46 and review Adam's coworker relationship with God. Check here when you have done so.** ❏

4. The following list describes ways you can participate in experiencing a restored coworker relationship with God. Match the statement about God on the left with your expected response on the right. Write a letter beside the number of the corresponding statement.

God:

___ 1. God is present.
___ 2. God provides for workers needs.
___ 3. God reveals His will.
___ 4. God initiates work.
___ 5. God works.
___ 6. God is Sovereign.

Christ Expects Me to:

a. Obey God's will.
b. Join God in His work.
c. Acknowledge God's presence.
d. Depend on God's provision.
e. Follow God's lead.
f. Cooperate under God's sovereignty.

To have a proper coworker relationship with God, you must let God be God. In a sense the items on the left above are part of God's job description. God is present. He provides for His workers. He establishes the purposes for the work (His will). He takes the initiative. He participates in the work, and He is Lord—He is Sovereign. The world's agenda will encourage you to take assignments from God's job description, rather than your own. When self rules your life, that is what you do. When you repent, you quit attempting to accomplish God's work by yourself. You begin accepting His assignments for the things He wants to accomplish through you.

Your job description in this coworker relationship calls for you to acknowledge that you are part of a team—coworkers together with God. So you acknowledge His presence. You learn to depend on Him for your needs rather than being driven to meet those needs yourself. You obey God's will and work on His purposes. You follow God's lead and work on His time table, not your own. This requires you to wait on the Lord rather than taking the initiative yourself. In summary you trust God as your Sovereign Ruler and you cooperate with Him. (Answers: 1-c,2-d,3-a,4-e,5-b,6-f.)

➡ **5. On page 49 we summarized the characteristics of a coworker relationship with God. A copy of that list is in the left margin. Read through the seven characteristics of the relationship and underline an important word in each one to help you remember the focus of each.**

As Christ restores a workplace, He is going to be restoring those characteristics to your own coworker relationship with God. Let's take a brief look at each characteristic.

Christ Restores a Relationship Based on Love. Because of love, God sent His Son Jesus Christ to provide the penalty for your sin. According to 1 John 4:19, we love God because He first loved us. When you respond to God's love, a powerful love relationship is established that is real, personal, and intimate.

Christ Restores a Proper Order of Authority. God is Sovereign. He is the Authority above all others. He is the Ruler of men and nations—and the whole universe. Part of Christ's restoration of the relationship requires that you submit to God's authority over all of your life including your work life. Under God's supreme authority, you will have proper respect and submission to those humans who have been given authority over you. If, however, you must choose between obedience to God or to man, you will do right by choosing to obey God. (See Acts 4:1-31 for an example from the early church.)

➡ **6. What are two things Christ restores when He restores the coworker relationship between you and God?**

a love. . ._____

proper order of. . . _____

The world's agenda will encourage you to take assignments from God's job description rather than your own.

When you repent, you quit working off God's job description and begin working off your own in a proper relationship with God.

Characteristics of a Coworker Relationship with God

1. Relationship Based on Love
2. Proper Order of Authority
3. Mutual Respect and Trust
4. Clear Division of Labor
5. Atmosphere of Peace and Harmony
6. Clearly Defined Guidelines
7. Regular Evaluation and Communication

Christ Restores a Mutual Respect and Trust. When you get in a right relationship with God, you will respect Him and trust Him. You will be able to walk by faith as He leads you. Paul said, *"All who are under the yoke of slavery should consider their masters worthy of full respect, so that God's name and our teaching may not be slandered"* (1 Tim. 6:1). Regardless of whether your superiors are believers or not, you should treat them with respect due their position. As more and more people in the workplace are changed by Christ, you will find that you can trust others because of God given integrity. You will find that you can share a mutual respect for others because your relationship with others will function as God intended.

Christ Restores a Clear Division of Labor. We discussed this point earlier related to Adam's coworker relationship with God. You must allow God to function as Creator, Initiator, and Sovereign. We sin when we try to take over God's job description instead of attend to our own. God also has assignments for you to carry out in your workplace. He will not do your work when you refuse to do it. He may look for someone else, but He may not have anyone else. You must be prepared to assume your work assignment from God for your workplace.

➡ **7. What are two more things Christ restores when He restores the coworker relationship between you and God?**

mutual. . ._____

clear division of. . ._____

Christ Restores an Atmosphere of Peace and Harmony. In the normal workplace today, the world's agenda is in constant conflict with the Kingdom Agenda. Sin and the consequences of sin cause broken relationships, unhealthy stress, and conflict. Christ comes into such a work environment as the Prince of Peace. Relationships are restored and love for God and others prevails. A spirit of servanthood develops cooperation and harmony. Though this seems like an ideal workplace that is impossible to achieve, Christ can begin working like leaven in a lump of dough. The influence of Godlike love can spread from one part to another until it has permeated the whole. Peace, however, can be yours regardless of the circumstances around you. You can experience inner peace that Christ gives, even when the storms of life swirl around you. His Kingdom Agenda would call for growing in peace and harmony in the context of love.

Christ Gives Clearly Defined Guidelines. The Bible is important because God gives guidelines for right living in the Scriptures. You cannot know right from wrong by your human reason. That is how Satan tempted Eve, and her human reason led her to make a wrong choice. A believer must function by revelation (God's revealed will) rather than by human reasoning. We will look at this more in detail in tomorrow's lesson concerning right conduct. God does give specific guidelines that are right and best for your workplace.

Christ Participates in Regular Evaluation and Communication. Time in prayer and studying the Scriptures will be invaluable for God to reveal His guidelines for your work. Christ will use the plumb line of Scripture to measure your life and actions. He will evaluate you and your work based on His standards and not based on what everybody else is doing. He uses the Word to cleanse and purify your life (see Eph. 5:25-26).

Regular communication with God in prayer also is a necessity. God

Regardless of whether your superiors are believers or not, you should treat them with respect due their position.

We sin when we try to take over God's job description instead of attend to our own.

A believer must function by revelation (God's revealed will) rather than by human reasoning.

Ephesians 5:25-26
"Christ loved the church and gave himself up for her to make her holy, cleansing her by the washing with water through the word."

wants a relationship with you and that requires time together. We will see in week 6 that prayer ought to become a major work strategy for you. Your desire is to get to the end of life and be able to hear God say, *"Well done, good and faithful servant! . . . Come and share your master's happiness!"* (Matt. 25:23).

➡ **8. What are three more things Christ restores when He restores the coworker relationship between you and God?**

atmosphere of. . . _____

clearly defined. . ._____

regular. . . _____

Christ Changes Your Relationships with Others

> When you move into a right relationship with God, your relationship with others will change also. When you are filled with the presence of Christ and His love, that love overflows to those around you.

When you move into a right relationship with God, your relationship with others will change also. When you are filled with the presence of Christ and His love, that love overflows to those around you. Through His Word, Christ also has given some clear guidelines for the way you treat others. When those guidelines are followed, relationships between people can be healed. Right relationships between coworkers in your workplace will make a significant difference.

➡ **9. Read the following Scriptures. Under each one, write a phrase, title, or statement that summarizes how you should relate to others. I have completed the first one for you.**

John 13:34-35 • *"A new command I give you: Love one another. As I have loved you, so you must love one another. By this all men will know that you are my disciples, if you love one another."*

Summary: _____ *Love One Another* _____

Matthew 7:12 • *"In everything, do to others what you would have them do to you, for this sums up the Law and the Prophets."*

Summary: _____

Luke 6:27-28 • *"But I tell you who hear me: Love your enemies, do good to those who hate you, bless those who curse you, pray for those who mistreat you."*

Summary: _____

Matthew 6:14-15 • *"If you forgive men when they sin against you, your heavenly Father will also forgive you."*

Summary: _____

Luke 6:36 • *"Be merciful, just as your Father is merciful."*

Summary: _____

Matthew 5:23-24 • *"If you are offering your gift at the altar and there remember that your brother has something against you, leave your gift there in front of the altar. First go and be reconciled to your brother; then come and offer your gift."*

Summary: _____

Matthew 5:38-42 • *"You have heard that it was said, `Eye for eye, and tooth for tooth.' But I tell you, Do not resist an evil person. If someone strikes you on the right cheek, turn to him the other also. And if someone wants to sue you and take your tunic, let him have your cloak as well. If someone forces you to go one mile, go with him two miles. Give to the one who asks you, and do not turn away from the one who wants to borrow from you.*

Summary: _____

This is by no means a complete list. However, can you imagine a workplace where everyone lived by these guidelines? Christ restores relationships and calls His people to love others—even their enemies. He calls for forgiving spirits, for mercy, and for reconciliation. He is the One who gave us the Golden Rule to treat others as we would want to be treated. He calls us to resolve conflict with evil persons in loving ways rather than by seeking revenge. Only the nature of Christ and the love of Christ in you can enable you to live that way. But when He does, it makes a difference in the workplace. When the love of Christ shows in your life, people will know you are His disciple.

> When the love of Christ shows in your life, people will know you are His disciple.

PRAYER STRATEGY

➡ **Take time now to pray about your relationship to God and to others in your workplace.**

- Do you love the Lord with all your being (heart, soul, mind)? Tell Him how much you love Him and why. Invite Him to show you any ways you may need to love Him more. [Consider setting aside some time in the next few days to take a walk with the One you love. Just spend some unstructured time walking and talking with Him.]
- Ask the Lord to reveal any relationships you have with others in your workplace that are not right. Repent of any sin He shows you, seek His forgiveness, and ask Him how you need to respond to the person or persons involved. Write notes to yourself in the margin.
- Ask the Lord if He wants you to demonstrate love toward anyone specific in your workplace by meeting some need they may have. If He reveals a need that another person has, do what He enables you to do to meet that need in Christ's name. Demonstrate the love of Christ.

DAY 5

Christ Changes Conduct and Productivity

Kingdom Agenda
"The kingdom of God is not a matter of eating and drinking, but of righteousness, peace and joy in the Holy Spirit, because anyone who serves Christ in this way is pleasing to God and approved by men" (Rom. 14:17-18).

➡ **Read the "Kingdom Agenda" in the margin. Pause for a moment of prayer. Ask the Lord to enable you to live a life of righteousness, peace, and joy in your workplace. Ask that you be able to do so in such a way that He would be pleased and that you would be approved by men.**

Conduct

When Jesus spoke to Zacchaeus and *"salvation"* came to his house, his conduct as a tax collector changed. Rather than be greedy, he became generous to the poor. He decided to make things right with anyone he had taxed unfairly. When Christ changed his life, his conduct changed.

➡ **1. When Christ changes lives, He changes relationships also. What is one more thing Christ changes?**

• Christ changes lives. • Christ changes relationships.

• Christ changes _____

As we saw yesterday, those who are followers of Christ and His commands treat other people differently—their relationships are different. Among other things, disciples of Christ. . .

___ • love other people by meeting needs in tangible ways.
___ • respect those in authority over them.
___ • seek to develop mutual respect and trust for coworkers.
___ • seek to relate to others in peace and harmony.
___ • do good to others and treat them the way they want to be treated.
___ • pray for others.
___ • forgive those who offend them.
___ • show mercy toward others.

➡ **2. Read through this list again. Which of these would be the most clearly different from the way people in your workplace currently relate? Write a #1 and a #2 on the lines at the left of the top TWO ways that would be different.**

This does not mean that an unbeliever cannot exhibit some or many of these virtues. But the life of Christ that is manifest through a genuine believer will be different than that of a natural man or woman in some measurable ways.

Making the Good News Attractive at Work

Paul wrote a letter that has a terrific message about conduct for Christians in the workplace. Let me guide you through a study of Paul's message to Titus.

Paul sent a letter to a coworker in the ministry—Titus. Paul and Titus evidently had started some churches on the island of Crete. Paul left Titus there to *"straighten out what was left unfinished and appoint elders in every town"* (Titus 1:5). This was a tough assignment. Already some people were teaching false doctrine for personal financial gain. The greater problem was that the people of Crete had a terrible reputation in the world. An ancient poet had said, *"Cretans are always liars, evil brutes, lazy gluttons"* (Titus 1:12). Paul said this was true about the people of Crete. But Christians must be different than that. He gave a couple of reasons:

"Our people must learn to devote themselves to doing what is good, in order that they may provide for daily necessities and not live unproductive lives" (Titus 3:14).

. . .so that in every way they will make the teaching about God our Savior attractive (Titus 2:10).

➥ **3. Why should Christians devote themselves to doing what is good? Complete these phrases.**

To provide for _____

and not live _____

make the teaching about God _____

The Christians of Crete needed to change their conduct to reflect the character of Christ in them. They needed to devote themselves to doing what is good to provide for daily necessities and be productive. They needed to live in such a way that the message about Christ as our Savior would be attractive. Do you realize that the way you live and work can be used by God to attract others to Christ? God wants to put you on public display to show what a difference Christ makes in a life. Paul also described those who do not believe and therefore are not pure:

> *To the pure, all things are pure, but to those who are corrupted and do not believe, nothing is pure. In fact, both their minds and consciences are corrupted. They claim to know God, but by their actions they deny him. They are detestable, disobedient and unfit for doing anything good.* (Titus 1:15-16).

God wants to put you on public display to show what a difference Christ makes in a life.

➥ **4. What are some words that Paul uses to describe *"those who are corrupted and do not believe"*?**

_____

5. Suppose a person claims to know God. How can this person deny that he or she knows God?

_____

Those who do not believe in Christ are corrupted in mind and conscience, impure, detestable, disobedient, unfit for doing anything good. A person who lives like that and then claims to know God, denies knowing God by his very actions.

➥ **6. If a person in your workplace claims to be a Christian and then lives like the world, how do people respond? Check all that apply.**
❑ a. They ridicule the church and Christ: "If that is what being a Christian means, I don't want to have any part of it."
❑ b. They use this hypocrite as an excuse to reject Christ: "Why should I be a Christian? Look at _____. He's a Christian and I live a better life than he does. He's just a hypocrite."
❑ c. They reject Christ and the church as irrelevant: "Christians are not different than anybody else. If they want to waste their time with that religion stuff, it's okay by me."

❑ d. Other: _____

Hypocrisy and bad examples from Christians can be the greatest hindrances to the spread of Christ's Kingdom. Christians in the workplace must be different as they allow Christ to live through them. Paul wanted Titus to teach these Christians in Crete to honor Christ by their actions. But first he challenged Titus to practice what he was to teach:

In everything set them an example by doing what is good. In your teaching show integrity, seriousness and soundness of speech that cannot be condemned, so that those who oppose you may be ashamed because they have nothing bad to say about us. (Titus 2:7-8).

➡ **7. Do you want your workplace to change and function the way God intends for a workplace to function?** ❏ YES ❏ NO
8. If you answered yes, are you willing to be an example to other Christians and to the world so that no one will have anything bad to say about you or other Christians? Write out a response to the Lord

_____

_____

_____

Christ wants to restore your workplace, regardless of whether it is a religious organization that has drifted or a "secular" corporation, whether it has five employees or 50,000. He needs a place to start. I pray that you and perhaps others in your group will be the starting point for Christ's redemptive work. Now lets look at what Titus was to teach the Christians of Crete:

➡ **9. As you read the following Scripture, underline the people Titus was to teach. Circle words that describe the behavior desired. I have underlined and circled one each as an example.**

You must teach what is in accord with sound doctrine. Teach the older men to be temperate, worthy of respect, self-controlled, and sound in faith, in love and in endurance.

Likewise, teach the older women to be reverent in the way they live, not to be slanderers or addicted to much wine, but to teach what is good. Then they can train the younger women to love their husbands and children, to be self-controlled and pure, to be busy at home, to be kind, and to be subject to their husbands, so that no one will malign the word of God.

Similarly, encourage the young men to be self-controlled (Titus 2:1-6).

Teach slaves to be subject to their masters in everything, to try to please them, not to talk back to them, and not to steal from them, but to show that they can be fully trusted, so that in every way they will make the teaching about God our Savior attractive.

For the grace of God that brings salvation has appeared to all men. It teaches us to say "No" to ungodliness and worldly passions, and to live self-controlled, upright and godly lives in this present age, while we wait for the blessed hope—the glorious appearing of our great God and Savior, Jesus Christ, who gave himself for us to redeem us from all wickedness and to purify for himself a people that are his very own, eager to do what is good (Titus 2:9-14).

Titus 2:9
"Teach slaves to be subject to their masters in everything, to try to please them, not to talk back to them, and not to steal from them, but to show that they can be fully trusted, so that in every way they will make the teaching about God our Savior attractive."

Remind the people to be subject to rulers and authorities, to be obedient, to be ready to do whatever is good, to slander no one, to be peaceable and considerate, and to show true humility toward all men (Titus 3:1).

I want you to stress these things, so that those who have trusted in God may be careful to devote themselves to doing what is good. These things are excellent and profitable for everyone. (Titus 3:8).

obedient, good
peaceable, considerate
humble, self-controlled
upright, godly
trustworthy, temperate
kind, respected, loving
persistent, sober, pure
subject to authority

Paul's instructions called for these different groups to be obedient, good, peaceable, considerate, humble, self-controlled, upright, godly, trustworthy, temperate, respected, loving, persistent, sober, pure, and subject to authority. If Christians worked like this in the workplace, people would eventually notice the difference. Christians should be honest and trustworthy. They should be hard workers and productive. They should be kind and considerate to others and maintain right relationships with them in public and in private. They should show proper respect for lines of authority. Like Pharaoh said of Joseph, people in the workplace should say, *"Can we find anyone like this man, one in whom is the spirit of God?"* (Gen. 41:38).

Christ Restores Productivity

Joseph is a good example of someone who experienced what I call a prosperity of effort. Because God was present and at work in Joseph's life, God caused what Joseph did to prosper. Joseph was careful to give credit to God for all that He was doing. Those around Joseph recognized God's blessing and favor on his life. His daily productivity was one of the ways God created favor for Joseph in the eyes of those who had authority over him—like Potiphar and the prison warden.

When sin entered the original workplace, God cursed the ground because of Adam's sin. Thorns and thistles would decrease productivity, and Adam's work would be difficult and painful. When Christ restores a person to a right relationship with God, He also begins to restore what sin took away. Christ restores productivity to a redeemed life.

➡ **Read John 15:1-8 in the left margin and notice the way a right relationship with Christ (the Vine) yields fruitfulness (productivity). Then answer these questions.**

10. In verse 8, why does Christ want your life to be fruitful?

_____

11. How much fruit can you bear by yourself? (vv. 4 and 5)

_____

12. What kind of relationship do you need to have with Christ—the vine in order to bear fruit? (vv. 5 and 7)

_____

13. What does God the Father do as the Gardner to make a branch more fruitful? (v. 1)

_____

Some people might try to spiritualize this verse to apply only to spiri-

John 15:1-8

"¹I am the true vine, and my Father is the gardener. ²He cuts off every branch in me that bears no fruit, while every branch that does bear fruit he prunes so that it will be even more fruitful. ³You are already clean because of the word I have spoken to you. ⁴Remain in me, and I will remain in you. No branch can bear fruit by itself; it must remain in the vine. Neither can you bear fruit unless you remain in me.

"⁵I am the vine; you are the branches. If a man remains in me and I in him, he will bear much fruit; apart from me you can do nothing. ⁶If anyone does not remain in me, he is like a branch that is thrown away and withers; such branches are picked up, thrown into the fire and burned. ⁷If you remain in me and my words remain in you, ask whatever you wish, and it will be given you. ⁸This is to my Father's glory, that you bear much fruit, showing yourselves to be my disciples"

Christ makes you fruitful in order to show the world that you are His disciple.

Galatians 5:22-24
"The fruit of the Spirit is love, joy, peace, patience, kindness, goodness, faithfulness, gentleness and self-control. Against such things there is no law. Those who belong to Christ Jesus have crucified the sinful nature with its passions and desires."

Matthew 5:13-14
"You are the salt of the earth . . ..

You are the light of the world."

tual matters or the church. But in verse 8 you see that Christ makes you fruitful in order to show the world that you are His disciple. You do not have to be a Christian to be productive in a job. Unbelievers can be productive in their work. But Christ wants to have such an intimate relationship with you that you appear to be one with Him. You in Him and He in you. Apart from that relationship you cannot be fruitful for Kingdom purposes.

Productivity may be recognized because you choose to work hard and honestly. Being able to share why you work that way can influence your workplace. God may also choose to reveal things to you that your employer needs. Like Joseph helped Pharaoh when no one else could, God may choose to reveal through you a solution, a direction, a caution, or some other valuable information that your employer or boss needs. God is able to work through you in such a way that He gets the attention of those you work for and with.

Productivity also is recognized through the fruit of the Spirit that is evident in those who cooperate with God. A Christian's response to circumstances around him or her is often radically different than the way a natural and worldly person would respond. When you display love, joy, peace, patience, kindness, goodness, faithfulness, gentleness, and self-control (Gal. 5:22-23) people notice the difference. This productivity of a life that yields spiritual fruit becomes salt and light (Matt. 5:13-14) in a world that operates off a self-focused agenda.

Keep in mind, however, that God has eternity in view. At times circumstances will appear negative and unproductive. Like Joseph you may face setbacks along the way. Yet God has an ultimate purpose in mind. You must trust Him, obey Him, and remain in an intimate relationship with Him always. You also need to realize that what appears to be a set-back may be God pruning (cutting away) a part of your life that needs to die so that the rest can become more fruitful.

PRAYER STRATEGY

➡ **Take time now to pray. Review what God has been saying to you about a restored workplace.**
- Ask the Lord to reveal ways that He wants your conduct to change so that Christ will be revealed to others.
- Pray for other Christians in your workplace that God will call them to the kind of holy conduct that Christ will be honored.
- Pray that God would increase your productivity in your workplace for the sole reason that you want Christ to be glorified through you.
- Pray that God would begin revealing things through you or other Christians in your workplace that will cause your employer to prosper.
- Ask the Lord to prepare you to respond whenever someone asks you to explain what is happening in your life and work. Prepare to trust Him for the words and to give Him the credit.

Notes

_____

_____

_____

_____

_____

_____

_____

_____

_____

_____

_____

_____

_____

_____

_____

_____

_____

_____

_____

_____

FOR FURTHER STUDY

➡ **Read the following Scriptures and look for qualities of Christlikeness or Christian virtues that should characterize a Christian even in the workplace. Make a list in the margin or underline them.**

1 Corinthians 1:10 • *I appeal to you, brothers, in the name of our Lord Jesus Christ, that all of you agree with one another so that there may be no divisions among you and that you may be perfectly united in mind and thought.*

1 Thessalonians 5:16-18 • *Be joyful always; pray continually; give thanks in all circumstances, for this is God's will for you in Christ Jesus.*

2 Chronicles 15:7 • *"As for you, be strong and do not give up, for your work will be rewarded."*

2 Chronicles 16:9 • *For the eyes of the LORD range throughout the earth to strengthen those whose hearts are fully committed to him.*

2 Corinthians 3:4-6 • *Such confidence as this is ours through Christ before God. Not that we are competent in ourselves to claim anything for ourselves, but our competence comes from God. He has made us competent as ministers of a new covenant—not of the letter but of the Spirit; for the letter kills, but the Spirit gives life.*

2 Corinthians 8:21 • *For we are taking pains to do what is right, not only in the eyes of the Lord but also in the eyes of men.*

2 Timothy 2:15 • *Do your best to present yourself to God as one approved, a workman who does not need to be ashamed and who correctly handles the word of truth.*

Ephesians 5:1-2 • *Be imitators of God, therefore, as dearly loved children and live a life of love, just as Christ loved us and gave himself up for us as a fragrant offering and sacrifice to God.*

Exodus 20:8-11 • *Remember the Sabbath day by keeping it holy. Six days you shall labor and do all your work, but the seventh day is a Sabbath to the LORD your God. On it you shall not do any work . . .For in six days the LORD made the heavens and the earth, the sea, and all that is in them, but he rested on the seventh day. Therefore the LORD blessed the Sabbath day and made it holy.*

Mark 9:41 • *I tell you the truth, anyone who gives you a cup of water in my name because you belong to Christ will certainly not lose his reward.*

Romans 12:9-21 • *Love must be sincere. Hate what is evil; cling to what is good. Be devoted to one another in brotherly love. Honor one another above yourselves. Never be lacking in zeal, but keep your spiritual fervor, serving the Lord. Be joyful in hope, patient in affliction, faithful in prayer. Share with God's people who are in need. Practice hospitality.*

KINGDOM STRATEGY
MEETING 4

*U*se the following suggestions to guide a one-hour small-group discussion of *The Kingdom Agenda* covering the lessons in this week's study. For general instructions for the group facilitator, see page 156.

This Week's Learning Objective
You will understand how Christ restores the workplace and demonstrate your commitment to the Kingdom Agenda.

Opening Prayer (2 minutes)
• Begin with prayer acknowledging God's presence.
• Ask the Holy Spirit to be your Teacher.
• Thank Christ for changing your lives.
• Ask the Lord to reveal to you His plans and ways for restoring the workplaces represented by your group.

Getting Better Acquainted (8 minutes)
Ask volunteers to each share <u>briefly</u> one experience or example of ways Christ has had a positive influence or impact on their workplaces.

Content Review (10 minutes)
Ask members to turn in their books to the Overview of Week 4 on page 77. Using the time suggested, review the following items of content from this week's lessons:
• Ask members to recite this week's Scripture-memory verse together—2 Corinthians 5:19-20. Remind them that they may use any Bible translation they prefer for memorizing verses. This week's verse is from the *King James Version.*
• Ask: Which one of the summary statements from week 4 was most meaningful to you and why?
• Ask: What are some of the ways Christ works to restore a workplace?
• Ask: How do you go about returning to the Kingdom Agenda through repentance?
• Ask: In a restored coworker relationship with God, how do you respond to God in the following cases:

-God is present.   -God provides.
-God reveals His will.   -God works.
-God initiates work.   -God is Sovereign

Discussion Questions (25 minutes)
Look over the following list of questions and lead the group to discuss those that you think would be most meaningful or helpful to your group. Watch your time (invite members to help you), so that you will allow adequate time for prayer at the end of the session. You may want to ask members to help you select the most helpful questions for discussion.

1. What does our Scripture-memory verse have to say about what God is doing in the world? How has He chosen to involve us in His work?
2. On pages 78 and 79 a list of bulleted items describe the work Christ came to do. Which of those works would have a positive influence in your workplace?
3. What is *repentance* and why is the fruit of repentance important?
4. In activity #4 on page 80, what did you describe as the fruit of repentance for the actions in a-d?
5. Instead of worrying about food and clothes, what is a disciple of Christ supposed to do? (See Matt. 6:25-33 on p. 83.)
6. How is Christ related to a believer and what difference does Christ make in a person's life and work?
7. (On p. 86) Which Scripture about overcomers was most meaningful to you and why?
8. [Ask members to evaluate their responses to #4 on page 88.] If God were to evaluate your Christian life based on what He sees of you at work, what would He conclude about your relationship with God?
9. What are some ways that Christ restores relationships between you and others? (Day 4: pp. 91-95)
10. What are the top two ways that relationships at work are different than the commands given to disciples? (#2 on p. 96)
11. How do people at your workplace respond when Christians live in worldly ways? (#6 on p. 97)
12. What did you learn from the study of Paul's letter to Titus in Day 5 (pp. 96-100) that was most meaningful?
13. What are the characteristics, virtues, or actions of a follower of Christ that could be most dif-

ferent and visible in a workplace?

14. If you were to become more productive in your workplace because of God's working through you, what would be the evidence of that productivity? (for example: more products produced, increased sales, or students making betters scores, etc.)

Priority Praying (15 minutes)

Conclude the session by spending time as a group praying for each other.

- Ask members to share with the group one of the following work-related concerns for the group to pray about. Ask them to keep the prayer requests brief; or, better yet, ask members to prayer for their own request and encourage others to join in. Concerns might include:

    -What I sense God wants me to do differently.

    -Christians at work who are poor testimonies for Christ because of their lifestyle.

    -People who need the Lord as Savior for whom God seems to be giving a burden to pray.

- Invite members to pray for these specific areas. You may use sentence prayers, conversational prayer, or pray in any other way you feel led. Give members permission to pray as many times as they choose. Remind them that they do not have to pray aloud if they choose not to.

- Invite members to use the space in the right column to record work-related prayer requests for group members so they can pray about them during the coming week.

WORK-RELATED PRAYER REQUESTS

Week 5 The Kingdom Worker

Yuri was just a child when he and his family immigrated to Venezuela from Russia. He had been educated in Venezuela, married Norelis, a Venezuelan girl, and started a business in Caracas, the capital city. When we met Yuri, he was a hard working person filled with dreams of success. He was not a Christian. His wife, Norelis,however, was a believer. Yuri soon began to ask a lot of questions about God.

One day, soon after we met them, we went to lunch with them in downtown Caracas. We talked, at length about Christ and shared how He had made a difference in our lives. That night, in his home, Yuri knelt down with his wife and prayed, surrendering his life to Christ. It was the beginning of a lifetime of changes for Yuri.

Just a few days after Yuri became a Christian, his business failed. Suddenly, he faced the reality of a huge debt - with no way to pay it. A typical reaction in that culture might have been to leave the city and all the debts behind. But Yuri made a decision that he admits he would never have made before he came to know Christ. He did not leave Caracas. He went, instead to his largest supplier, the one whom he owed the most money and told him the truth! Then Yuri offered to pay off his debt, over a period of time, as soon as he was able to find another job.

To his surprise, the man did not get angry, as Yuri expected. In fact, he was so impressed by Yuri's honesty and determination to face his debts with responsibility, that he offered Yuri a job - more than a job,really - he offered him a chance to become a partner in his business and a plan which would allow him to gradually pay off the debt!

Yuri was so excited when he shared the news with us! He told us:

"I just knew that I must do what Christ wanted me to do. But if this had happened before I became a Christian, I doubt that I would have handled it this way!"

One of the qualities of a "Kingdom Worker" is a growing confidence in God's ways and His work - a growing TRUST in God's activity in your life, including your work life! It is being obedient to what you know is God's will and trusting Him with the outcome. A working faith is a developing, growing faith. When Yuri faced a difficult situation early in his career, he did what he knew Christ would have him do. He had no idea what would happen, but one thing is for sure, he trusted God with the results.

OVERVIEW OF WEEK 5

This Week's Scripture-Memory Verse

"You are the light of the world. . . . let your light shine before men, that they may see your good deeds and praise your Father in heaven" (Matt. 5:14,16).

This Week's Lessons

Day 1: A New Character
Day 2: Kingdom Integrity
Day 3: A Working Faith
Day 4: Motivated by Christ's Love
Day 5: A Divine Network

Summary Statements from Week 5

- The condition of your heart allows God to become the Author of your daily activities.
- He wants you to recognize your need for Him.
- He wants you to grieve over sin in your life.
- He wants you to be humble, lowly, and submissive to His work in your life.
- He wants you to seek righteousness and holiness as a priority.
- God wants you to look just like Christ—to have His Spirit and His mind, to act like Him and talk like Him.
- He wants you to treat others with mercy and forgiveness.
- He wants your heart and your desires to be pure.
- He wants you to be a peacemaker and a reconciler in times of conflict.
- He wants you to endure persecution for doing right.
- A person with integrity in the workplace can be trusted to keep promises, tell the truth, stand up for right, have pure motives, and keep confidential matters private.
- *"I know, my God, that you test the heart and are pleased with integrity"* (1 Chron. 29:17).
- God calls you to cooperate with Him and allow Him to mold and shape your life.
- As you commit your actions to the Lord, He can use that to change your thoughts and desires.
- Faith in God leads to obedience.
- Your witness is a natural overflowing of your daily relationship with God.
- Faith produced work. Love motivated the work. And hope gave them endurance for their work.
- The world's motivators are fragile, temporal, and unreliable.
- The greatest motivation in a Christian's life should be his or her love for God.

- God is present in you, enabling you to serve Him out of love.
- He can give you wisdom, knowledge, or understanding about a work issue that you do not possess.
- He knows the future and can guide you to choose the right option based on the responses of others
- Christians need to experience the dynamic power Christ can produce in a workplace where His people are united. You need a relationship with the other Christians in your workplace.
- God is Sovereign. He is the Initiator. Do not take matters into your own hands and try to make things happen or to manipulate people.
- Be prepared to join God when He shows you what He is doing.

IMPORTANT IDEAS

Being Restored to the Kingdom Agenda
Step 1: Reorient Your Life to the Sovereignty of God.
Step 2: Set Aside Your Own Agenda by Dying to Self.
Step 3: Accept a Kingdom Work Strategy.

The Beatitudes
1. Poor in spirit
2. Mourn
3. Meek
4. Hunger and thirst for righteousness
5. Merciful
6. Pure in heart
7. Peacemakers
8. Persecuted because of Christ

Four Facts About Faith
1. A little faith is enough to accomplish much.
2. When your faith is weak, you can turn to God for help.
3. Christ works greater things through those who have faith in Him.
4. Christ begins and perfects your faith.

Coworkers in Your Divine Network
- Christ Jesus and His Holy Spirit
- Members in Your Church
- Christians in Your Workplace
- Christians Outside Your Workplace with Whom You Interact as Part of Your Work
- Christians in the Same Occupation or Type of Business

DAY 1   A New Character

Kingdom Agenda

"You are the light of the world. . . . let your light shine before men, that they may see your good deeds and praise your Father in heaven" (Matt. 5:14,16).

and

"When Jesus spoke again to the people, he said, 'I am the light of the world. Whoever follows me will never walk in darkness, but will have the light of life'" (John 8:12).

➡ **Read the "Kingdom Agenda" in the margin. Pause for a moment of prayer. Ask the Lord to help you die to self so that Christ and His light will shine through you. Begin to pray that your good deeds (Christ working through you) at your workplace will bring glory and praise to your heavenly Father**

1. As a review of last week's lessons, see if you can list at least three changes Christ brings about in restoring the workplace to God's original intention.

Christ changes _____

Christ changes _____

Christ changes _____

Christ changes _____

In restoring the workplace, Christ calls you to repent and surrender to God's sovereign rule. He begins by changing lives. He changes relationships between you and God and between you and others. He changes conduct as you obey His commands and live according to God's ways. Christ changes productivity as you abide in Him (the Vine) and He produces much fruit through your life.

Christ changes productivity as you abide in Him (the Vine) and He produces much fruit through your life.

Three Steps

When you respond to Christ and His work in you, He is able to work through you for the glory of His Father. I see three steps Christ guides you to take in this process:

Step 1: Reorient Your Life to the Sovereignty of God.

Step 2: Set Aside Your Own Agenda by Dying to Self.

Step 3: Accept a Kingdom Work Strategy.

These three steps are summarized by Jesus: *"If anyone would come after me, he must deny himself and take up his cross daily and follow me"* (Luke 9:23). When you turn (repent) to follow Christ, you are reorienting your life to His sovereign rule in your life (step 1 above). You set aside your own personal agenda by denying self and dying to self. Then you are prepared to take up your cross, which represents God's will or Kingdom Agenda for your life.

When Christ works in your life in the process of restoring the workplace, He changes who you are and what you do. Your human tendency will be to focus on what you can DO differently (step 3 above). We are much more interested in doing than being (step 2 above). Christ, however, will work on preparing your life to be one through whom He can work. His first priority is on your "being" the person He wants you to be in the workplace.

Christ, however, will work on preparing your life to be one through whom He can work.

➡ **2. See if you can arrange the following three words in proper order to show what Christ emphasizes first, second, and third. Write these**

three works on the proper lines below: "being," "doing," "repent."

First:_____

Second:_____

Third:_____

Christ's first message was *"repent."* You must first turn from self-centered and worldly ways to Him and His kingdom ways. Last week we looked at what repentance meant. This week we want to look at the Kingdom worker—that's you. What kind of person does Christ want you to BE? As Christ focused on being before doing, we will focus our lessons this week more on "being." We will look at character, integrity, faith, and love. We will also take a look at the divine network Christ creates between you and other believers to accomplish His kingdom purposes. Next week we will turn our focus to the Kingdom work—the "doing."

Kingdom Job Description

We have already talked about the fact that we try to take over God's job description as if it were ours. Christ reorients us to work on our own job description. I see much of that job description in the Sermon on the Mount in Matthew 5—7. There are two dimensions to the Kingdom Job Description. One dimension focuses on "development" (being) and the other on "execution" (doing).

The Beatitudes

Jesus began his sermon by first focusing on the character of a Kingdom worker. He described the type of heart attitudes—the character—that is required to work according to His Kingdom Job Description. These attitudes are called the Beatitudes. They reflect the ingredients of a heart and life in which God is truly Sovereign. The condition of your heart allows God to become the Author of your daily activities. Jesus has given us God's description of inner character. The Beatitudes are the essential prerequisites for a Kingdom assignment.

➡ **3. As you read Matthew 5:3-12 in the margin, underline the eight attitudes that are blessed by God. Through this passage, let Christ paint a mental picture of what your life ought to look like. Then He will be able to chip away all that does not reflect this character.**

This description of character should become your developmental compass as well as a daily checklist for evaluating your Kingdom focus. These heart attitudes are God-given developmental goals. Let's take a brief look at each one.

Poor in Spirit. Blessed are those who recognize their great need for Christ and trust Him for every provision. They realize that they can do nothing of Kingdom value apart from Him. They realize that Christ is their life. They cannot live apart from His Spirit.

Mourn. Blessed are those who are grieved by the sin in their lives and in the lives of others. Blessed are the ones who allow Christ to use brokenness in their lives to "chip away" self so that godliness remains.

Meek. Blessed are those who are gentle spirited. They are not self-assertive. They do not act out of self-interest. They are responsive and sub-

Matthew 5:3-12
"Blessed are the poor in spirit, for theirs is the kingdom of heaven. Blessed are those who mourn, for they will be comforted. Blessed are the meek, for they will inherit the earth. Blessed are those who hunger and thirst for righteousness, for they will be filled. Blessed are the merciful, for they will be shown mercy. Blessed are the pure in heart, for they will see God. Blessed are the peacemakers, for they will be called sons of God. Blessed are those who are persecuted because of righteousness, for theirs is the kingdom of heaven.

"Blessed are you when people insult you, persecute you and falsely say all kinds of evil against you because of me. Rejoice and be glad, because great is your reward in heaven, for in the same way they persecuted the prophets who were before you."

The Beatitudes

1. Poor in spirit
2. Mourn
3. Meek
4. Hunger and thirst for righteousness
5. Merciful
6. Pure in heart
7. Peacemakers
8. Persecuted because of Christ

missive to God's molding and shaping of their lives. This is not weakness, but power under control of the Master.

Hunger and Thirst for Righteousness. Blessed are those who want to be holy and right with God more than anything else. They shun evil. They seek to be right with God and with others as if they would starve to death without it!

➡ **4. In each pair below check the one statement that is most like you.**

❑ a1. I recognize my need for Christ and look to Him to give me life.
❑ a2. I can make it on my own. I only need Christ when things get really bad.

❑ b1. I weep and grieve over my sin and submit to God's discipline as a good thing.
❑ b2. I'm satisfied with life and don't get bent out of shape over sin. I'm only human.

❑ c1. Christ must increase and I must decrease. I don't try to assert myself. I strive to be lowly and humble like Christ.
❑ c2. I like being first, important, and in charge. I won't let anybody push me around. I have my rights.

❑ d1. I can't seem to get enough of God's Word and I love spending time with the Lord. I really want to be like Christ and live in a way that pleases Him.
❑ d2. I am very busy with my job, my family, my hobbies, and taking care of my things (house, car, yard). I don't have much time for church, Bible study, prayer, or spending time with God's people.

Look back over your responses. Were you able to check the first statement in each pair or did you have to check the second? These may not be the best contrasts for the Beatitudes, but they should help you begin to think about the kind of character that Christ wants you to have. He wants you to recognize your need for Him. He wants you to grieve over sin in your life. He wants you to be humble, lowly, and submissive to His work in your life. He wants you to seek righteousness and holiness as a priority. Let's look at four more Beatitudes.

Merciful. Blessed are those who have pity and show compassion to people who are needy and distressed. This is not just a feeling but action that seeks to relieve the need or the distress.

Pure in Heart. Blessed are those who have pure motives. In Jewish thought the heart is the center of the will. Pure means unmixed or not polluted. Seeking first the Kingdom and God's glory for His sake is a pure motive. There is no place for selfish and self-centered motives in a pure heart.

Peacemakers. Blessed are those who seek peace and reconciliation when relationships are broken. Some people seem to agitate others and get into disputes or arguments easily. Others face problems by closing their eyes and ears and hoping they will go away. Others actively seek to resolve conflict in order to see the peace of Christ reign. Those who make peace are blessed.

Persecuted Because of Christ. Blessed are those who are so like Christ they are persecuted. These people prefer God's approval over the approval of others. They will not compromise their faith just to avoid ridicule, in-

He wants you to recognize your need for Him.

He wants you to grieve over sin in your life.

He wants you to be humble, lowly, and submissive to His work in your life.

He wants you to seek righteousness and holiness as a priority.

sults, or persecution. They will stand for Christ and what is right even when it may be costly.

➡ **5. In each pair below check the one statement that is most like you.**

❑ a1. When I see people who are needy or distressed, I just have to do whatever I can to help out. I treat them as I would want to be treated if I were in their place.

❑ a2. I have to take care of myself. Other people should take care of themselves. I'm not my brother's keeper. Let someone else help them.

❑ b1. My desire is to please God and bring glory to Christ through all that I do. I love Him and want to serve Him faithfully because He first loved me.

❑ b2. I'm doing my best to get ahead. I don't mind compromising here and there if it can make me look good.

❑ c1. When I am thrust into the middle of conflict, my desire is to see peace, harmony, and unity prevail for God's glory. I turn to the Lord—the Prince of Peace—for help to bring resolution to the conflict in a godly manner.

❑ c2. I would rather fight than switch. I like to keep things stirred up— that makes life more interesting. I enjoy playing "the devil's advocate" just for the sake of argument.

❑ d1. The more I seek to be like Jesus, the more ridicule I receive. People at work are critical of my faith. They argue about my convictions and tease me for my commitment to Christ.

❑ d2. I keep quiet about my relationship to Christ. I think I hide it pretty well, because nobody accuses me of being a Christian. I avoid taking a stand for Christ if anybody would attack me for my stand.

> He wants you to treat others with mercy and forgiveness.
>
> He wants your heart and your desires to be pure.
>
> He wants you to be a peacemaker and a reconciler in times of conflict.
>
> He wants you to endure persecution for doing right.

Again, these may not be the best contrasts for the last four Beatitudes, but they should help you think about the kind of character that Christ wants you to have. Ultimately God wants you to look just like Christ—to have His Spirit and His mind, to act like Him and talk like Him. He wants you to treat others with mercy and forgiveness. He wants your heart and your desires to be pure. He wants you to be a peacemaker and a reconciler in times of conflict. He wants you to endure persecution for doing right. Anything in your life that does not reflect Christ needs to be removed. That needs to begin in your heart, in your attitudes, and in your values. Then your character will be reflected in your outward actions and words.

PRAYER STRATEGY

➡ **Take time now to pray and ask the Lord to guide your character development so you will be a vessel that He can use in Kingdom work.**

- Ask the Lord to speak to you through the Scriptures to reveal the Christlike character that He desires of your life.
- Ask the Holy Spirit to enable your understanding of the Beatitudes. Ask Him to reveal anything in your mind or heart that needs to change.
- Give God permission to do whatever He knows is needed to mold and shape your character to reflect Christ.

For Further Study
➡ **Read the following Scriptures that describe different aspects of character that God wants in your life. Pray through each one. On the line above the Scripture write a title that summarizes the trait or traits that God desires in you. I have titled the first one for you.**

Summary Title: _____*Humility of a Child*_____
Matthew 18:3-4 • *I tell you the truth, unless you change and become like little children, you will never enter the kingdom of heaven. Therefore, whoever humbles himself like this child is the greatest in the kingdom of heaven.*

Summary Title: _____
James 3:17 • *The wisdom that comes from heaven is first of all pure; then peace-loving, considerate, submissive, full of mercy and good fruit, impartial and sincere.*

Summary Title: _____
James 1:2-4 • *Consider it pure joy, my brothers, whenever you face trials of many kinds, because you know that the testing of your faith develops perseverance. Perseverance must finish its work so that you may be mature and complete, not lacking anything.*

Summary Title: _____
Galatians 5:22-24 • *The fruit of the Spirit is love, joy, peace, patience, kindness, goodness, faithfulness, gentleness and self-control. Against such things there is no law. Those who belong to Christ Jesus have crucified the sinful nature with its passions and desires.*

Summary Title: _____
1 Peter 3:14-16 • *Even if you should suffer for what is right, you are blessed. "Do not fear what they fear; do not be frightened." But in your hearts set apart Christ as Lord. Always be prepared to give an answer to everyone who asks you to give the reason for the hope that you have. But do this with gentleness and respect, keeping a clear conscience, so that those who speak maliciously against your good behavior in Christ may be ashamed of their slander.*

Summary Title: _____
1 Thessalonians 4:7 • *For God did not call us to be impure, but to live a holy life.*

Summary Title: _____
2 Peter 1:5-9 • *For this very reason, make every effort to add to your faith goodness; and to goodness, knowledge; and to knowledge, self-control; and to self-control, perseverance; and to perseverance, godliness; and to godliness, brotherly kindness; and to brotherly kindness, love. For if you possess these qualities in increasing measure, they will keep you from being ineffective and unproductive in your knowledge of our Lord Jesus Christ. But if anyone does not have them, he is nearsighted and blind, and has forgotten that he has been cleansed from his past sins.*

DAY 2 Kingdom Integrity

Kingdom Agenda

"In everything set them an example by doing what is good. In your teaching show integrity, seriousness and soundness of speech that cannot be condemned, so that those who oppose you may be ashamed because they have nothing bad to say about us" (Titus 2:6-8).

Psalm 15:1-5

"LORD, who may dwell in your sanctuary? Who may live on your holy hill? He whose walk is blameless and who does what is righteous, who speaks the truth from his heart and has no slander on his tongue, who does his neighbor no wrong and casts no slur on his fellowman, who despises a vile man but honors those who fear the LORD, who keeps his oath even when it hurts, who lends his money without usury and does not accept a bribe against the innocent. He who does these things will never be shaken."

This person keeps his promises.

A Person of Integrity:

_____

➡ **Read the "Kingdom Agenda" in the margin. Pause for a moment of prayer. Ask the Lord to help you understand and appreciate the importance of integrity in the cause of the Kingdom.**

Part of the character of a Kingdom worker is integrity. The word integrity comes from a Latin word which means "wholeness," "completeness," or "perfection." In the Sermon on the Mount Jesus said, "Be perfect, therefore, as your heavenly Father is perfect" (Matt. 5:48). This is one of those qualities that we will never measure up to on our own. It is a quality of living shaped by Christ's character within us.

➡ **1. Read Psalm 15 in the margin. List below several characteristics of Kingdom integrity revealed in this passage.**

_____

_____

_____

A person of integrity according to David is one who is blameless, does what is righteous, is truthful and does not slander, treats others rightly, despises vile men, honors those who fear the Lord, keeps his promises, does not take advantage of the poor, and accepts no bribes that would prevent justice. David writes *"He who does these things will never be shaken"* This is God's promise to people of integrity.

Integrity means honesty, truthfulness, or trustworthiness. You may have heard of a person with integrity described this way, "His word is his bond." In other words, this person keeps his promises. Jesus commanded His followers to possess this character trait:

"You have heard that it was said to the people long ago, `Do not break your oath, but keep the oaths you have made to the Lord.' But I tell you, Do not swear at all: either by heaven, for it is God's throne; or by the earth, for it is his footstool; or by Jerusalem, for it is the city of the Great King. And do not swear by your head, for you cannot make even one hair white or black. Simply let your `Yes' be `Yes,' and your `No,' `No'; anything beyond this comes from the evil one" (Matt. 5:33-37).

➡ **2. Suppose you were asked to describe a person who had integrity in your workplace. How would you describe him or her?**

_____

_____

_____

3. Can you name a person in your workplace that you would say is a person with genuine integrity? Write his or her name in the margin.

4. Check the statements below that would indicate a person of integrity. Place an "X" beside those statements that may indicate a person who does not have integrity.

❑ a. When you say it is so, it is so.

❑ b. Say whatever the customer (or supervisor) wants to hear.

❑ c. Refuse to compromise on basic issues of right and wrong.

❑ d. Back out of commitments if you realize they are becoming too costly.

❑ e. Pad your expense report with inflated charges just in case you forgot to include an expense.

❑ f. Refuse to spread gossip about others that may or may not be true.

❑ g. Do everything within your power to follow through on commitments.

> *A person with integrity in the workplace can be trusted to keep promises, tell the truth, stand up for right, have pure motives, and keep confidential matters private.*

A person with integrity in the workplace can be trusted to keep promises, tell the truth, stand up for right, have pure motives, and keep confidential matters private. Did you check a, c, f, and g? I would put an "X" beside b, d, and e. King David prayed and said to the Lord, *"I know, my God, that you test the heart and are pleased with integrity"* (1 Chron. 29:17).

➡ **5. If God were to test your heart right now, would He find integrity there? Ask the Lord to examine your heart and reveal the condition of your heart in each of the following areas. Write a number beside the trait on the left using the numbers of the evaluations on the right.**

____ a. Honest	1. You show integrity here.
____ b. Truthful	2. You need to work on your integrity here.
____ c. Trustworthy	3. You are failing in your integrity here.
____ d. Pure motives	
____ e. Keeps promises	
____ f. Does what is right	
____ g. Upholds justice	
____ h. Does not slander	

> *Today's workplace provides a good opportunity for Christians to be radically different than most of the world in the area of integrity.*

Just meeting a person who tells the truth and keeps his or her word is truly unusual in today's workplace. Today's workplace provides a good opportunity for Christians to be radically different than most of the world in the area of integrity.

Building Integrity

Integrity is a reflection of inner character which has been shaped over time by the thoughts of God. Integrity does not appear spontaneously in the middle of volatile circumstances or under great pressure. When Christians find themselves under the pressure of difficult circumstances, many choose to compromise what they know to be right. They take the route of least resistance.

True integrity is developed by the Spirit of God, one thought at a time. Its strength in time of trial rests not upon the power of the human spirit, but rather the power of the Spirit of God. We are all fellow strugglers in a world that has not yet been fully redeemed. Most of us are like Paul when he said, *"What I do is not the good I want to do; no, the evil I do not want to do— this I keep on doing"* (Rom. 7:19). The strength we need consistently to make right choices in our lives can only be found in Jesus Christ! Integrity, morality, and ethics are born out of an authentic relationship with the living God.

The key to letting God create a heart of integrity in your life is recognize

Philippians 2:13
"It is God who works in you to will and to act according to his good purpose."

your inadequacy and Christ's sufficiency. He can enable you to live as He commands (see Phil. 2:13). When you turn to Christ and His Holy Spirit for help, you have taken the first step toward becoming a person of integrity. How can you cooperate with God as He develops integrity in your life? Let me walk you through the following diagram.

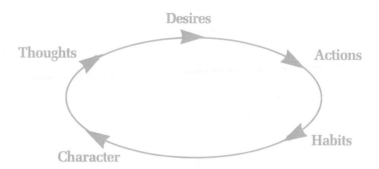

Character is developed over a period of time. It can be either good or bad depending on how it measures up to God's standards. Character development begins in the mind with your thoughts.

• When you dwell on thoughts they may lead to desires.
• Desires, if not carefully examined, can lead to actions.
• When actions are repeated enough, they lead to habits.
• Habits that are practiced develop into character.
• Character can then influence the kinds of thoughts that you permit.

. . . And the cycle continues molding and shaping your character, your values, and your lifestyle.

➡ **6. Suppose you sensed that God wanted to change a flaw in your character—something that is wrong or lacking in His sight. Where do you think He would begin? Check your response.**
  ❏ a. He would forgive me and everything would automatically be changed.
  ❏ b. He would point out my bad habits and tell me to quit.
  ❏ c. He would tell me to change specific actions—stop some and start others.
  ❏ d. He would change my desires so that I would want to do right.
  ❏ e. He would cleanse and renew my thought life.
  ❏ f. He could begin at any one of these points.

God is Sovereign and all-powerful. He could begin to change your character any way He wanted to. He could miraculously change you, or He could begin a lengthy process of renewing your character. Consider the woman caught in adultery (John 8:3-11). She had a character flaw that led to sexual immorality. Living in adulterous relationships reveals a deeply rooted character problem. In this woman's case Jesus forgave her and commanded her to be different.

Getting rid of a sinful character may happen much more quickly, however, than developing a godly character to replace it.

Getting rid of a sinful character may happen much more quickly, however, than developing a godly character to replace it. If you have an integrity problem that results in sinful behavior, Christ could say to you: *"Neither do I condemn you. . . . Go now and leave your life of sin"* (John 8:11). Leaving your sin can be immediate, but developing a new character will take time. You must cooperate with God as He renews your character. He has given you the freedom to choose obedience or rebellion. God calls you to cooperate with Him and allow Him to mold and shape your life.

➡ **Read the following Scriptures and answer the questions after each one.**

I urge you, brothers, in view of God's mercy, to offer your bodies as living sacrifices, holy and pleasing to God—this is your spiritual act of worship. Do not conform any longer to the pattern of this world, but be transformed by the renewing of your mind. Then you will be able to test and approve what God's will is—his good, pleasing and perfect will (Rom. 12:1-2).

➡ **7. What are you to offer to God as a living sacrifice?**

_____

8. How are you to respond to the "pattern of this world"? Fill in the blank:
"Do not _____ to the pattern of this world."

9. How are you to be transformed?

_____

It is God who works in you to will and to act according to his good purpose (Phil. 2:13).

➡ **10. In Philippians 2:13 above, what does God work in you? Fill in the blanks:**
"God who works in [me] to _____ and to _____ according to his good purpose."

Commit thy works unto the LORD, and thy thoughts shall be established (Pro. 16:3, KJV)

➡ **11. If you commit your works (actions) to the Lord, what can be established?**

_____

> Give Him full access to all of your life including your thought life.

You can cooperate with God by first offering your whole being to God as a living sacrifice. Hold nothing back from Him. Give Him full access to all of your life including your thought life. God does not want you to molded by the world's agenda (pattern). He wants your mind and thoughts to be transformed. That is next to impossible apart from God's working in you. But, as you yield to Him and cooperate with Him, He can cause you to desire (to will) to do His will. Once the desire is established, He enables you to act according to His will and purposes.

Sometimes God may work at that same process in reverse. He may reveal a sinful behavior and command you to change your actions. You may not want to do what God instructs you to do, but you choose to obey Him anyway. As you commit your actions to the Lord, He can use that to change your thoughts and desires.

> As you commit your actions to the Lord, He can use that to change your thoughts and desires.

Suppose you had grown up in a very deprived environment and you had never tasted ice cream. Just looking at ice cream for the first time, may not cause you to want any. But then suppose you taste the ice cream. You act first. You decide that ice cream tastes good, and soon your desire for ice cream changes. This is a very simple analogy. But God may give you a command to keep your promises (vows). You obey Him even though you don't want to. In the process of obeying God, God may develop a healthy pride in the fact that you can be trusted. People learn that you can be trusted to keep your word. Before long you realize that God is right about keeping vows and you don't want to do anything to break a promise. Sometimes God works this way:

1. God renews your mind—your thoughts and desires.
2. Based on your desires you change your actions.
3. As your actions change you develop healthy and right habits.
4. Consistently walking in this pattern your character is changed to reflect godly character.

1. God renews my thoughts and desires.
2. I change my actions.
3. I develop right habits.
4. My character begins to reflect Godly character.

➡ **12. Based on this pattern, place these words in order below:**
   actions;   habits;   thoughts (desires)

   new _____ → new _____ → new _____ → new character

At other times God may work in this way:

1. God commands you to take a right action (perhaps replacing a wrong one).
2. As you obey God, He begins to change your desires and thoughts.
3. With renewed desires you continue the right actions.
4. These right actions lead to the development of habits and character.

1. God commands a right action.
2. I choose to obey and God begins to change my desires.
3. I continue right actions.
4. God develops right habits and character.

➡ **13. Based on this pattern, place these words in a different order.**
   actions;   habits;   thoughts (desires)

   new _____ → new _____ → new _____ → new character

God may begin by changing actions, or He may begin by changing thoughts and desires. In either case God will be working in you to direct you. Your job is to cooperate with God by obeying Him. At times what God commands may not make sense. Your human reason may tell you to act just the opposite. At those times you need to obey God and trust the outcome to Him.

➡ **14. Consider starting the following long-term assignment:**
   • Begin to making a personal list of actions or habits that you realize are not right.
   • Ask yourself why you are doing what you are doing, and write your response under a heading: "DESIRES/MOTIVES."
   • Begin to search the scriptures to find God's thoughts about what you are doing. Write those verses down and begin to pray them each day. Memorize these verses and review them in your mind several times each day.
   • The next time you face temptation in that area of your life, stop and pray God's thoughts. Then choose to obey Him.

PRAYER STRATEGY

➡ **Take time now to pray.**
   • Ask God to point out any actions or habits of yours that reflect a lack of integrity or morality. Make notes in the margin or on separate paper.
   • Confess your sin to the Lord and ask for His forgiveness and restoration.
   • Ask the Lord to begin revealing what you are to think and do in order for these actions and habits to change. This will probably include some things you must stop doing.
   • Ask the Lord to speak through the Scriptures and prayer to cause you to want to do His will. Then depend on the Lord to enable you to obey.

DAY 3 A Working Faith

"Trust in the LORD with all your heart and lean not on your own understanding; in all your ways acknowledge him, and he will make your paths straight" (Pro. 3:5-6).

➡ **Read the "Kingdom Agenda" in the margin. Pause for a moment of prayer. Commit to the Lord your trust. Decide not to lean on your human understanding. Ask the Lord to enable you to walk by faith in His straight paths.**

According to Scripture, *"Without faith it is impossible to please God, because anyone who comes to him must believe that he exists and that he rewards those who earnestly seek him"* (Heb. 11:6). Faith is trusting God when your human senses cannot see the way. *"Faith is being sure of what we hope for and certain of what we do not see"* (Heb. 11:1). Faith in your workplace will require that you:

• Trust in God's presence when you do not sense that He is near.
• Trust in God's purpose when His redemptive work seems impossible.
• Trust in God's protection when you are under attack and want to turn to purely human means for protection.
• Trust in God's provision when you do not see where the resources or abilities will come from.
• Trust in God's ways when human reason would call the ways foolish or tell you to do things differently.

➡ **1. As you think about your own work life, in which of the following areas do you seem to have difficulty trusting God? Check all that apply.**
  ❑ a. I have trouble believing that God's is present in my workplace.
  ❑ b. I have trouble believing that God can redeem the people and the environment where I work.
  ❑ c. I have trouble believing that God will protect me when I do what is right.
  ❑ d. I have trouble believing that God will provide for my needs and that He will enable me to accomplish His work.
  ❑ e. I have trouble believing that God's ways are the right ways to accomplish Kingdom work.
  ❑ f. Actually, I have trouble believing that God cares about my workplace and can do anything through me that would be of value.

Four Facts About Faith
1. A little faith is enough to accomplish much.
2. When your faith is weak, you can turn to God for help.
3. Christ works greater things through those who have faith in Him.
4. Christ begins and perfects your faith.

Four Facts About Faith

If you had to check one or more of the items above (maybe even all of the items above), don't be discouraged. There are some exciting truths about faith you need to know.

First: A little faith is enough to accomplish much. Jesus said: *"I tell you the truth, if you have faith as small as a mustard seed, you can say to this mountain, 'Move from here to there' and it will move. Nothing will be impossible for you"* (Matt. 17:20). The amount of your faith is the problem. You either have faith or you practice unbelief. With a little faith you can see "mountains" move.

Second: When your faith is weak, you can turn to God for help. On one occasion the disciples asked Jesus, *"Increase our faith!"* (Luke 17:5). You, too, can ask Christ to increase your faith.

A father once asked Jesus to heal his demon possessed son. Jesus said, *"Everything is possible for him who believes"* (Mark 9:23). The father needed faith, but he realized his faith was weak. So he said, *"I do believe; help me overcome my unbelief!"* (Mark 9:24). Jesus helped him and then healed his son. When you have weak faith, you can ask Christ to help you overcome your unbelief.

Third: Christ works greater things through those who have faith in Him. He said to his disciples:

Anyone who has faith in me will do what I have been doing. He will do even greater things than these, because I am going to the Father. And I will do whatever you ask in my name, so that the Son may bring glory to the Father. You may ask me for anything in my name, and I will do it (John 14:12-14).

Fourth: Christ begins and perfects your faith. When you surrender to Him as Lord and fix your attention on Him, Christ helps your faith. The writer of Hebrews said it this way, *"Let us fix our eyes on Jesus, the author and perfecter of our faith"* (Heb. 12:2).

➡ **2. Which of the four truths about faith (listed in the margin) are most encouraging to you and why?**

_____

_____

_____

A Formula for Faith

Your faith is not dependent on who you are. Your faith is in God and who He is. Faith can grow and increase as you cultivate your love relationship with God. Here is a formula for a working faith:

> **Knowing → Loving → Trusting → Obeying**

Knowing. Faith has a foundation in knowing God. To know God is not just to know about Him even though that helps, too. Knowing God comes as you experience Him at work in and around your life.

Loving. When you come to know and experience God in real and personal ways, you will love Him. You will love Him because He first loved you. We will study more about this love tomorrow. It is a strong motivation for following the Kingdom Agenda.

Trusting. As your love grows for your heavenly Father, you realize that you can trust Him. You realize that He loves you so deeply that He will always seek what is for your good. He can even take "bad" things and work them together for good (see Rom. 8:28). When you know that God is love, that His will is best, and that His ways are always right, you can trust Him with ever widening aspects of your life.

Obeying. When you know, love, and trust the Lord, you will obey Him. Those who do not obey do not love (see John 14:15,24). Obedience to your Sovereign Lord is the Kingdom Agenda.

➡ **3. Where is your relationship with the Lord with regard to your workplace? Do you still need to know Him? Are you still needing to cultivate a love relationship with Him? Are you loving but not yet trusting Him?**

Four Facts About Faith
1. A little faith is enough to accomplish much.
2. When your faith is weak, you can turn to God for help.
3. Christ works greater things through those who have faith in Him.
4. Christ begins and perfects your faith.

Romans 8:28
"In all things God works for the good of those who love him, who have been called according to his purpose."

John 14:15,24
"If you love me, you will obey what I command....
"He who does not love me will not obey my teaching."

Are you still needing to learn to obey Him? Which of these areas do you sense God wants to work on most in your work life? Circle it.

Knowing   Loving   Trusting   Obeying

Developing Your Faith

Faith in God leads to obedience.

James said, *"As the body without the spirit is dead, so faith without works is dead also"* (Jas. 2:26,KJV). Faith in God leads to obedience. Obedience is a demonstration of your faith. The formula we looked at above is really more like a cycle than a line. When you trust God and obey Him, He accomplishes through you more that you can do alone. When you experience God doing God-sized things around you, you come to know Him better. You come to love Him more and your faith is increased to trust Him for even greater things. Therefore, little steps of faith and obedience can develop a working faith that trusts God to "move mountains." Below are some ways you need to trust God at work.

Trust in God's Presence

1 Corinthians 6:19

"Do you not know that your body is a temple of the Holy Spirit, who is in you, whom you have received from God?"

Trust in God's Presence. God is present at your workplace whether you sense His presence or not. He is present in you. Your body is the temple (dwelling place) of the Holy Spirit (see 1 Cor. 6:19). He is present to work, to guide, to protect, to enable, and to encourage.

➡ **Pause for a minute of prayer. Ask the Lord to increase your trust in His presence in your workplace. Decide to take time to pray throughout your work day (eyes open or closed as the conditions allow). Use this action to help you remember that He is present and available.**

Check here when you have prayed: ❏

Trust in God's Purpose

Trust in God's Purpose. Fine-tuning your faith as a Kingdom worker calls you to trust in God's purpose to reconcile the world to Himself. No matter how difficult or impossible the task may seem, *"with God all things are possible"* (Matt. 19:26).

When you trust that God is able to redeem people and your workplace, you can join God in His redemptive work. This reconciliation is accomplished through Christ and your willingness to work according to the Kingdom Agenda. You become a Kingdom lobbyist in the lives of others. Your witness is a natural overflowing of your daily relationship with God. You have the privilege of demonstrating Christlike love to others in His name. But the fruit is the Lord's work. He brings forth fruit through your life.

Your witness is a natural overflowing of your daily relationship with God.

➡ **Pause for a minute of prayer. Ask the Lord to increase your trust in His redemptive purpose. Agree to accept any assignment He may give you, even if it is to work with the least likely person.**

Check here when you have prayed: ❏

Trust in God's Protection

1 John 4:18

"There is no fear in love. But perfect love drives out fear. . . . The one who fears is not made perfect in love."

Trust in God's Protection. When King David wrote the words, *"The Lord is my shepherd"* (Ps. 23:1) he revealed a living faith in God's protection. It was the shepherd who stood between the sheep and pending destruction. It was the shepherd who was vigilant to protect the sheep from circumstances that they were totally unaware of. It is God who stands between you and all the evil that surrounds your life. Perfect love will cast out fear (see 1 John 4:18).

You need to realize that living like Christ in the workplace may be met with opposition. It may bring persecution. It might even cost you your job some day. You must depend on God to protect you so you will make the hard decisions to do right. You also need to depend on God to be your avenger. Paul says, *"Do not take revenge, my friends, but leave room for God's wrath, for it is written: 'It is mine to avenge; I will repay'"* (Rom. 12:19).

➡ **Pause for a minute of prayer. Ask the Lord to increase your trust in His protection in your workplace.**

Check here when you have prayed: ❏

Trust in God's Provision

Trust in God's Provision. Adam trusted God to be His Provider. As a Kingdom worker, you, too, need to trust God to provide for your needs. Jesus said:

> *Therefore I tell you, do not worry about your life, what you will eat or drink; or about your body, what you will wear. Is not life more important than food, and the body more important than clothes? Look at the birds of the air . . . your heavenly Father feeds them. . . .*
>
> *And why do you worry about clothes? See how the lilies of the field grow. . . . God clothes the grass of the field. . . . So do not worry, saying, "What shall we eat?" or "What shall we drink?" or "What shall we wear?" For the pagans run after all these things, and your heavenly Father knows that you need them. But seek first his kingdom and his righteousness, and all these things will be given to you as well* (Matt. 6:25-33).

You also must trust God to provide the spiritual resources you to do His work. Without Him you can do nothing (John 15:5). Remember with Him present in you, He can do through you anything He chooses to accomplish.

➡ **Pause for a minute of prayer. Ask the Lord to increase your trust in His provision for your needs. Confess any worry you may have. Throw all your cares on the Lord.**

Check here when you have prayed: ❏

Trust in God's Ways

Trust in God's Ways. Today's "Kingdom Agenda" Scriptures says, *"Trust in the LORD with all your heart and lean not on your own understanding; in all your ways acknowledge him, and he will make your paths straight"* (Pro. 3:5-6). If you want to know and do God's will, you need to trust His ways and not rely on your own understanding. God has said:

> *"My thoughts are not your thoughts, neither are your ways my ways," declares the LORD. "As the heavens are higher than the earth, so are my ways higher than your ways and my thoughts than your thoughts"* (Isa. 55:8-9).

As you trust God's ways and obey, you will realize that His ways are always right and best. Even when you disagree or don't understand, obey. Then God will accomplish what He had in mind in the way that produces the greatest fruit.

➡ **Pause for a minute of prayer. Ask the Lord to increase your trust in His ways in your workplace. Agree now to follow His ways.**

Check here when you have prayed: ❏

PRAYER STRATEGY

➥ **Take time now to pray about your working faith.**

- Ask the Lord to increase your faith in areas where it may be weak.
- If you are having trouble trusting Him, ask the Lord to reveal Himself to you in ways that will help you to know Him and love Him.
- Surrender your life to His sovereign will and purposes. Give Him permission to lead you anywhere and any way He chooses in your work. Commit yourself on the front end to obey Him whatever He should ask you to do.

DAY 4 Motivated by Christ's Love

Kingdom Agenda
"Christ's love compels us. . . . that those who live should no longer live for themselves but for him who died for them and was raised again" (2 Cor. 5:14-15).

Hebrews 11:6
"Without faith it is impossible to please God, because anyone who comes to him must believe that he exists and that he rewards those who earnestly seek him."

James 2:26
"As the body without the spirit is dead, so faith without works is dead also" (KJV).

➡ **Read the "Kingdom Agenda" in the margin. Pause for a moment of prayer. Thank God for the love of Christ that He demonstrated on the cross. Ask the Lord to help you live for Christ because of His love.**

Yesterday you studied about the importance of faith. Without it you cannot please God (Heb. 11:6). You also learned that faith that is not expressed by good deeds is dead (Jas. 2:26). Faith and good deeds are important parts of living a Christlike life. One other virtue is important if faith is to have any value. Paul said, *"If I have a faith that can move mountains, but have not love, I am nothing"* (1 Cor. 13:2).

➡ **1. Match the words on the right with the descriptions on the left.**

___ a. It is required to please God.	1. Good deeds
___ b. Without it, faith is worthless.	2. Faith
___ c. They show the sincerity of faith.	3. Love
___ d. It can move mountains.	

God accomplishes mighty works through those who have faith. Good deeds are an expression of a sincere faith. But great faith without love is worthless. (Answers: a-2, b-3, c-1, d-2). Paul put faith and love together when he described the Kingdom work of the Christians in Thessalonica. He said, *"We continually remember before our God and Father your work produced by faith, your labor prompted by love, and your endurance inspired by hope in our Lord Jesus Christ"* (1 Thess. 1:3). Faith produced work. Love motivated the work. And hope gave them endurance for their work. Today's lesson turns our focus to the importance of love as a motivator for your work in the Kingdom.

The World's Motivation
The world will attempt to use the desires of your human nature to motivate you to do a good job or work hard. Work on the Kingdom Agenda is motivated by the love of Christ.

➡ **2. What are some of the ways your employer tries to motivate you to do a good job or work hard? Check all that apply.**

❑ contest prizes	❑ criticism	❑ encouragement
❑ financial bonus	❑ pay raise	❑ performance reviews
❑ praise	❑ promotions	❑ public awards
❑ recognition	❑ reprimands	❑ trips

The world has many different ways to try to influence your behavior on the job. Some of the motivation is negative. Criticism, reprimands, and perhaps even public ridicule may be used to cause you to work harder. A promotion, pay raise, or bonus may appeal to your desire for more money. Recognition, praise, and awards may appeal to your desire for esteem. Striving after these can bring satisfaction in a temporary way. The world's motivators are fragile, temporal, and unreliable. For instance, have you ever gotten a merit increase but been upset because yours was not as large as someone else's?

The world's motivators are fragile, temporal, and unreliable.

None of these motivators are necessarily wrong. But they may encour-

The world's motivators can actually draw you away from an intimate relationship with God.

age you to turn your focus to self. When the world's motivators influence you to become self-centered, you turn from being God-centered. Working hard for the wrong reasons can be worthless to the Kingdom and cause you to feel empty and frustrated. The world's motivators can actually draw you away from an intimate relationship with God.

The Kingdom's Motivation

The agenda of the Kingdom points to a different motivation for your work. Jesus revealed the best motivation in a Christian's life when he talked with Simon Peter on the seashore after the resurrection. Peter had gone fishing (his old career). Jesus had a Kingdom assignment for Peter. Peter was to be a major leader in the early church. Notice why Jesus wanted Peter to serve in the Kingdom:

> When they had finished eating, Jesus said to Simon Peter, "Simon son of John, do you truly love me more than these?"
> "Yes, Lord," he said, "you know that I love you."
> Jesus said, "Feed my lambs." . . .
> "Take care of my sheep." . . .
> "Feed my sheep" (John 21:15-17).

➡ **3. What was it in Peter that would cause him to want to serve Jesus by taking care of His sheep? Check one.**
❑ a. Peter needed a good salary and benefits package.
❑ b. Peter wanted a high position and a good title.
❑ c. Peter wanted to go down in history as a famous person.
❑ d. Peter loved Jesus.

Love for Christ was to be Peter's source of motivation for the Kingdom work ahead. Nothing less would satisfy or last. In fact, Jesus revealed that this motivation would eventually lead to Peter's death. The love of Christ would be sufficient to keep Peter on track all the way to a martyr's death on a cross. Peter did serve faithfully, and he was crucified upside down on a cross for his Lord.

1 John 4:19
"We love because he first loved us."

The greatest motivation in a Christian's life should be his or her love for God. The reason we love God is because He first loved us (1 John 4:19). This love is what motivates us to serve Him. Paul said: *"Christ's love compels us. . . . that those who live should no longer live for themselves but for him who died for them and was raised again"* (2 Cor. 5:14-15). This is the passage where Paul went on to explain that we have been given the ministry of reconciliation. We are ambassadors for Christ. Christ's love for us and our love for Him compels us to serve Him faithfully.

The greatest motivation in a Christian's life should be his or her love for God.

John 14:15
"If you love me, you will obey what I command."

➡ **4. Where does the love begin that motivates you to serve in the Kingdom? Check one.**
❑ a. It starts with Christ's love for me. I love because He loved me.
❑ b. It starts with me. I'm just a loving kind of person.

2 Corinthians 5:20
"We are therefore Christ's ambassadors, as though God were making his appeal through us. We implore you on Christ's behalf: Be reconciled to God."

Your love for Christ began with Christ's love for you that He demonstrated most clearly on the cross (a). The love of Christ motivates your service in two ways. First, you love Christ so much you want to obey Him (John 14:15). Second, because Christ's love is in you, you love others and want to see God's redemptive purposes accomplished in their lives. His love compels you to lead others to Christ (2 Cor. 5:20). Actually, Christ is the one in you who loves others through you! It is Christ's love that shows.

The Kingdom's motivation teaches you to love God and others. It is a strong and dependable motivation that can last a lifetime. The motivation is not dependent on you alone. God is present in you, enabling you to serve Him out of love. When you serve the Lord because you love Him, every act of service draws you closer to Him. You grow in your love for Him.

> **God is present in you, enabling you to serve Him out of love.**

➡ **5. In each pair below, write a "W" for characteristics of the World's motivation and a "K" for the characteristics of the Kingdom's motivation.**

_____ 1a. Encourages me to love God and others.
_____ 1b. Encourages me to love self.

_____ 2a. Is strong, dependable, and long-lasting.
_____ 2b. Is fragile, unreliable, and short-lived.

_____ 3a. Is dominated and guided by human nature and my desires.
_____ 3b. Is empowered and directed by God's divine nature and His desires.

_____ 4a. Draws me away from intimacy with God.
_____ 4b. Draws me toward a deeper love relationship with God.

Christ's love causes you to love God and others. That becomes the greatest motivator for your service in the Kingdom Agenda. It is strong, dependable, and long-lasting. Your service in the Kingdom is empowered and directed by God's divine nature and His desires. His love draws you toward a deeper love relationship with God (K = 1a, 2a, 3b, and 4b).

The World's motivators, however, encourage you to focus on self and love for self. They are fragile, unreliable, and can be short-lived. The world's motivators are dominated by human nature and your human desires. This can set you up to be manipulated by others if you are not careful. Striving after the world and the things of the world can draw you away from an intimate love relationship with God (W = 1b, 2b, 3a, and 4a).

Reasons to Do Your Best on the Job

In New Testament times, Christian leaders like Paul and Peter gave specific instructions for work. Their instructions were primarily directed to the slave and master relationship. Though you are not a slave or a slave-owning master, these words of instruction can apply to your workplace.

➡ **6. As you read the following Scriptures look for reasons to do your best on the job. Underline them. You also ought to look for specific things you should do or not do. List them in the margin.**

Ephesians 6:5-9 • *Slaves, obey your earthly masters with respect and fear, and with sincerity of heart, just as you would obey Christ. Obey them not only to win their favor when their eye is on you, but like slaves of Christ, doing the will of God from your heart. Serve wholeheartedly, as if you were serving the Lord, not men, because you know that the Lord will reward everyone for whatever good he does, whether he is slave or free.*

And masters, treat your slaves in the same way. Do not threaten them, since you know that he who is both their Master and yours is in heaven, and there is no favoritism with him.

Things to Do

_____

_____

_____

_____

Things to Not Do

_____

_____

_____

_____

_____

Things to Do

_____

_____

_____

_____

_____

_____

_____

_____

Things to Not Do

_____

_____

_____

_____

_____

_____

_____

_____

_____

Colossians 3:22-24 • _Slaves, obey your earthly masters . . . with sincerity of heart and reverence for the Lord. Whatever you do, work at it with all your heart, as working for the Lord, not for men, since you know that you will receive an inheritance from the Lord as a reward. It is the Lord Christ you are serving._

Titus 2:9-10 • _Teach slaves to be subject to their masters in everything, to try to please them, not to talk back to them, and not to steal from them, but to show that they can be fully trusted, so that in every way they will make the teaching about God our Savior attractive._

Colossians 4:1 • _Masters, provide your slaves with what is right and fair, because you know that you also have a Master in heaven._

1 Peter 2:18-25 • _Slaves, submit yourselves to your masters with all respect, not only to those who are good and considerate, but also to those who are harsh. For it is commendable if a man bears up under the pain of unjust suffering because he is conscious of God. But how is it to your credit if you receive a beating for doing wrong and endure it? But if you suffer for doing good and you endure it, this is commendable before God. To this you were called, because Christ suffered for you, leaving you an example, that you should follow in his steps. "He committed no sin, and no deceit was found in his mouth." When they hurled their insults at him, he did not retaliate; when he suffered, he made no threats. Instead, he entrusted himself to him who judges justly. He himself bore our sins in his body on the tree, so that we might die to sins and live for righteousness; by his wounds you have been healed. For you were like sheep going astray, but now you have returned to the Shepherd and Overseer of your souls._

You will discuss your findings in these passages in your Kingdom Strategy Meeting this week.

PRAYER STRATEGY
➡ **Take time now to pray about your work.**
- Thank the Lord for demonstrating His love for you on the cross.
- Ask Him to help you show your love for Him by the way you serve your employer. Ask Him to enable you to work as if you were serving Christ.
- Ask the Lord what you can do differently at work so that your love for Christ and love for others will be revealed to those who watch your life.
- Ask the Lord to help you work in such a way that the teachings about the Lord will be attractive to others.

DAY 5   A Divine Network

Kingdom Agenda

"Let us consider how we may spur one another on toward love and good deeds. Let us not give up meeting together, as some are in the habit of doing, but let us encourage one another—and all the more as you see the Day approaching" (Heb. 10:24-25).

➡ **Read the "Kingdom Agenda" in the margin. Pause for a moment of prayer. Ask the Lord to help you understand ways that you can help encourage other Christians in your workplace to demonstrate love and good deeds.**

God does not intend for the Kingdom worker to work all alone. He has put in place a divine network that plays a vital role in your work. Today, I want you to begin to see the divine network God may have already given you. I also want you to begin watching, praying, and waiting on the Lord for other coworkers that God may bring into that network. Your divine network will include some or all of the following:

COWORKERS IN YOUR DIVINE NETWORK
• Christ Jesus and His Holy Spirit
• Members in Your Church
• Christians in Your Workplace
• Christians Outside Your Workplace with Whom You Interact as Part of Your Work
• Christians in the Same Occupation or Type of Business

Christ Jesus and His Holy Spirit
We have already seen that Christ Jesus is a Coworker with you in your workplace. He is not just a figurehead, silent partner, or imaginary friend. He is real, and He is ready to be involved actively in Kingdom work at your workplace. Just as a reminder:
• He is the vine and you are a branch though which He bears fruit (John 15).
• God is reconciling the world to Himself through Christ, and Christ is in you (2 Cor. 5:18-20; Col. 1:27, 2:9-10).
• When you are yoked with Christ, the work is well fitted and the burden is light (Matt. 11:28-30).

We have also studied about the Holy Spirit. He is the Spirit of Christ that has taken up residence in you. He has the assignments for:
• Revealing spiritual truth (1 Cor. 2:10-16).
• Guiding your prayers when you don't know what to ask (Rom. 8:26-27).
• Providing knowledge, wisdom, counsel, power, and understanding (Isa. 11:1-2)
• Providing power and boldness for witnessing (Acts 1:8, 4:31)
• Convicting of guilt regarding sin, righteousness, and judgment (John 16:8-11).

➡ **1. Based on what you know about Christ and the Holy Spirit, what are some of the ways they could make a difference in your work and your workplace? List two or three ways.**

_____

_____

_____

He can give you wisdom, knowledge, or understanding about a work issue that you do not possess.

He knows the future and can guide you to choose the right option based on the responses of others.

Matthew 16:18
"I will build my church; and the gates of hell shall not prevail against it." (KJV)

The ways Christ and His Spirit can work through you are limitless. He can give you wisdom, knowledge, or understanding about a work issue that you do not possess. He knows the future and can guide you to choose the right option based on the responses of others. No one else could predict those responses with complete accuracy the way Christ can. He can guide you to do the right thing and receive God's blessing in behalf of your company. He can change the hearts and minds of people. He can influence relationships. He can guide your witness and give you boldness. Christ and His Spirit are essential partners in your divine network.

Members in Your Church

When you are born again, God adds you to the body of Christ. The body of Christ is a local church that has many members who work together to see God's purposes accomplished around them. The body of Christ is intended to work together so that every member can be strong in the work Christ (the Head of the Body) may assign. Christ builds His church in such a way that even the gates of Hell will not stand against it's advance (Matt. 16:18). Members in the body can be involved with you in your workplace assignment in a number of ways. They can:

- Pray for you and the concerns you face in your work.
- Give you godly and biblical counsel concerning issues or decisions at work.
- Help you discern what God wants to do in your workplace.
- Encourage you when the going gets tough.
- Correct you if you stray from Christlike behavior.
- Provide a place for you to share testimonies about what God is doing in the workplace.
- Rejoice with you when God wins a victory through you.
- Help you make disciples of those who are born again.

➡ **2. Who has God placed in your church that already is (are) part of your divine network? This could be prayer partners, teachers, members of a class or group, your pastor, deacons, or other brothers and sisters in Christ who help you with work-related issues. List the name or names and ways God uses them to help you in your work.**

_____

_____

_____

3. What are some of the ways you think God could use your church more effectively to help members live by the Kingdom Agenda in their workplaces?

_____

_____

_____

4. Do you sense that God is leading you to be involved in helping someone else in your church regarding his or her workplace?

Who? _____

How? _____

Christians in Your Workplace

Often Christians have remained isolated from other Christians in their workplace. Sometimes they have been silent about their relationship to Christ. Many Christians in the workplace may not even know the others who are believers. That needs to change. In fact that is one reason we wrote this course. Christians need to experience the dynamic power Christ can produce in a workplace where His people are united. You need a relationship with the other Christians in your workplace. God may want to do something through you all, that He will not or cannot do through only one.

➡ **5. Has God revealed to you people at work who are Christians and part of your divine network? If so list their names below or in the margin.**

_____

_____

_____

> Christians need to experience the dynamic power Christ can produce in a workplace where His people are united. You need a relationship with the other Christians in your workplace.

Your divine network in your workplace can do things that your church cannot do. As you gather with other Christians in your workplace, you can share and pray with a different insight and knowledge. For instance Christians in the your workplace can:

• Pray for those in authority over you.
• Pray for specific individuals who need to know Christ.
• Take specific problems to the Lord in prayer seeking God's directions.
• Share what you are seeing of God's activity. Often each person may describe what only looks like a confusing piece of a jig-saw puzzle. But when others share what they see of God's activity, a beautiful and clear plan may begin to unfold.
• Discuss the application of Scripture to work practices.
• Confess sin to the Lord in behalf of your company and seek God's directions about how to seek change.
• Join in united prayer to seek God's work strategy for your workplace.
• Pray for each other and specific work concerns. These may relate to relationships, decisions, problems, and so forth.

➡ **6. What is one time and/or way God has worked in your workplace through Christians working together? If you cannot think of one, what is one way you believe God wants to work through Christians working together in your workplace?**

_____

_____

_____

Christians Outside Your Workplace

Depending on the kind of work you do, you may find God has a divine network outside your workplace that He will use to influence your workplace.

➥ **7. Begin trying to think of people that you may relate to who are Christians, but who are not in your specific workplace. Ask God to help you. List their names or company name in the margin. Let the following list start your thinking:**

❏ Christians in corporate headquarters or sister companies or plants
❏ Vendors who provide products or services for your company
❏ Customers
❏ Salespersons
❏ Government or agency officials
❏ Transportation personnel
❏ Chamber of Commerce representatives
❏ Others?

Ask the Lord to reveal the members of this divine network. Begin watching for them to surface in answer to prayer. As you relate to outside people in your work, listen for hints that may indicate that a person is a Christian. Be attentive to what others say or do. God may use an outside person to answer a prayer or give a word of direction. Remember, too, that this network is two-way. God may want to use you in the workplace of someone else with whom you relate.

This divine network of outside people may serve to give counsel or directions. They may become prayer partners. They may be the means God has to answer prayer or accomplish a project. They may be in a position to influence others in your company in ways you cannot. They may become a means God uses to bless your company in financial ways that bring glory to Him.

➥ **8. What is one time and/or way God has worked in your workplace through Christians from the outside? If you cannot think of one, what is one way you believe God wants to work through this divine network outside your workplace?**

_____

_____

_____

Christians in the Same Occupation or Type of Business

One other source of people in your network is people who are in the same type of occupation or type of business. If you are an assembly line worker, accountant, attorney, janitor, physician, or banker, you could better understand the Kingdom Agenda by talking and praying with people in the same occupation. This could be the most exciting and valuable part of your divine network apart from Christ Himself. People who do the same kind of work you do will be able to understand:

• problems you face
• the difficult ethical, moral, and legal decisions you must make
• reasons you get weary, bored, or hurt
• times you may be pressured to compromise your faith

You also can benefit from relationships with Christians in the same type of business but with different occupations. These might include businesses like:

• manufacturers

> You could better understand the Kingdom Agenda by talking and praying with people in the same occupation.

- banking and financial institutions
- non-profit organizations
- government entities
- missions organizations
- denominational agencies
- educational institutions
- retail sales companies
- construction companies

➡ **9. In what type of business do you work?** _____

10. Name two or three other companies, organizations, or institutions that share a similarity with your company.

_____

_____

Christians in similar lines of work can benefit from sharing and praying together. For instance, people related to medical professions will share some common concerns. A group with a medical doctor, a dentist, a pharmacist, a nurse, a hospital chaplain, and a hospital administrator might be able to share and pray in meaningful ways. God might even use one group member to be the answer to another's prayers.

➡ **11. With which of the following do you already have a divine network relationship where you share, pray, and maybe even work together? Check all that apply.**
- ❏ Members in my church
- ❏ Christians in my workplace
- ❏ Christians outside my workplace
- ❏ Christians in the same occupation or type of business

Read the following Scriptures and list two reasons why God might want you involved in your divine network.

"Any kingdom divided against itself will be ruined, and a house divided against itself will fall" (Luke 11:17).

"He who is not with me is against me, and he who does not gather with me, scatters" (Luke 11:23).

12. What are two reasons God might want you involved in your divine network?

_____

_____

_____

God is Sovereign. He is the Initiator. Do not take matters into your own hands and try to make things happen or to manipulate people.

Working with Your Network
As you think about what God may do through this network, keep in mind that God is Sovereign. He is the Initiator. Do not take matters into your own hands and try to make things happen or to manipulate people. Allow God

Be prepared to join God when He shows you what He is doing.

to take the initiative. Depend on Him to guide and direct. But you need to be ready to receive what God gives. Be prepared to join God when He shows you what He is doing. Make the necessary adjustments and obey Him.

PRAYER STRATEGY

➡ **Take time now to pray about your divine network.**
- Acknowledge that Christ Himself and His Spirit are present and want to work through you.
- Ask God to reveal those people who are a part of His Kingdom Network for your life. Pray for each one of them. Ask God how He might want you to bring this Network together or how this network needs to work.

FOR FURTHER STUDY

➡ **Read the following Scriptures that speak about the value of other people in the work of the Kingdom. Make notes in the margin about specific things God may say to you about your network.**

Proverbs 15:22 • *Plans fail for lack of counsel, but with many advisers they succeed.*

Proverbs 20:18 • *Make plans by seeking advice; if you wage war, obtain guidance.*

Proverbs 19:20 • *Listen to advice and accept instruction, and in the end you will be wise.*

Proverbs 27:17 • *As iron sharpens iron, so one man sharpens another.*

Ecclesiastes 4:9-12 • *Two are better than one, because they have a good return for their work: If one falls down, his friend can help him up. But pity the man who falls and has no one to help him up! Also, if two lie down together, they will keep warm. But how can one keep warm alone? Though one may be overpowered, two can defend themselves. A cord of three strands is not quickly broken.*

Matthew 18:19-20 • *If two of you on earth agree about anything you ask for, it will be done for you by my Father in heaven. For where two or three come together in my name, there am I with them.*

For Further Study

➡ **Read the following Scriptures that describe different aspects of character that God wants in your life. Pray through each one. On the line above the Scripture write a title that summarizes the trait or traits that God desires in you.**

Summary Title: _____

Hebrews 12:14-15 • *Make every effort to live in peace with all men and to be holy; without holiness no one will see the Lord. See to it that no one misses the grace of God and that no bitter root grows up to cause trouble and defile many.*

Summary Title: _____

Philippians 4:4-6 • *Rejoice in the Lord always. I will say it again: Rejoice!*

NOTES

_____

_____

_____

_____

_____

_____

_____

_____

_____

_____

_____

_____

_____

_____

NOTES

_____

_____

_____

_____

_____

_____

_____

_____

_____

_____

_____

_____

_____

_____

_____

_____

_____

_____

_____

_____

_____

Let your gentleness be evident to all. The Lord is near. Do not be anxious about anything, but in everything, by prayer and petition, with thanksgiving, present your requests to God.

Summary Title: _____
Proverbs 22:11 • *He who loves a pure heart and whose speech is gracious will have the king for his friend.*

Summary Title: _____
Romans 12:3 • *For by the grace given me I say to every one of you: Do not think of yourself more highly than you ought, but rather think of yourself with sober judgment, in accordance with the measure of faith God has given you.*

For Further Study
➥ **Read the following Scriptures. Talk to the Lord about what He may want to say to you through them. Let God speak to you about honesty and integrity in your life. Write notes to yourself in the margin.**

Proverbs 10:9 • *The man of integrity walks securely, but he who takes crooked paths will be found out.*

Proverbs 13:6 • *Righteousness guards the man of integrity, but wickedness overthrows the sinner.*

Ecclesiastes 5:4-5 • *When you make a vow to God, do not delay in fulfilling it. He has no pleasure in fools; fulfill your vow. It is better not to vow than to make a vow and not fulfill it.*

Psalm 25:21 • *May integrity and uprightness protect me, because my hope is in you.*

Proverbs 22:1 • *A good name is more desirable than great riches; to be esteemed is better than silver or gold.*

Proverbs 11:1 • *The LORD abhors dishonest scales, but accurate weights are his delight.*

1 Chronicles 29:17 • *I know, my God, that you test the heart and are pleased with integrity. All these things have I given willingly and with honest intent. And now I have seen with joy how willingly your people who are here have given to you.*

Psalm 26:1-3 • *Vindicate me, O LORD, for I have led a blameless life; I have trusted in the LORD without wavering. Test me, O LORD, and try me, examine my heart and my mind; for your love is ever before me, and I walk continually in your truth.*

KINGDOM STRATEGY
MEETING 5

Use the following suggestions to guide a one-hour small-group discussion of *The Kingdom Agenda* covering the lessons in this week's study. For general instructions for the group facilitator, see page 156.

This Week's Learning Objective
You will understand the required nature of a Kingdom worker and demonstrate your surrender to God's transformation of your own character into Christlikeness.

Opening Prayer (2 minutes)
- Begin with prayer acknowledging God's presence.
- Ask the Holy Spirit to be your Teacher.
- Ask the Lord to continue revealing the kind of character that would be pleasing to Him in a Kingdom worker.
- Ask the Lord to increase your faith and strengthen you to die to self daily so that Christ may reveal Himself through you in your workplaces.

Getting Better Acquainted (8 minutes)
Ask volunteers each to share briefly one experience where God used an experience at work to develop their character or teach them His ways. Some may want to share a testimony about what the Lord has done this week to direct their character development.

Content Review (10 minutes)
Ask members to turn in their books to the Overview of Week 5 on page 105. Using the time suggested, review the following items of content from this week's lessons:
- Ask members to recite this week's Scripture-memory verse together—Matthew 5:14,16.
- Ask: Which one of the summary statements from week 5 was most meaningful to you and why?
- Ask: What are the three steps through which a person can go to be restored to God's Kingdom Agenda for their work life?
- Ask: What character traits and attitudes are found in the Beatitudes that would make the strongest impact on a watching world in your workplace?
- Ask: What are four facts about faith and why are these encouraging to you as you seek to please God by your walk of faith.
- Ask: Where do the people come from that make up the divine network God has for you and your workplace?

Discussion Questions (25 minutes)
Look over the following list of questions and lead the group to discuss those that you think would be most meaningful or helpful to your group. Watch your time (invite members to help you), so that you will allow adequate time for prayer at the end of the session. You may want to ask members to help you select the most helpful questions for discussion.

1. What does our Scripture-memory verse mean about being light to the world? How will that light affect those around us when they see our good deeds?
2. Of the three steps listed on page 106, which requires the greatest or most difficult change?
3. In activities #4 and #5 on pages 108-109, which responses were the most convicting? Which of the Beatitudes seems to be the most difficult?
4. Which of the Beatitudes is most needed in your workplace and why?
5. Why is Kingdom integrity important in the life of a Kingdom worker? What are the characteristics of a person of integrity?
6. In #1 on page 116, which area do you seem to have the greatest difficulty trusting God?
7. How did you respond to #2 on page 117 and why?
8. In which one of the areas of trusting God do you have the greatest difficultly? (See pp. 118-119.) Which is the easiest for you?
9. Can you describe a series of experiences through which God has guided you in a way that has developed greater faith? What are some ways He has developed your faith?
10. What are the ways your supervisor or employer tries to motivate you to do a better job? Have those ever backfired and demotivated you?
11. What are the Kingdom reasons for doing your best work in your job? (See pp. 123-124.)
12. What are some of the ways Christ and the Holy Spirit could make a difference in your work and workplace? (#1 on p. 125)
13. What is your church currently doing to help you be your best on the job in your workplace? What do you sense they could do that would help you the most?
14. What are some ways God has already worked through your Kingdom Agenda group or your divine network to assist you on the job?
15. [For those who may have completed the "For Further

Study" assignments on pages 130-131.] What truths from the Scriptures have spoken to you this week about how you should live out your faith on the job?

Priority Praying (15 minutes)
Conclude the session by spending time as a group praying for each other.
- Ask each member to share with the group one burden or concern about his or her work life for which he or she would like the group to pray. Ask them to consider areas of character development in which God may be working.
- Ask members to divide into smaller groups of two, three, or four and pray for each other. Ask them to use conversational prayer and pray as many times as they feel led. Focus your praying on one person at a time. Then turn your prayers toward another.
- Invite members to use the space in the right column to record work-related prayer requests for group members so they can pray about them during the coming week.
- As time permits allow members to share answers to prayers that have been prayed over the past five weeks. You may even want to discuss getting together for a time of fellowship or a prayer meeting to devote more time to sharing and prayer.

WORK-RELATED PRAYER REQUESTS

Week 6 The Kingdom Work

Murphy recently began a private law practice. At first it was difficult to decide what fees to charge and what causes he should take. One day, he was trying to decide about two particular cases which had been presented to him. The problem was that neither of the prospective clients had the ability to pay him much for his services. Yet they both needed an attorney. He decided to consult with a more experienced attorney to see what he would advise in these situations.

His friend reviewed the cases and advised him against taking them. "Yes, they have been wronged. Obviously they need help, but you are in private practice now, Murphy. You have got to make money. Besides that, these cases will be time-consuming and keep you from being able to handle other cases. If I were you, I just would not do it."

Based on his friend's advice, Murphy resolved to call the people and tell them he would not be able to take their cases. That Friday night, Murphy attended a Kingdom Agenda Conference. About midway through the session, he abruptly got up and left the room. Later, he told me what had happened.

That morning as he was doing his morning Bible study, he read the following passage:

Now Ahaziah had fallen through the lattice of his upper room in Samaria and injured himself. So he sent messengers, saying to them, "Go and consult Baal-Zebub, the god of Ekron, to see if I will recover from this injury."

But the angel of the LORD said to Elijah the Tishbite, "Go up and meet the messengers of the king of Samaria and ask them, 'Is it because there is no God in Israel that you are going off to consult Baal-Zebub, the god of Ekron?'

Therefore this is what the LORD says: 'You will not leave the bed you are lying on. You will certainly die!'" So Elijah went (2 Kings 1:2-4).

Murphy said the Lord had convicted him through the passage. "God seemed to be asking the same question of me," Murphy said. "I realized that, by trusting the advice of the other attorney who was not a believer, I had been consulting "Baal" instead of God! I realized that there was a God in Israel, and there is a God in me. He wants to work in and through my life, and I must trust Him and give Him access to what He desires."

Murphy realized that God wanted him to take these two cases for people who had been wronged and needed help to get justice. He had left the conference to go and call the prospective clients and tell them he would take their cases. He agreed to serve for whatever they were able to pay. He didn't want to take any chances with obedience to the word from the Lord.

God taught Murphy a valuable lesson about making Kingdom decisions. God wants to be consulted. Most of us, however, are more like Ahaziah. We consult the "Baals" of our society—following the world's agenda—to find out what we should do.

We need to learn to turn to the Lord for our Kingdom job assignments. As we seek His directions, He will help us understand what He is doing and how we are to be involved. That frequently will be different than the counsel of the world. We need to learn to trust Him and then wait for His response. When the directions come from the Lord, we must make the necessary adjustments and obey the Lord. Then God is able to work through us to accomplish His kingdom purposes.

OVERVIEW OF WEEK 6

This Week's Scripture-Memory Verse
"Jesus came to them and said, 'All authority in heaven and on earth has been given to me. Therefore go and make disciples of all nations, baptizing them in the name of the Father and of the Son and of the Holy Spirit, and teaching them to obey everything I have commanded you. And surely I am with you always, to the very end of the age'" (Matt. 28:18-20).

This Week's Lessons
Day 1: Kingdom Assignments
Day 2: Your Kingdom Job Description
Day 3: Prayer as a Primary Work Strategy
Day 4: Building Redemptive Relationships
Day 5: The Kingdom Influence in the Workplace

Summary Statements from Week 6
- God does not give jobs just so you can earn a paycheck.
- He wants to work through you to see His kingdom rule come in the hearts and lives of the people around you.
- When you join God in doing Kingdom work, you will even see change in the social, moral, and ethical fabric of your workplace.
- When God has been permitted to mold and shape you to be the kind of servant He needs, then He can begin using you to accomplish Kingdom work.
- For most of the people who study this course, Christ wants to leave you in your present job and workplace—but as a different person with a Kingdom focus.
- Because you are part of a team and not a loner, assignments in the Kingdom Agenda will be different for different people.
- Some work assignments may lay a foundation for someone else to come along and complete the work.
- As God's fellow workers, which part of the process you are assigned doesn't matter. God is the one who gets the credit.
- Mission Statement: To join Christ in a coworker relationship with God, where God is Sovereign and I am cooperative.
- The greatest victories will be won in your prayer life.
- Prayer ought to be one of your primary work strategies.
- Your right relationship with God depends on your forgiving those who have sinned against you.
- You never <u>have</u> to sin. You always have a choice.
- Paul sacrificed and paid a price to build redemptive relationships. He identified himself with others so he could help them understand the gospel from their unique perspective.
- Paul's primary tool was to preach Christ and allow God to demonstrate the Spirit's power to change lives.
- The Kingdom influence through your lives can have far reaching affects that touch your entire workplace.
- God may accomplish mighty or miraculous things through His coworkers that will affect the entire company and bring great credit to the Lord.
- God is the One who produces growth and brings a harvest.

IMPORTANT IDEAS

Four Facts About the Kingdom Work
Fact 1: God is present and working in your workplace.
Fact 2: God chooses to do His work through people.
Fact 3: God is able to accomplish His purposes.
Fact 4: When you join God and obey Him, you and others experience God in your workplace.

Being Restored to the Kingdom Agenda
Step 1: Reorient Your Life to the Sovereignty of God.
Step 2: Set Aside Your Own Agenda by Dying to Self.
Step 3: Accept a Kingdom Work Strategy.

Career Assignments
1. New Career
2. New Focus on Your Present Career
3. New Location for Your Present Career

The Model Prayer of the Kingdom
1. Acknowledge God's Sovereignty
2. Accept God's Agenda in Place of My Own
3. Trust in God's Provision
4. Build Redemptive Relationships
5. Trust in God's Protection
6. Do All for God's Glory

DAY 1 Kingdom Assignments

Kingdom Agenda

"Jesus came to them and said, 'All authority in heaven and on earth has been given to me. Therefore go and make disciples of all nations, baptizing them in the name of the Father and of the Son and of the Holy Spirit, and teaching them to obey everything I have commanded you. And surely I am with you always, to the very end of the age'" (Matt. 28:18-20).

➡ **Read the "Kingdom Agenda" in the margin. Pause for a moment of prayer. Ask the Lord to help you understand your work assignment in spreading His Kingdom.**

God does not give jobs just so you can earn a paycheck. God has a redemptive mission that He intends to accomplish through you. The Great Commission (Matt. 28:18-20) that you just read is a call to make disciples—followers of Jesus Christ. Your workplace is a place where God wants to carry out His plan to reconcile people to Himself through Christ. Your work is a place where you can experience God working through you to redeem a lost world. Review four facts we studied in week 1 about Kingdom work:

> **Four Facts About the Kingdom Work**
> Fact 1: God is present and working in your workplace.
> Fact 2: God chooses to do His work through people.
> Fact 3: God is able to accomplish His purposes.
> Fact 4: When you join God and obey Him, you and others experience God in your workplace.

➡ **1. What is one of God's PRIMARY purposes for your work? Check one.**
❑ a. He wants me to earn a paycheck to support my family.
❑ b. He wants to work through me to accomplish His plan of redemption in the lives of people around me.
❑ c. He wants me to experience God at work through me.

God wants to redeem a lost world.

God does want to provide for you and your family through your work, but that is not His primary purpose. He does want you to experience Him working through you, but that is a side benefit. God wants to redeem a lost world. He wants to work through you to see His Kingdom rule come in the hearts and lives of the people around you.

Therefore, every job has a Kingdom job description that reflects God's purposes. God has specific assignments for you. In order for you to know and be empowered to do your Kingdom work, you need to develop a prayer relationship with God. Prayer must become a major part of your work strategy. God will guide you and use you to build redemptive relationships through which He will work to draw people to His Son Jesus Christ. When you join God in doing Kingdom work, you will even see change in the social, moral, and ethical fabric of your workplace.

When you join God in doing Kingdom work, you will even see change in the social, moral, and ethical fabric of your workplace.

➡ **2. What needs to become a major part of your work strategy?**

_____

3. What are some of the changes God wants to bring about through your life and work?

_____

You may feel very inadequate for that work. Seeing people come to Christ and seeing change in the social, moral, and ethical fabric of your workplace sounds too big for any one person. By yourself, you are inadequate. Apart from Him, you can do nothing of Kingdom value. But you are not alone! The Spirit of Christ is present in you to do the work. He will accomplish Kingdom assignments through you in such a way that God receives glory and His Kingdom rule advances. For this reason you need an intimate love relationship with God in prayer, so He can guide you clearly to know and do His will.

Accept a Kingdom Work Strategy

Last week we looked at three steps that are summarized in Luke 9:23. Jesus said, *"If anyone would come after me, he must deny himself and take up his cross daily and follow me."* Those steps are:

Step 1: Reorient Your Life to the Sovereignty of God.
Step 2: Set Aside Your Own Agenda by Dying to Self.
Step 3: Accept a Kingdom Work Strategy.

Up until now, we have focused more on the first two steps. You must see God as Sovereign and choose to follow Him obediently. You must follow His lead and trust Him for your needs. In order to let Christ be Lord and Sovereign, you have had to set aside your own agenda and die to self.

This week's lessons will focus on Kingdom work. This is the "doing" part of the Kingdom Agenda. When God has been permitted to mold and shape you to be the kind of servant He needs, then He can begin using you to accomplish Kingdom work. You must accept the assignments God has for you—the Kingdom work. And you must do this work in Kingdom ways. Accepting a Kingdom work strategy means:

- Not attempting to satisfy your needs apart from God.
- Not taking credit for the creative and redemptive activity of God.
- Giving God the credit.
- Doing much of what you do in secret so that the credit does not come back to you.
- Trusting God to provide.
- Trusting God's protection.
- Setting aside the world's definition of success and doing all that you do for the glory of God.
- Being competent for Christ's glory.
- Loving God more than yourself.
- Loving others in the same sacrificial way that Christ loves you.
- Cooperating with God.
- Your death to self . . . and Christ resurrected as the Lord of your life!

This is all a part of the Kingdom Agenda—God's plan to bring about Christ's rule in the hearts and lives of people.

➡ **4. Have you surrendered to God's Kingdom Agenda for your life and work?** ❑ Yes ❑ No

5. What evidence could you offer that shows you are seeking to live by the Kingdom Agenda? How is your work life different?

_____

_____

6. After five weeks of study and meeting together with other believers, what one thing has God said or done that has been most meaningful, helpful, or life-changing?

Being Restored to the Kingdom Agenda

Step 1: Reorient Your Life to the Sovereignty of God.

Step 2: Set Aside Your Own Agenda by Dying to Self.

Step 3: Accept a Kingdom Work Strategy.

You must accept the assignments God has for you—the Kingdom work. And you must do this work in Kingdom ways.

_____

_____

Career Assignments

Career Assignments

When you begin to think about Kingdom work, you probably want to know the "what" and the "where" of your work. The following paragraphs identify three types of career assignments Christ may give.

New Career. Kingdom assignments may vary from person to person. God knows how He wants to use each person. Sometimes Christ may call you to a whole new career like He did Peter, Andrew, James and John. They left their fishing businesses and moved into full-time work that eventually was church-related. God may call some of you to change careers and become missionaries, pastors, church staff, evangelists, or some other church-related career. He may move you to a different type of work.

➡ **7. What is one type of career assignment to which Christ may call you?**

_____

New Focus for Your Present Career. He may call you to a new career. More often, Christ wants to change people and leave them in their workplace to reveal the difference Christ can make. This is what Jesus did with Zacchaeus. Zacchaeus did not quit being a tax collector after He was born again. He was just a very different kind of tax collector. Jesus healed or cast demons out of many people. When they wanted to follow Him, He instructed them to go home and tell the great things God had done for them. They didn't have to change jobs to join in the Kingdom Agenda. For most of the people who study this course, Christ wants to leave you in your present job and workplace—but as a different person with a Kingdom focus.

➡ **8. What is a second type of career assignment Christ may give you?**

_____

New Location for Your Present Career. Yes, He may leave you right where you are with a new focus doing Kingdom work in your current workplace. At other times, Christ may give you an assignment that changes the location of your work, but not the basic type of work. In Scripture Aquila and Priscilla were tentmakers. They worked as tentmakers in Rome until the Jews were run out of town. Paul met them and worked as a tentmaker with them in Corinth. They were still tentmakers, but they were permitted to join Paul in his missionary work. Later, they moved their business to Ephesus where they trained Apollos in _"the way of God more adequately"_ (Acts 18:26).

➡ **9. What is a third type of career assignment Christ may give you?**

_____

The Kingdom Agenda is not about where you work, nor whether your work is classified by the world as "secular" or "sacred." It is not dependent on whether you work around Christian people or unbelievers. It is all about a very special relationship you have through Jesus Christ with your heavenly Father. In that relationship God will reveal what He is doing. You then are invited to join Him in His work.

Types of Kingdom Assignments

Because you are part of a team and not a loner, assignments in the Kingdom Agenda will be different for different people. Some will be more public, while others will be unseen ministries. Some work assignments may lay a foundation for someone else to come along and complete the work. Paul described assignments this way:

> *Neither he who plants nor he who waters is anything, but only God, who makes things grow. The man who plants and the man who waters have one purpose, and each will be rewarded according to his own labor. For we are God's fellow workers (1 Cor. 3:7-9).*

Some may plow, plant, water, or harvest. As God's fellow workers, which part of the process you are assigned doesn't matter. God is the one who gets the credit. He will reward you for your labor. The assignments may be very different. Here are some examples from Scripture:

- Act justly, love mercy, and walk humbly with God (Mic. 6:8)
- Be a faithful manager of resources entrusted to you (1 Cor. 4:2).
- Be prepared to give a reason for the hope that is in you (1 Pet. 3:15)
- Be rich in doing good, generous, and willing to share (1 Tim. 6:17-19).
- Demonstrate love toward your neighbor (Jas. 2:8)
- Give a *"cup of cold water"* in Christ's name (Matt. 10:42).
- Give to the needy (Matt. 6:1-4).
- Live godly lives among pagans so they will glorify God (1 Pet. 2:11-12).
- Live in peace with all men and be holy (Heb. 12:14).
- Look after orphans and widows in their distress (Jas. 1:27).
- Love one another and show the world you are His disciples (John 13:34-35).
- Love your enemies (Matt. 5:43-48).
- Make disciples teaching them to obey everything Christ commands (Matt. 28:19-20).
- Meet needs of others as a servant and as a slave (Matt. 20:25-28).
- Minister to Christ by meeting the needs of others (Matt. 25:34-40).
    - give food to the hungry
    - give water to the thirsty
    - invite strangers in
    - give clothes to the naked
    - look after the sick
    - visit the prisoner
- Plead with others to be reconciled to Christ (2 Cor. 5:20).
- Preach the good news to all creation (Mark 16:15).
- Set an example by doing good, showing integrity and sound speech (Titus 2:6-8).
- Shine spiritual light for those in spiritual darkness (Matt. 5:14-16).
- Show Christian unity among believers, so the world will know that Jesus is God's Son (John 17:20-23).
- Speak up for those who cannot defend themselves (Prov. 31:8-9).
- Submit yourselves to every authority and show respect (1 Pet. 2:13-17).
- Turn a sinner from the error of His way (Jas. 5:19-20).

PRAYER STRATEGY

➡ **Take time now to pray about God's Kingdom assignments for you.**
- Ask the Lord to draw you ever deeper into a love relationship with Him.
- Ask the Lord to reveal Himself, His purposes, and His ways to you.
- Ask the Lord to open your eyes and ears to see and hear where He is working in your workplace.
- Agree to obey the Lord, whatever the assignment may be.

139

DAY 2 Your Kingdom Job Description

Kingdom Agenda
"Jesus said, 'Peace be with you! As the Father has sent me, I am sending you'" (John 20:21).

➡ Read the "Kingdom Agenda" in the margin. Pause for a moment of prayer. Ask the Lord to help you understand that you have been sent into the world to work just as Jesus was sent.

Joining God at Work

➡ 1. Turn to page 29 and review Jesus' Kingdom Work. How would you summarize how Jesus came to know and do the will of His Father?

_____

_____

Jesus watched to see what His Father was doing and that is what He would do. Jesus joined the Father where He was at work. That is a way for you to function also. Watch to see where God is working around you, and when He shows you, join Him.

How would you know if God were working around you? Only God can reveal His activity in such a way that you know He is the author of it. You need Him to open your spiritual eyes to see what He is doing. You should anticipate that He will do just that. When He shows you His activity, join Him. It might look something like the following:
• a person seeking after spiritual understanding
• a person under the conviction of sin
• a person who needs to experience the unconditional love of God
• a person suffering from the consequences of sin and judgment
• a person who is lonely
• a person who asks about the reason you are different
• a burden God gives in prayer for a specific need or individual
• instructions from Scripture that call you to obedience
• a request for your help that you know only God could provide

➡ 2. Has God invited you to be involved with Him in his work since you have begun this study? When? what? how?

_____

_____

Following Jesus' Example

➡ 3. Read the following Scriptures. Note in the margin insights God may give you regarding how Jesus lived by the Kingdom Agenda. Pray and ask God how you can allow Christ in you to live out that same Kingdom Agenda in your life.
• Jesus (at age 12) said to His parents: *"How is it that ye sought me? wist ye not that I must be about my Father's business?"* (Luke 2:49,KJV)
• Jesus prayed to His Father just prior to the cross: *"I have brought you glory on earth by completing the work you gave me to do"* (John 17:4).
• *"But the world must learn that I love the Father and that I do exactly what my Father has commanded me"* (John 14:31).
• *"For I have come down from heaven not to do my will but to do the will of him who sent me"* (John 6:38)

- *"My teaching is not my own. It comes from him who sent me"* (John 7:16)
- *"When you have lifted up the Son of Man, then you will know that I am the one I claim to be and that I do nothing on my own but speak just what the Father has taught me. The one who sent me is with me; he has not left me alone, for I always do what pleases him"* (John 8:28-29)
- *"Do not believe me unless I do what my Father does. But if I do it, even though you do not believe me, believe the miracles, that you may know and understand that the Father is in me, and I in the Father"* (John 10:37-38).
- *"I did not speak of my own accord, but the Father who sent me commanded me what to say and how to say it. I know that his command leads to eternal life. So whatever I say is just what the Father has told me to say"* (John 12:49-50).
- *"Don't you believe that I am in the Father, and that the Father is in me? The words I say to you are not just my own. Rather, it is the Father, living in me, who is doing his work"* (John 14:10).
- *"The world must learn that I love the Father and that I do exactly what my Father has commanded me"* (John 14:31).
- *"I gave them the words you gave me and they accepted them. They knew with certainty that I came from you, and they believed that you sent me"* (John 17:8).

➡ **4. If you were to live and work by the Kingdom Agenda like this in your workplace, what would you need to do differently? How would you have to think, act, and speak in order to live in a similar way at your work? Write responses below.**

_____

_____

_____

_____

_____

Normally a job description includes a purpose or mission statement for the job, qualifications, and specific responsibilities. Here is an outline for your Kingdom Job Description:

> **Mission Statement**
> To join Christ in a coworker relationship with God, where God is Sovereign and I am cooperative.

➡ **1. Review the characteristics of a coworker relationship with God on pages 49-51. Which of these areas do you sense God would like to work on to improve your relationship with Him? Why?**

_____

_____

_____

```
┌─────────────────────────────────────────────┐
│              Qualifications                   │
│  1. A Coworker Relationship with God          │
│  2. Character of Christ (The Beatitudes)      │
│  3. A Working Faith                           │
└─────────────────────────────────────────────┘
```

➥ **2. Review the Beatitudes on pages 107-109. Which of these heart attitudes or character traits would God want to develop more perfectly in your life? Why?**

_____

_____

3. Review "Developing Your Faith" on pages 118-119. Which of these areas of trust do you sense God would want to deepen in your life? Why?

_____

_____

```
┌─────────────────────────────────────────────┐
│              Responsibilities                 │
│  1. Work with Integrity                       │
│  2. Serve in the Spirit of Christ             │
│  3. Build Redemptive Relationships            │
│  4. Seek Righteousness and Justice            │
└─────────────────────────────────────────────┘
```

➥ **4. Review yesterday's lesson about Kingdom assignments (pp. 138-139). With which, if any, of those assignments do you sense God is calling you to be involved in with Him? Why?**

_____

_____

PRAYER STRATEGY

➥ **Take time now to pray about the work assignments God has for you.**
- Ask the Lord to open your spiritual eyes to identify His work around you, so you can join Him.
- Pray about specific assignments to which you already sense God has called you.
- Pray that the Lord will show others in your group how they are to be involved with Him in His work.
- Ask the Lord to continue to enlarge your divine network.

DAY 3 Prayer as a Primary Work Strategy

Kingdom Agenda

"Ask and it will be given to you; seek and you will find; knock and the door will be opened to you. For everyone who asks receives; he who seeks finds; and to him who knocks, the door will be opened" (Matt. 7:7-8).

➡ **Read the "Kingdom Agenda" in the margin. Pause for a moment of prayer. Ask the Lord to help you understand this prayer promise and learn to experience its reality in your workplace.**

You may not realize just how involved God is in your life until you begin to pray and meet God. The greatest victories will be won in your prayer life. Prayer is the very place where human nature is crucified, and God—with His divine nature—is restored to His sovereign position in your life.

This strategic meeting with God is an opportunity for God to reorient your agenda to His agenda. Prayer is an ideal time to exchange:
- your fears for Christ's faith
- your self-focus for Christ's other-focus
- your inadequacies for Christ's sufficiency
- your loneliness for God's unconditional love
- your limited knowledge for God's unlimited knowledge and wisdom
- your limited power for God's unlimited power
- your limited sight for God's eternal insight

➡ **1. How would you evaluate your prayer life at the present time? Check one of the responses below or write your own on the lines provided.**

❑ a. I have wonderful times of fellowship, worship, and conversation with the Lord. Many of my work related concerns are resolved in prayer. God reveals what He is doing at my workplace so I can join Him.

❑ b. Prayer is fine for those who have time. I can't waste much time praying, or I would never get anything done. Anyway, God expects me to "put feet on my prayers." I don't want to just talk. I want to work.

❑ c. I have to work very hard to be disciplined to pray. For some reason, no matter how hard I try, I seldom see any answers to my prayers. I want to be committed to prayer, but it is a struggle.

❑ d. Other: _____

_____

Prayer Is Essential

Prayer is not just a formality you go through before you can get on to the real work of the Kingdom (b). It is not just an expected religious activity you "ought" to do, like exercising or taking showers. It doesn't have to be sterile or dead. Prayer can be one of the most meaningful and important parts of your life.

Prayer is a relationship with God. It is a time where you are invited to the nerve center of the universe. There in God's throne room, you can orient yourself to God and what He is doing to redeem His world. In God's presence you can discuss with Him your concerns about work. In prayer God will give you guidance, correction, or comfort. Prayer is the time where you can cultivate the kind of intimate personal love relationship that God desires with you. Prayer ought to be one of your primary work strategies.

Can you imagine going to work and never getting any directions about what you are to do or how you are to do it? Can you imagine showing up for work every day where no boss or supervisor ever comes around to answer your questions? In a sense that is what many Christians face in their Kingdom work. Without a prayer relationship with God, you cannot know what to do or how to do it. Without an abiding relationship with God in prayer, you will never know His power and presence working through you in the way He desires.

➥ **2. Why should prayer be one of your major work strategies in Kingdom work? Check all the answers that apply.**

❑ a. Prayer is where I get instructions for the work I am to do in the Kingdom.

❑ b. Prayer is where God reveals how I am to go about my work in a way that will accomplish His purposes and bring Him glory.

❑ c. Prayer is where I find peace in God's presence to cope with the storm that rages around. In prayer God becomes my resting place.

❑ d. Prayer is a time I can pray for others or for problems at work and see God answer by meeting needs, providing solutions, or changing circumstances.

❑ e. All of the above and more.

Did you check "e" and all of the items above it? Good! Prayer is a relationship with God where all those things can take place—and so much more. Prayer is a relationship where you get in touch with the unlimited resources of God! If you have not experienced God that way in prayer, don't feel like you must lower prayer to your level of experience.

➥ **3. Ask the Lord to teach you the value of a prayer relationship with Him. Pray the prayer of the disciples:** *"Lord, teach us to pray"* **(Luke 11:1).**

Jesus' Model Prayer

Jesus gave his disciples a model prayer, after which they could pattern their prayer life. They would pray according to his Kingdom pattern and experience a daily reorientation to God's Agenda for their lives. Each petition or phrase of the prayer reflects some essential ingredient of the Kingdom Agenda.

➥ **Read the model prayer (Matt. 6:9-13) in the margin.**

Matthew 6:9-13, KJV

(v. 9) "Our Father which art in heaven, Hallowed be thy name."

(v. 10) "Thy kingdom come. Thy will be done in earth, as it is in heaven."

(v. 11) "Give us this day our daily bread."

(v. 12) "Forgive us our debts, as we forgive our debtors."

(v. 13a) "Lead us not into temptation, but deliver us from evil."

(v. 13b) "Thine is the kingdom, and the power, and the glory, for ever."

Jesus provided you with an agenda for prayer which will help you experience and understand the priorities of His Kingdom. Through this intimate prayer relationship with Him, God will begin to shape His Kingdom Agenda within you. In the model prayer I see an outline for you to orient your life and work to God's agenda each day.

➥ **4. See if you can match the following aspects of the Kingdom Agenda with the six sections of the Lord's Model Prayer. Write a verse number from the prayer in the margin beside each of the following aspects of the Kingdom Agenda.**

___ a. Build Redemptive Relationships
___ b. Trust in God's Provision
___ c. Acknowledge God's Sovereignty
___ d. Do All for God's Glory
___ e. Trust in God's Protection
___ f. Accept God's Agenda in Place of My Own

You may not have gotten all the answers correct, but here they are: a-12; b-11; c-9; d-13b; e-13a; f-10. Next we are going to look at each of these aspects of the Kingdom Agenda and how you can follow the model prayer in orienting your life to Christ's Kingdom.

• **Acknowledge God's Sovereignty:** *"Our Father which art in heaven, Hallowed be thy name."* Jesus begins the model prayer focusing on the sovereignty and holiness of God. Each day you need to acknowledge that God is Sovereign. He is in an exalted position in heaven. He is ruler of the universe, but He is also approachable as a Father. Praying for God's name to be "hallowed" is to treat Him and His name as holy and not common.

• **Accept God's Agenda in Place of My Own:** *"Thy kingdom come. Thy will be done in earth, as it is in heaven."* One of the greatest struggles in the Christian life is not in <u>understanding</u> God's will. The greater struggle is choosing to <u>obey</u> His will. In this prayer you confess that you want God's agenda to be done instead of your own. You pray for His will at the beginning. God wants you to say, "Yes, Lord," even before He tells you what He desires. Strive to reach the point of saying, "No matter what you desire today, my answer is yes. I want your will to be done—no matter what it is."

➡ **5. Pause to pray these two ways.**
- Acknowledge that God is Sovereign. Thank Him for being a Father.
- Meditate on the fact that He is holy. Since you carry His name as "Christian," pray that your actions today will maintain the holiness of His name and not tarnish it.
- Tell God how much you want His will to be done, because you know His will is best.
- Ask Him to work in and around you today to see His Kingdom purposes accomplished.

• **Trust in God's Provision:** *"Give us this day our daily bread."* The world's agenda focuses on working hard to provide for yourself. But God is Sovereign over every aspect of life. He causes the sun to shine and the rain to fall. He can bless, and He can curse. Everything that you have that is good has come from His hand (Jas. 1:17).

James 1:17
"Every good and perfect gift is from above, coming down from the Father of the heavenly lights, who does not change like shifting shadows."

When you pray for your daily provision you are showing an attitude of being "poor in spirit." You acknowledge that you need God, that you are depending on Him and not yourself. This is a way of learning dependence on God for your daily needs. Not only can you pray for bread (food), but you can pray for every other need you have for the day. You can pray this prayer several times during the day as different needs arise. When God provides, be sure to thank Him.

➡ **6. What are some of the genuine needs (not greeds) you have today?**

_____

Pause and ask God to provide for your needs.

• **Build Redemptive Relationships:** *"Forgive us our debts, as we forgive our debtors."* Here, Jesus was not talking about financial debts. He was referring to sin debts. When you sin, you have a debt you cannot pay. Christ provided for your forgiveness on the cross. In this prayer you are asking to be forgiven for your current sin debts. Keeping sin confessed and cleansed up to date is a vital part of your being rightly related to God.

Your right relationship with God depends on your forgiving those who have sinned against you.

Jesus also taught His disciples to pray for right relationships with others. This is a reminder that you need to be forgiven. You also need to evaluate any way others may have sinned against you. Are you carrying a grudge? Are you bitter? Do you have an unforgiving spirit? Then you need to get that relationship right. Your right relationship with God depends on your forgiving those who have sinned against you.

➡ **7. Has anyone at work (or other place) sinned against you, offended you, taken advantage of you, or harmed you in any way? Have you forgive that person? If not, make a list (in the margin) of people with whom you have a broken relationship. Ask God for the grace to forgive them from your heart. If you are not ready to forgive, then read the stern caution from Jesus in the margin (Matt. 6:14-15).**

Matthew 6:14-15
"If you forgive men when they sin against you, your heavenly Father will also forgive you. But if you do not forgive men their sins, your Father will not forgive your sins"

Prayer helps you enter into building redemptive relationships with others just as God, through Christ, has built a redemptive relationship with you. Sometimes forgiving someone (when the world's agenda tells you to get even or fight back) is a clear way to reveal Christ in you. When people ask how you can respond as you do, you have an open invitation to share Christ.

• **Trust in God's Protection:** *"Lead us not into temptation, but deliver us from evil."* Do you face temptations at work? Are you tempted in your thought life? Are you tempted to sin with your tongue by what you say? Are you tempted to do immoral, unethical, or illegal things to get the job done or stay in good graces with the boss? By praying this prayer, you confess your weakness. You express your need for God's help. You determine at the beginning of the day that you want to choose to do right. Paul said:

> *If you think you are standing firm, be careful that you don't fall! No temptation has seized you except what is common to man. And God is faithful; he will not let you be tempted beyond what you can bear. But when you are tempted, he will also provide a way out so that you can stand up under it* (1 Corinthians 10:12-13)

You never <u>have</u> to sin. You always have a choice.

You never <u>have</u> to sin. You always have a choice. It may be a very difficult choice. Obedience to God may be costly. But God will provide a way for you to stand up under temptation and come through it without sin.

➡ **8. Pause to pray and ask the Lord to strengthen you to resist temptation today. If you know of areas where you are regularly tempted, describe those to the Lord and ask for His help in facing them today. Don't worry about tomorrow. Focus your prayers on today.**

• **Do All for God's Glory:** *"Thine is the kingdom, and the power, and the glory, for ever."* Jesus ends this prayer with an awesome reminder. God is Sovereign. He is all powerful. He can bring to pass what He purposes. He can enable and strengthen you for all He wants to do through you today. Just remember that everything is for His glory, not your own. Your life is to bring glory to Christ and the Father. Keep that thought throughout the day so that you will never claim credit for the things God does. Be like Joseph and give God full credit when He works through you.

PRAYER STRATEGY

➡ **Take time now to pray through the model prayer one more time.**
- Acknowledge God's sovereignty.
- Accept God's agenda in place of your own.
- Ask for God's provision for today's needs.
- Ask for His forgiveness and pray about building redemptive relationships with others who may have sinned against you.
- Ask for God's strength and protection to endure temptation without sin.
- Praise the Lord and commit yourself to giving Him glory today.

DAY 4 Building Redemptive Relationships

Kingdom Agenda
"I have become all things to all men so that by all possible means I might save some. I do all this for the sake of the gospel, that I may share in its blessings" (1 Cor. 9:22-23).

➡ **Read the "Kingdom Agenda" in the margin. Pause for a moment of prayer. Ask the Lord to help you understand ways that you may build redemptive relationships with others and see them come to Christ as Savior and Lord.**

Paul's Example

In this passage to the church at Corinth, Paul describes his strategy for his Kingdom work. He made the necessary adjustments in his life to build redemptive relationships with other people for the sake of the gospel. Let's take a closer look at Paul's approach to building redemptive relationships.

➡ **Read the following Scripture and look for the ways Paul built redemptive relationships. Underline the people he sought to reach. Then answer the questions that follow.**

> *Though I am free and belong to no man, I make myself a slave to everyone, to win as many as possible. To the Jews I became like a Jew, to win the Jews. To those under the law I became like one under the law (though I myself am not under the law), so as to win those under the law. To those not having the law I became like one not having the law (though I am not free from God's law but am under Christ's law), so as to win those not having the law. To the weak I became weak, to win the weak. I have become all things to all men so that by all possible means I might save some. I do all this for the sake of the gospel, that I may share in its blessings* (1 Cor. 9:19-23).

"I have become all things to all men so that by all possible means I might save some."

1. Paul was free in Christ. Why did he make himself a slave to everyone?

_____

2. What was Paul's primary strategy for building redemptive relationships? Check one.

❑ a. He caught people in times of weakness and manipulated them into making a decision for Christ.

❑ b. He argued and fought with people to convince them to become Christians.

❑ c. He set up a church and waited until people came to him seeking help. Then he led them to Christ.

❑ d. He identified himself with others so he could understand life from their perspective. Then he shared the good news of the gospel in terms they understand. He became a servant to help them into the Kingdom.

Paul sacrificed and paid a price to build redemptive relationships.

Paul sacrificed and paid a price to build redemptive relationships. He identified himself with others so he could help them understand the gospel from their unique perspective. He wanted to win them to Christ, and he anticipated that he would share in the joy (blessings) that would result. Paul reminded the church at Corinth how he did this in their city:

When I came to you, brothers, I did not come with eloquence or superior wisdom as I proclaimed to you the testimony about God. For I resolved to know nothing while I was with you except Jesus Christ and him crucified. I came to you in weakness and fear, and with much trembling. My message and my preaching were not with wise and persuasive words, but with a demonstration of the Spirit's power, so that your faith might not rest on men's wisdom, but on God's power (1 Cor. 2:1-5).

➡ **3. What was Paul's primary "tool" for helping the Corinthians come to faith in Christ? Check one.**

❏ a. Paul allowed Christ to live through him in such a way that people saw a demonstration of the Spirit's power. The focus of his message was on the sacrificial death of Jesus Christ.

❏ b. Paul used his speaking skills, human wisdom, and persuasive words to convince people intellectually to turn to Christ. The focus of his message was practical lessons on how they could enjoy life.

4. Which of the following was most true about Paul's public image? Check one.

❏ a. Paul appeared proud, confident, and superior.

❏ b. Paul appeared humble, weak, fearful, and trembling.

5. In which of the following do you believe Paul was placing his confidence?

❏ a. He was confident in himself and his human abilities.

❏ b. He was confident in Christ and His Spirit's power to change lives.

> Paul's primary tool was to preach Christ and allow God to demonstrate the Spirit's power to change lives.

Paul's primary tool was to preach Christ and allow God to demonstrate the Spirit's power to change lives. He was not proud. He did not assume a superior position. Paul was humble and recognized that he could do nothing without Christ. His confidence rested in Christ alone.

Jack's Example

Jack had worked in pharmaceutical sales for several years. He is a Christian and has found many opportunities to share Christ in his work. Jack believes strongly in building relationships with people and trusting the Holy Spirit to initiate the right times to share his faith with others. God touched Jack's life deeply through one of those "God initiated" experiences.

One day Jack was sitting in the waiting room of a doctor's office hoping to make his sales contact with the doctor soon. A young man sitting next to him was looking at an issue of *Sports Illustrated*. Jack began talking to the young man about basketball. Eventually their discussion led to the reason the young man was there. He told Jack that he had leukemia and the doctor had told him that things didn't look good.

They talked further about the doctor's bleak prognosis. Jack asked the young man if he had peace about what would happen to him if he were to die. The young man said he wasn't sure what would happen. He said that he knew there was a God, but he didn't think God really loved him or He wouldn't have given him this horrible disease. He told Jack he had gone to church a few times when he was younger, but he didn't really know much about God.

Jack got the young man's address and telephone number and made an appointment to have lunch with him the next day. Over the next four months, Jack and the young man really got close. The young man attended the SEC tournament with Jack and practically became another member of Jack's family. During those months together, the young man accepted Christ as his Savior and Lord. Jack tried to disciple the young man right up to the last few days of his life. Jack was with him that night when he stepped into glory! The pain that Jack felt when the young man died was intense, since they had become so close. The joy of knowing that God had used him to guide this young man to Christ brought hope and thanksgiving in the midst of tears. The young man's family was so grateful for Jack's friendship with their son. They experienced God as they saw their son transformed from an angry heart of despair to a loving heart of hope.

Jack joined God, invested his life into the life of a young man who desperately needed the Lord. He met a stranger, made a friend, invested his own precious time, shared his faith, and witnessed the awesome power of God transcend a hopeless situation and redeem the life of another. Jack joined God as the Heavenly Father drew this young man to faith in Christ.

➡ **6. Think about your workplace or places (as in Jack's case). Has God ever invited you to join Him in building a redemptive relationship with a person at work? If so who and how? What were the results?**

_____

_____

_____

Some Guidelines for Developing Redemptive Relationships
There are several ways God calls us to build redemptive relationships with those people He places in our lives at work. The following guidelines, taken from the Sermon on the Mount, should help you recognize God's initiative and help make you aware of His invitation to build redemptive relationships with others:

Love Your Enemies

Love Your Enemies
In the Sermon on the Mount Jesus commanded:

> *"You have heard that it was said, 'Love your neighbor and hate your enemy.' But I tell you: Love your enemies and pray for those who persecute you, that you may be sons of your Father in heaven. He causes his sun to rise on the evil and the good, and sends rain on the righteous and the unrighteous"* (Matthew 5:43-45).

You don't have to work very long in the marketplace to realize that you will face people who treat you as though you are their enemy. They may be jealous of you, think they are better than you, be focused only upon themselves, or just be plain mean. I always see this type of person as God's invitation for me to join him in a human relations strategy of unconditional love. This is literally the opposite way of dealing with difficult people than the world takes.

Before you push back away from the workbook and say, "This guy doesn't realize how difficult it is to relate to people who consider themselves your enemy", remember, the Kingdom Agenda is a dynamic partnership. The world is usually so shocked by this strategy of loving your enemy that they literally are disarmed. This strategy requires you to place your faith in God to provide, protect, and influence the situation to accomplish

His objective. Watch for opportunities and God's invitation to love your enemies.

➥ **7. Do you have any enemies at work? Do you sense God's invitation to demonstrate an unconditional love toward any one of them? If so, who?**

_____

The Golden Rule

"Do to others what you would have them do to you."

Jesus gave us one clear guideline for building redemptive relationships with the people His Father brings into our lives: *"In everything, do to others what you would have them do to you, for this sums up the Law and the Prophets"* (Matthew 7:12). This has been called the Golden Rule. He taught us to relate to others in the way that you would want them to relate to us.

➥ **8. So what does that mean to you? How would you want others to relate to you? Take a few moments to consider these ways you would want to be treated. List others that come to your mind in the margin.**

Others:

_____

_____

_____

_____

- If you see a person with a need, do what you can to meet that need.
- If you see someone who needs help, help.
- If someone is sick, visit.
- If someone is grieving over the loss of a loved one, comfort.
- If someone needs forgiving, forgive.
- If someone is lonely, be a friend.
- If someone achieves success, rejoice with him or her.
- If someone does a quality job, praise his work.
- If someone fails, encourage him or her.

Invest Your Life in Others

Paul wrote to the church at Thessalonica. He described the way he demonstrated his love for the people. Paul said:

> *We were gentle among you, like a mother caring for her little children. We loved you so much that we were delighted to share with you not only the gospel of God but our lives as well* (1 Thess. 2:7-8).

Paul not only shared the gospel with the people; but, because of love, he also shared his very life with them. Paul worked hard and long hours to make sure that he was not a burden to the people. He sought to demonstrate his love by investing his very life in their lives.

Let God open your eyes to see where He may be working around you. Let him invite you to build relationships with others. Don't be surprised if He chooses someone who would be your last choice. He will probably invite you into a situation that requires faith. Trust Him. Pray and depend on Him to reveal the way you are to respond.

PRAYER STRATEGY

➥ **Take time now to pray about building redemptive relationships.**
- Ask the Lord to open your eyes to see where He is at work.
- Pray for specific individuals in your workplace and pay attention if God begins to give you a special burden for one particular person.
- Ask the Lord to enable you to love your enemies.
- Ask the Lord to enable you to love other unselfishly and to treat them the way you would want to be treated. Invite the Lord to love them through you.

DAY 5   The Kingdom Influence in the Workplace

Kingdom Agenda
"The kingdom of heaven is like yeast that a woman took and mixed into a large amount of flour until it worked all through the dough" (Matt. 13:33).

➡ Read the "Kingdom Agenda" in the margin. Pause for a moment of prayer. Ask the Lord for faith, hope, and endurance to see God's Kingdom Agenda have that kind of influence in your workplace.

Yeast Influences the Whole
The influence of the Kingdom will not be readily apparent to a casual observer. Jesus described the Kingdom like yeast in a lump of dough. You don't even see it. But, over time, the yeast permeates the whole lump causing it to rise when it is baked. You and other Christians in your workplace may seem small and insignificant in number or influence. But the Kingdom influence through your lives can have far reaching affects that touch your entire workplace. God may start by changing one life. That one touches another and his or her life is changed. Those two touch others through redemptive relationships and more are changed. God is able to transform an entire workplace when He is allowed to work fully through just one person or small group that is full surrendered to His sovereign will.

➡ 1. What is one thing that the Kingdom is like? _____

Light and Good Deeds Bring Glory to Your Father
"You are the light of the world . . . . Let your light shine before men, that they may see your good deeds and praise your Father in heaven" (Matt. 5:14,16). Jesus Christ is the light of the world. Jesus also called you "the light of the world." You are light because He dwells in you. Light reveals things. Light will influence your workplace as others see your good deeds and glorify your Father. However, some people do not like light because it reveals their evil deeds. Sometimes your light and godly righteousness may cause others to feel very uncomfortable. Don't compromise in order to make them comfortable. God can use that conviction of sin to influence them to repent and turn to Christ. Your conduct and productivity can influence your workplace for God's glory.

➡ 2. How can light have both a positive influence for the Kingdom and also cause people to resist the light?

_____

_____

Matthew 13:31-32
He told them another parable: "The kingdom of heaven is like a mustard seed, which a man took and planted in his field. Though it is the smallest of all your seeds, yet when it grows, it is the largest of garden plants and becomes a tree, so that the birds of the air come and perch in its branches."

Mustard Seed—Matthew 13:31-32
Kingdom influence may begin with only one person. It may begin very very small and seemingly insignificant. When God begins to cause it to grow, it can become something great that touches many lives and in many far-reaching places. Remember that a mustard seed of faith is all that is required to move mountains. God may accomplish mighty or miraculous things through His coworkers that will affect the entire company and bring great credit to the Lord.

➡ 3. Can you think of a time or a way that something small grew to become a very influential part of the Kingdom work? When and how did it happen?

_____

_____

Mark 4:26-29

He also said, "This is what the kingdom of God is like. A man scatters seed on the ground. Night and day, whether he sleeps or gets up, the seed sprouts and grows, though he does not know how. All by itself the soil produces grain—first the stalk, then the head, then the full kernel in the head. As soon as the grain is ripe, he puts the sickle to it, because the harvest has come."

Growing Seed—Mark 4:26-29

Apart from God, you can do nothing. As God works through you, He can do anything. The influence of the Kingdom is not dependent on all your hard work and your extra effort. Though you will be involved in the work, and it may be difficult at times. God is the One who produces growth and brings a harvest. Trust Him and work together with Him. Be patient to wait on His initiative. Obey His every command or commission. Then be prepared for a harvest of righteousness.

➡ **4. Which stage do you sense you are in at your place of employment? Check one.**
- ❏ a. plowing hard ground
- ❏ b. planting seeds
- ❏ c. watering and waiting
- ❏ d. taking care of growing plants
- ❏ e. reaping a harvest

Where To From Here?

I pray these last six weeks have been very meaningful and fruitful for your life and work. This may have just been the beginning of what God wants to do to begin restoring your workplace to His original intention.

➡ **5. Look over the following list and begin thinking and praying about what the Lord may want you to do next to work together with Him.**
- ❏ continue meeting and praying with my small-group to encourage one another and counsel each other
- ❏ start another small-group to expand the number of people working together to influence your workplace or profession
- ❏ get some additional discipleship training in the following area (underline):
  - knowing and doing God's will
  - praying as a work strategy
  - demonstrating love
  - building redemptive relationships
  - sharing my faith with others
  - learning to disciple others in their faith
- ❏ join God in the invitations He is calling me to at work

- ❏ other: _____

_____

PRAYER STRATEGY

➡ **Take time now to pray about the next steps God has in store for you and your workplace.**
- Thank the Lord for specific ways He has guided you or spoken to you during this study.
- Renew your surrender to do all He has called you to do.
- Ask Him to reveal His will for the coming weeks in your work. Ask Him what next steps to take.
- Ask the Lord to expand your divine network for His purposes.
- Ask the Lord to take His glory. Give Him permission to do anything He chooses to get glory through your life.
- Ask the Lord to restore your workplace for His glory.

How to Become a Christian

Perhaps as you have studied *The Kingdom Agenda,* you may realize that you don't have a real and personal love relationship with God. Do you desire to have that kind of experience? If so, that desire inside you is the work of your heavenly Father drawing you to a love relationship with His Son, Jesus Christ. God created you for a love relationship with Him. You will never know true peace and joy apart from that intimate love relationship. It is a real and personal relationship with the God of the universe. It also is an eternal relationship. It can begin now, and it will continue in heaven for all eternity.

If God is drawing you to Himself, would you respond to Him? Because of sin, all humanity is separated from God and spiritually dead. Scripture indicates that the *"wages of sin is death"* (Rom. 6:23*a*). God, however, has paid the penalty (wages) for your sin through the death of Christ on the cross. Yes, He loved you that much! He wants your love and devotion in return. *"The gift of God is eternal life in Christ Jesus our Lord"* (Rom. 6:23*b*).

God says in the Bible, *"If you confess with your mouth, 'Jesus is Lord,' and believe in your heart that God raised him from the dead, you will be saved"* (Rom. 10:9). When Jesus began His earthly ministry, His message was: *"Repent for the kingdom of heaven is near."* To repent, you turn from your self-centered life to a Christ-centered life where He rules in your mind and heart. You agree that you are a sinner in need of a Savior. You can ask Christ to be that Savior right now.

You can turn to a love relationship with God. He is listening. Just talk to Him. Tell Him of your desire to know and experience Him. Agree with Him about your sin and your need for His forgiveness and cleansing. Ask Him to forgive you. Surrender your will to Him, and make Him Lord of your life. When you do, God will place His Spirit in you. You will be a new creation. Your old life will be put away and a newness of life will take its place (1 Cor. 5:17).

If you have prayed and entered into a love relationship with God, God wants to place you in the body of Christ—a local church. Contact a pastor or other leader in a church nearby. Tell him about your decision, and he will be able to help you follow through on your decision to follow Christ. If you need help with this or other spiritual decisions, talk to one of the members in your small group or another Christian. He or she will be happy to lead you to the Lord for help.

KINGDOM STRATEGY
MEETING 6

Use the following suggestions to guide a one-hour small-group discussion of *The Kingdom Agenda* covering the lessons in this week's study. For general instructions for the group facilitator, see page 156.

This Week's Learning Objective
You will understand your role in kingdom work and demonstrate your cooperation by joining God in His work in your workplace

Opening Prayer (2 minutes)
• Begin with prayer acknowledging God's presence.
• Ask the Holy Spirit to be your Teacher and to reveal the Kingdom work that God has for each individual.
• Thank the Lord for the experiences of the past six weeks, and ask Him to guide you

Getting Better Acquainted (8 minutes)
Give each member an opportunity to share the one thing that they have learned or experienced during the study that has been most meaningful or life changing. (See #6 on pages 137-138.

Content Review (10 minutes)
Ask members to turn in their books to the Overview of Week 6 on page 135. Using the time suggested, review the following items of content from this week's lessons:
• Ask members to recite this week's Scripture-memory verse together—Matthew 28:18-20.
• Ask: Which one of the summary statements from week 6 was most meaningful to you and why?
• Ask: What are some important facts about Kingdom work?
• Ask: What kind of career assignments may the Lord call you to?
• Ask: How does Jesus' model prayer provide a pattern for orienting yourself to the Kingdom Agenda?

Discussion Questions (15 minutes)
Look over the following list of questions and lead the group to discuss those that you think would be most meaningful or helpful to your group. Notice that the normal time for discussion has been cut this week in order to allow more time for prayer at the conclusion of the study. Watch your time (invite members to help you), so that you will allow adequate time for prayer at the end of the session. You may want to ask members to help

you select the most helpful questions for discussion.
1. What does our Scripture-memory verse have to say about our primary assignment in the Kingdom Agenda?
2. What are some of the kinds of changes God may bring to pass through your Kingdom work?
3. On page 137, (#5) what evidence have you observed in your work life that indicates a change in the way you are following the Kingdom Agenda?
4. What kind of career directions, if any, has the Lord given you during this study?
5. How has God invited you to join Him in His work during the past six weeks of this study? (#2, p. 140)
6. How did you respond to #4 on page 141? What things would you have to do differently to live out the Kingdom Agenda the way Jesus did?
7. What do you sense God is wanting to do in the near future to continue preparing you for Kingdom service?
8. Why is prayer such a critical part of your work strategy?
9. Have you experienced the value of prayer in your work life? How?
10. How can you use the model prayer to guide your prayer life toward a Kingdom focus?
11. What was Paul's primary strategy for building redemptive relationships? (pp. 147-148)
12. How did you respond to #6 on page 149?
13. How could loving your enemies in your workplace become a way of building a redemptive relationship?
14. What other means might God use to identify the person with whom He wants you to build a redemptive relationship?
15. What are some of the ways that the Kingdom can influence your workplace?
16. What do you sense God wants you (us) to do next to continue your focus on the Kingdom Agenda at your workplace?

Priority Praying (25 minutes)

Conclude the session by spending time as a group praying for each other.

• Place a chair in the center of the circle. Ask one member to share with the group the one last prayer request that he or she would like for the group to pray concerning his or her work life. Ask three or four individuals to gather around the person and pray for his or her work.

* Continue this same process until each member has been prayed for.

• Close the time of prayer holding hands in a circle. Invite members to pray conversationally one or two sentences each concerning the burdens you carry for each other, your workplaces, and your church.

WORK-RELATED PRAYER REQUESTS

FACILITATOR'S GUIDE

God created us and placed us in the body of Christ so that we could work together with other Christians to see God's kingdom come on earth as it is in heaven. We are interdependent upon one another. We cannot function as we ought without the rest of the body. *The Kingdom Agenda* has been designed and written to help Christians help each other to know and do God's will in their workplaces.

This course has been designed for use in small groups. Each small group will need a leader or facilitator to guide the group sessions. The following suggestions should help you understand the role of the facilitator and ways to lead the group to experience God in their workplaces. Before you read the following suggestions, you may want to review the "Introduction" on pages 10-13.

Your Role as a Small-Group Facilitator

Each small group should select a leader or facilitator for their sharing time. This could be the same person for the entire study or it could be a different person each week. The facilitator does not have to be a content expert. He or she will not be required to master the material in order to teach or lecture on the weekly topics. Your role is ti guide discussion, sharing, and praying related to the content that members will have studied during the week.

Following each week's lessons you will find a two-page outline for a "Kingdom Strategy Meeting." These suggestions should provide more than enough help for a one-hour small-group session. You should feel free to adapt the suggestions and questions for discussion to meet the specific work needs of your group. One of your primary roles is to guide the group to seek the Lord and His counsel regarding the Kingdom Agenda for your respective workplaces.

Preparing for *The Kingdom Agenda* Study

This workbook has been designed for self-paced interactive learning. That means that an individual can study the course at his or her own pace. The content is designed to interact with the student. Thus, a segment of content will be presented. Then a learning activity will call the student to respond. Where correct answers can be identified, the content following a learning activity will help the student review his or her answers.

The individual study, however, is not complete without a small-group session to process the learning and help with application. This small-group process will take at least seven weeks. The first group meeting will be an introductory session. Members will begin their individual study following that session. Then they will meet once each week for the following six weeks in "Kingdom Strategy Meetings."

Forming a Group

The ideal group for this study will be coworkers at a common workplace. As Christians in the same workplace gather to share and pray, they will be able to deal with very specific concerns and issues. The next most beneficial group will be people from the same occupation or profession. Other possible groupings are listed on page 12. Someone, perhaps you, should take the lead in forming a group. Ask God to guide you to enlist just the right people for your group.

Size of Group for Effective Learning

The sharing, discussion, and praying that will take place in the Kingdom Strategy Meetings needs to be personal and in-depth. If a group is too large, some people will feel left out or frustrated by not getting to share adequately. For this reason we suggest that you form groups for every six to eight people. Ten should be a maximum number in a group. If you have more than ten interested persons form groups for every six or eight. If you have several groups in the same workplace, profession, or church, you may want to schedule a couple of joint sessions so that people can share what God is teaching them.

Enlist Participants

Prayer is the place to begin enlisting participants. Ask the Lord to guide you to the people He would want in your group. You may want to share will fellow Christians about the course and watch to see if they express an interest in participating. You may already have a group meeting that may choose to use this study to facilitate discussion. Invite persons to participate. We do not encourage you to force people to participate. Because homework is involved, a participant needs to be committed to the process.

Order Resources

You will need one copy of *The Kingdom Agenda* for each group member. You may order these through your local bookstore. If you have difficulty finding the books in your area, you may write to Dayspring Discipleship Resources, P. O. Box 369, Murfreesboro, TN 37133-0369 for ordering information.

Collect Book Fees

Some Christian employers may want to provide this study as a training and development option for employees in which case the cost of books would be covered by the employer. Churches that coordinate small groups may want to cover some or all of the cost of books. However, in most cases members will be expected to buy their own books. You will want to announce the cost of the books as you enlist participants so that they will be prepared to pay for their books at the introductory session. Watch for persons who may need financial assistance. In those cases you may want to subsidize the cost of the book or provide one on a "scholarship" basis.

Develop a Time Schedule

You need to allow for an hour for each Kingdom Strategy Meeting. This could take place before work, after work, during a lunch hour (brown bagging lunch), or at some other convenient time. Be sure to plan you schedule in such a way that you are faithful to your employer. Do not take advantage of a Christian employer by running into work time. Some groups may even decide to meet twice during the week for briefer periods. Let the group members help you determine the optimum time for your meeting.

Help Members Memorize Scripture

Some members may not have memorized Scripture before. Give them some basic suggestions to help them memorize their weekly memory verses. These might include:
• Write the Scripture on a card for daily review.
• Read the verse aloud several times.
• Study the verse to understand what it means.
• Break the verse down into phrases and learn one at a time.
• Continue reviewing the verse for several weeks until you have mastered it.

Encourage Members to Keep a Journal

God will be guiding and speaking to members throughout this study. He may give specific suggestions about dealing with a particular problem. He may surface a Scripture that gives counsel for dealing with a difficult issue. Encourage members to keep a daily journal of what God is saying and doing in the workplace. This will prove to be a valuable tool for review, sharing, and discussion.

At some point in time, Kingdom Agenda Ministries is going to provide specific helps for different professions or occupations. We are also considering developing a newsletter to share helpful ideas or Scriptures that God has given to different groups. If members sense that God has given specific help or guidance, they may want to send a brief written testimony or explanation to Kingdom Agenda Ministries, P. O. Box 747, Murfreesboro, TN 37133-0747. If they do send testimonies or other written text to share with others, ask them to indicate with their correspondence permission to use the text for sharing with others.

Conducting an Introductory Session

Because members will need to complete the first week's lessons prior to your first strategy meeting, plan to conduct an introductory session prior to your first official session. (See p. 158.)

Conducting Kingdom Strategy Meetings

Suggestions for weekly small-group sessions are provided at the end of each week's lessons. These may be lead by the same person throughout the study, or different members could lead the sessions to share the leadership role. These sessions are designed so that little advance preparation will be required of the leader.

Each segment of the session has suggested time requirements. These add up to a 60 minute session. You may want to adjust these time allotments to best meet the needs of your group. One tendency will be to spend so much time for discussion that little time is left for prayer. Work diligently to avoid that temptation. Prayer, as you will learn, needs to be a major part of your work strategy. This may be the time God gives specific directions or answers to your group that no amount of discussion could achieve. Ask members to help you guard the closing prayer time. If necessary, set an alarm or timer to announce the close of discussion. Read the discussion questions before the session. Select the ones that will be most helpful for your group.

Spend time in personal prayer for yourself and your group so that you will be prepared for the session. Pray regularly for your group members.

May the Lord guide you and use you in a special way during these coming weeks!

INTRODUCTORY SESSION

Use the following suggestions to guide a one-hour introductory session for a study of *The Kingdom Agenda: Experiencing God in Your Workplace*. For general instructions for the group facilitator, see page 156.

This Session's Learning Objective
You will understand the requirements for individual and small-group study of *The Kingdom Agenda* and commit yourself to participating in the study for the next six weeks.

Arrival Activities
As prospective members arrive, greet them and ask them to do the following:
1. Fill out a name tag and place it on your clothing.
2. Write your name, home address, employer's name, occupation, and phone numbers (home and work) on an index card provided.
3. Take a copy of *The Kingdom Agenda* and begin reading the Introduction on pages 10-13.

   If members are paying for their books, collect the book fees at this time.

Opening Prayer
Begin the session with prayer.
- Thank the Lord for calling these members to participate in the study of *The Kingdom Agenda*.
- Ask the Lord to guide each of you to understand His Kingdom Agenda for your life and workplace.
- Ask the Holy Spirit to be your Teacher during the coming six weeks of your study.
- Ask the Lord to reveal exactly what His Kingdom is like and how all of you can surrender to His Sovereign rule in your lives.

Getting Acquainted
Ask each participant to introduce himself or herself. Ask them to include in their introduction the following:
- name and family information
- workplace (employer) and job title
- why you decided to participate in this study

Questions and Concerns About Experiencing God in Your Workplace
Ask members to identify questions and concerns they have about how they might experience God working in their workplaces. Using an overhead or chalkboard, write questions and concerns as they are mentioned.

Overview of *The Kingdom Agenda*
- Ask participants to identify key facts or information that they read about in the introduction.
- Divide into six groups (depending on the number of people attending this may be one or two persons per "group"). Assign one Week to each group. Ask the groups to quickly survey the lessons in their week and prepare a summary for the large group.
- Call on groups to report to the large group by giving a brief summary of the topics to be dealt with during your study.
- Encourage members to memorize the Scripture Memory Verse for each week.
- Suggest that members keep a journal of what God say to them during the study.
- Discuss plans for the weekly session time and place.
- If you have more people than one group can accommodate (over 10), discuss options for dividing into two or more groups. Focus on the ideal that people would be grouped by employer, occupation, or similarity of work first.
- Determine the number and membership of each group. If necessary, this can be done following the session and group facilitators can call group members during the week to inform them of their group assignments.

Sharing and Praying Together
Divide into groupings of 3 or 4 members each. Ask members to share with their small group an answer to the following question: *In your line of work or at your workplace, what is the greatest challenge you face concerning how you live and work as a Christian in the workplace.*

After members have answered this question, ask two volunteers from each group to close in prayer. Ask them to pray about the upcoming study and ask the Lord to teach them His ways and purposes for life at work.

COMMISSIONING SERVICE

*T*he body of Christ—the local church—has an important role in helping support, encourage, and equip Christians for Kingdom work in their workplaces. The workplaces represented by members in a church are some of the most fertile and ripe mission fields with which a church has contact. Churches need to join God as He calls people to missionary assignments in the workplace.

The local church should function as a missionary sending agency to the community. God has strategically placed His people in the world, so they can serve as ambassadors for His Kingdom. Every job assignment should be considered a mission point for the local church. Church members are called to take the church to the world. The local church should equip God's people to be Kingdom workers in the world.

As your church begins to recognize God's all upon His people, you will want to consider commissioning "marketplace missionaries" for service in their workplaces. For many Christians a commissioning service would focus their understanding on the fact that God has called them to be His witnesses where ever they go. The following suggestions may give you some ideas for planning and conducting a service for your church.

Who?
This service should be conducted when a maximum participation of your members can be achieved. Involve a number of laypersons in planning all the details of the service. This can be as simple or elaborate as you desire. You may want to involve some temporary committees to plan for publicity, program, follow-up, and so forth. Members who have already studied through *The Kingdom Agenda* would be a good group with which to begin discussions.

When?
This service may come after a series of sermons about faith in the workplace. You might want to use this service to invite members to join other Christians in a study of *The Kingdom Agenda: Experiencing God in Your Workplace*. You may use this service to conclude a study of *The Kingdom Agenda*, as members move into their workplaces to apply what they have learned. There they will follow God's leadership by His power to accomplish His Kingdom Agenda in their workplaces.

What?
Plan for the entire service to focus on representing Christ in the workplace.

- Select songs that call for obedience, integrity, giving your best, faith, love, and so forth.
- Prepare Scripture readings that speak to the workplace. Use some of the "Kingdom Agenda" Scriptures in this book. This could be a choral reading or readings by individuals.
- Dramatize some of the work experiences of Joseph, Daniel, Nehemiah, or Paul (or other). These could be dramatic monologues describing God's work through these individuals in their workplaces.
- Enlist two members to share testimonies about ways they have been able to join God in His activity at their workplace or through their work.
- Preach a message on the Great Commission and make specific application to making disciples as workers go to their workplaces. Keep this message God-centered (what God is wanting to do through His people), rather than man-centered (what man can do for God in his workplace). [I have included a sample outline for you on the following page.
- Extend an invitation for Christians to surrender to God's Sovereign leadership in their workplaces as they become marketplace (or workplace) missionaries.
- Use a "Worker's Covenant" as a prayer of commitment to the Lord.
- Invite people to join other Christians in a study of *The Kingdom Agenda*.

Message
Called to Be Marketplace Missionaries

Text: Matthew 28:16-20

I. God Calls Ordinary People

A. The world's agenda would set some of the following criteria for a missionary assignment:
- Must be a seminary graduate.
- Must be a person of influence, wealth, etc.
- Must have a good resume.
- Must have the right connections.

B. God calls ordinary people with one significant qualification.
- Jesus called a group made up of fishermen, a tax collector, and other ordinary men.
- Some even "doubted" and had little faith.
- They had one common trait—a cooperative and obedient heart.

C. God chooses the weak, powerless, and common people of this world so a watching world will come to know Him and see His power.

II. Our Assignment Is Given Under the Highest Authority—The King of God's Kingdom

A. Kingdom work is authorized by the King.

B. We must accept God's leadership and our role as ambassadors of the King.

C. Developing an effective prayer life is our greatest work strategy. In prayer and in God's Word, we recognize His leading and initiative. Prayer is where God shows us what He is about to do (John 5:19-20).

III. Our Assignment Is Clear—Build Redemptive Relationships.

A. God is calling us to make investments that yield a high return.
- LifeShare: Investing your life into those God brings into your life at work (1 Thess. 2:8).
- Jesus lived God's agenda as He took the time to invest a part of Himself into the lives of others (e.g. Zacchaeus, Woman at the well, Disciples, Centurion)

B. God is calling us to equip people in the Kingdom Agenda.
- "Baptize them in the name . . ."
- "Teach them to obey all . . ."

C. Jesus assures us of His presence always—even in our workplaces.

Worker's Covenant with God

PASTOR:

Father, we kneel before You today to make a covenant with You. We confess our acceptance of Your Sovereignty over all areas of our lives. You are our Sovereign Lord. We have come to know You because Jesus Christ—Your Son—has reconciled us to You. Through Him, You have given us life that is both abundant and eternal. Therefore, as coworkers in Your Kingdom we pray . . .

MARKETPLACE MISSIONARIES:
- I accept Your will and Your agenda as my own agenda.
- I pray for Your Kingdom to come and Your will to be done in my workplace as it is in heaven.
- I place my trust in You, Father, as the Provider of all my needs.
- I covenant with You, Lord, to build redemptive relationships with others as You have done with me.
- I place my trust in Your protection, Your presence, and Your purposes.
- For Yours is the Kingdom, and the power, and the glory for ever and ever. Amen.